December 2024 921

HOT KITCHEN

Margaret Ann Spence is the author of two novels, the award-winning *Lipstick on the Strawberry* and the award finalist *Joyous Lies*.

A graduate of Melbourne University, Margaret worked for Penguin Books (Australia) Ltd, and *Walkabout* magazine before moving to the United States to obtain a master's degree in journalism from Boston University. She worked in public relations, earned an MBA degree, and has published in newspapers and print and on-line magazines.

Retaining close ties with Australia, Margaret was appointed the Australian Honorary Consul in Boston 1990–2000. She moved to Phoenix, Arizona, on her marriage to the Australian scientist, John C.H. Spence, FRS. Following his death in 2021 Margaret splits her time between Arizona and Massachusetts, where her children live with their families.

https://www.margaretannspence.com

By the same author

Lipstick on the Strawberry
Joyous Lies

COLD WAR in a HOT KITCHEN

A memoir of mid-century Melbourne

Margaret Ann Spence

Wakefield
Press

Wakefield Press
16 Rose Street
Mile End
South Australia 5031
www.wakefieldpress.com.au

First published 2024

Map of Victorian goldfields: Proeschel, F & Philp, James B. (1853). Pocket map of the roads to all the mines in Victoria with the new mines and the cross roads from one mine to another: divided into squares of ten miles each to easily find out and mark the new mines which may be hereafter discovered in Victoria Retrieved March 19 2024, from http://nla.gov.au/nla.obj-231354593

Map of Western Australian goldfields: Western Australia. Department of Mines & Davies, A. B. (1958). Western Australia, 1958 Retrieved March 19 2024, from http://nla.gov.au/nla.obj-1485546174

Cover designed by Stacey Zass
Edited by Julia Beaven, Wakefield Press
Typeset by Jesse Pollard, Wakefield Press

ISBN 978 1 92304 243 8

NATIONAL LIBRARY OF AUSTRALIA   A catalogue record for this book is available from the National Library of Australia

CORIOLE
McLAREN VALE   Wakefield Press thanks Coriole Vineyards for continued support

To the memory of my parents, Ruth and Dick Edquist, and to their grandchildren and great-grandchildren.

Contents

Maps   viii

Introduction   1

Chapter 1   A Vein of Gold   5

Chapter 2   The World's Edge   10

Chapter 3   A Suit of Pale Blue   12

Chapter 4   The House on Florence Avenue   16

Chapter 5   Phosphorus and Father Christmas   21

Chapter 6   A Bookie's Daughter   24

Chapter 7   A Haven in Hampton   29

Chapter 8   Lords and Ladies   33

Chapter 9   Shaped by Early Grief   38

Chapter 10   Charlie and the Cherry Cake   44

Chapter 11   Cherry Blossoms   49

Chapter 12   The Family Grows Sideways   54

Chapter 13   The Move to Grange Road   59

Chapter 14   From Spinifex to Suburbia   64

Chapter 15   Seen But Not Heard   68

Chapter 16   Battle of Ideas   75

Chapter 17   Left and Right in Kew   81

Chapter 18   Gaslighting   92

Chapter 19   Our Cousin, Our Sister   97

Chapter 20   Running Through Her Days   102

Chapter 21   On Passchendaele Street   107

Chapter 22	The Stony Rises	115
Chapter 23	Hardship, Best Forgotten	128
Chapter 24	Up Above Comes Down Under	141
Chapter 25	Lifelong Friends	153
Chapter 26	Science at the Dinner Table	158
Chapter 27	Food of the Past, Food of the Future	168
Chapter 28	A Rightward Turn	176
Chapter 29	Private School, Public Transportation	184
Chapter 30	Holidays and Happy Times	192
Chapter 31	Cultsha	196
Chapter 32	My Mother's Secret Studies	205
Chapter 33	The Corporate Wife	208
Chapter 34	The Companionate Wife	213
Chapter 35	Aptitudes, Attitudes and Ambition	219
Chapter 36	A Journey Back in Time	224
Chapter 37	Ruination	239
Chapter 38	A Daughter of the Empire	244
Chapter 39	The White House in the Wild West	250
Chapter 40	Four O'Clock	259
Chapter 41	The Industry of Women	269
Acknowledgements		281
Notes		284
Bibliography		304
Index		314

Victorian goldfields

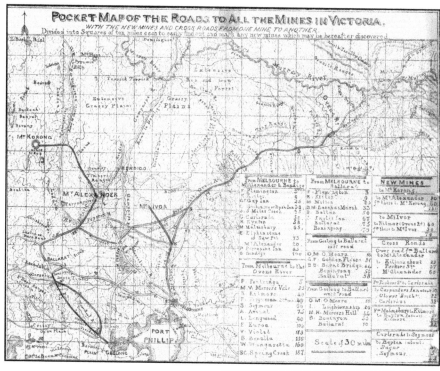

1 Ballarat
2 Bendigo
3 Geelong
4 River Loddon
5 Port Phillip

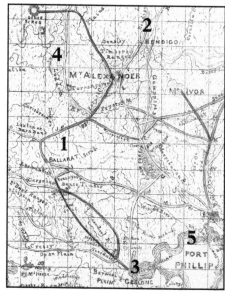

Western Australian goldfields

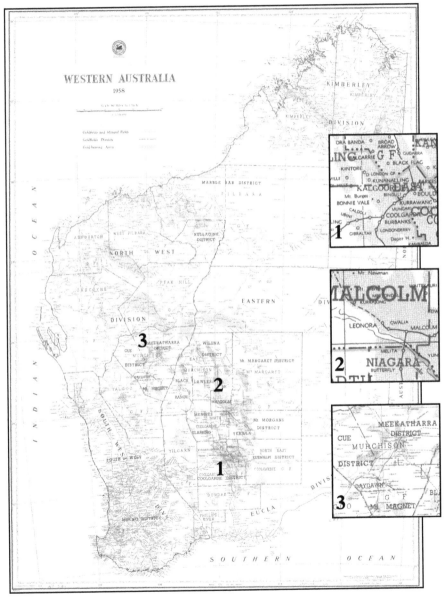

1 Kalgoorlie   **2** Leonora–Gwalia   **3** Murchison goldfields

Introduction

The most interesting history is often made by those going about their everyday lives. How they coped has spurred all inventors and visionaries who imagined how our world could be made better. *The Spirit of Progress*, a train named without irony, ran between Sydney and Melbourne during my childhood. It epitomised this Western viewpoint in tracks of steel thundering over a natural landscape which, before my ancestors landed on its shores, had changed scarcely at all. Australia, less than 250 years ago, existed on a different timescale and with respect for its natural rhythms.

While it is not the intention of this book to discuss the cultural clash between the Indigenous inheritors of this country and the colonists who invaded it, this personal history is spiked with the knowledge that a great deal of environmental degradation accompanied the extraction from the earth of prized metals. This business of mining called to my ancestors on both sides of the family tree. Whether they succeeded or not, this role made them symbols of Australia today, a land which still draws most of its good fortune from underground.

The pillaging of the earth caused by mining is obvious to those who live the life; the rest of us, treasuring our gold wedding rings, our dangling earrings, admiring the gold leaf of illuminated manuscripts, typing at our word processors or talking on our mobile phones (which use rare metals, including gold) are all complicit, if unaware.

My story is set one hundred years, more or less, from the time that my forebears first set foot in this land. The isolation of the Australian continent had not protected its people from the troubles of the wider world. Two world wars in the first half of the twentieth century reverberated for years. The immediate aftermath of World War II formed my early childhood experience, even though we lived far from the scene of its devastation. The world was different now, the old certainties gone.

The 1950s are regarded from today's viewpoint as a time of rigid conformity and blandness, a time when boredom was averted only by increasing material prosperity for the middle classes. That's not my recollection. In fact, the late 1940s and the early 1950s were a time of great world tension. Just recovering from World War II, the nations were sorting themselves into East and West; those that were communist or about to become communist, and those that lived by the belief system of capitalism. In 1949 and 1950, these systems were poised on the brink of a third world war, made potentially even more catastrophic because of the proven capability of the atom bomb.

It may seem strange that a very young child could absorb these tensions in a place so far removed from the scenes of the previous wars, and yet they were part of the air I breathed. Perhaps my parents were unusually aware of them. Certainly, they behaved differently from my friends' parents. They actively sought out and befriended the non-Anglo foreigners who came to Australia seeking refuge and new lives after the shattering of Europe.

Secondly, 'moral standards', which slipped so swiftly as my generation came of age, were already pulling at the fabric of probity in the supposedly prim 1950s. War had exposed humanity's dark side. Back home, those in charge (all male) tried to suppress these urges, especially in women. Censors made great efforts to keep out literature they deemed indecent, thus increasing its attraction.

Though proved perfectly capable in the workforce while the men were at war, women were now instructed to stay home. It is unbelievable, looking back, that society expected women to survive by the largesse of men, when so many men had been killed or maimed by a recent war.

Women were encouraged to stay home and populate, but home was not a haven for many. Resentment began as a gentle simmer, rippling and rising to a boil in the age of feminism a few decades later.

A subtle shift began as immigrants flooded the cities, bringing their exotic and wonderful foodways with them. As food began to interest the media, respect for its traditional preparers, women, began to rise. Paradoxically, kitchens became trendy as multiculturalism and feminism went hand-in-hand toward a new world. In our house, the kitchen became the metaphor—as well as the battleground—for competing ideas.

What should a home be? In the 'ideal' modern home, parents and children lived as a unit. My childhood differed from that of my peers. We were not a nuclear family. Sometimes we lived with my mother's relatives, or they lived with us. Vivid and warm personalities, they made these makeshift arrangements fun.

For a while, in our house two women lived simultaneously: Ruth, my sweet, gentle mother, and her sister, Nan, a glamorous, convention-breaking, witty journalist. Then, Eva, our paternal grandmother, known as Granny, a small person with a large sense of her own importance, came to stay, disrupting our lives for the next thirteen years.

Each of these three women presented a different role

model of how to be a woman, a wife and a mother. As the only girl child in a male-dominated household, it set my head spinning.

As adults, my brothers and I had questions about the odd nature of our upbringing. In 2007, needing to make sense of the tensions that pervaded our home, we travelled to the arid goldfields of Leonora and Gwalia in Western Australia. It was here that my grandfather, Victor, had risen from lowly beginnings to manage the Sons of Gwalia mine and later run the company from Melbourne. Seeing the old gold mine where our grandfather had been manager was a revelation, reminding us that all our forebears had been drawn to the mines and their promise of easy wealth.

On her wooden table beside the chintz-upholstered chair in which she spent her later days, my grandmother kept a copy of the *Rubaiyat of Omar Khayyam*.

Poised as we seem to be on the edge of another epochal change, this quote from the *Rubaiyat* sums it up.

> Drink wine and look at the moon
> and think of all the civilisations
> the moon has seen passing by.

Read on then, about a vanished world.

Chapter 1

A Vein of Gold

After the robbers stole all my parents' silver and jewellery, wrapping them for the getaway in the dining room's oriental rug, my father made me a necklace.

The burglars had not taken the large quartz stone in the glass-fronted cabinet in the living room. The stone had sat there, pale and veined like a woman's breast, for years. Its back was turned to the room modestly, to conceal the side shot through with ribbons of gold. My father joked that the robbers had not taken the most valuable thing in the house. Interested only in what they could fence, the thieves ignored the handbag-sized milk-coloured piece of quartz.

My pragmatic father decided, having lost all other mementos of almost half a century of life at 5 Grange Road, that this stone should be recycled. So typical of him to take a loss and turn it into a gain, a lesson learned in his sparse childhood. By 1993, the year of the robbery, my mother was suffering from Alzheimer's and showed little interest.

Our grandmother, who in 1950 bought the house we lived in, had also died, though the two front rooms of the house were not much changed. The dark Victorian furniture, her precious English porcelain, the Victorian-era books with their leather spines, were unappealing to the thieves, who snatched what could be easily sold.

From the gold in the big white rock, Dad had four identical

necklaces made, one for each of his children. I have not removed mine since he gave it to me, the gold reminding me of my father and symbolising the mystery of that big stone.

The beribboned rock came from one of the mines in the West Australian outback where my grandfather worked as a young man; a tantalising distant land of gold. Plane travel was expensive, and we could not drive 2000 miles across the desolate and dangerous Nullarbor Plain. So the rock and our aged grandmother Eva were a mystery. Neither was pretty, each contained a treasure. The rock held gold, Granny a cache of family lore, part narrative, part myth.

Born in 1913, my father, Richard Courtney Edquist, known as Dick, spent his early childhood in the dusty and remote goldfields of Western Australia, in the arid semi-desert to the east and north of Perth. Kalgoorlie, the centre of mining activity, lies over one of the world's richest gold deposits. Scattered further east and north are isolated settlements where my father's ingenious father built a reputation as he wrested profit from failing mines. Dad was ten when his father's job took him to the Sons of Gwalia mine, about 200 kilometres north of Kalgoorlie, thirteen when he travelled alone the 885 kilometres to boarding school in Perth. Self-reliance became his motto, and that of his parents, who both came from cities: Victor Edquist from Adelaide, Eva Litchfield from London. Each opted for an adventurous, difficult life in the deserts of Western Australia. As long as Granny lived with us, she protected the quartz in her sitting room from the children's touch, but we were aware of its role in our family history. Gold had captured my grandfather's teenage imagination and set him on his career. Victor's mother's first marriage was to a goldminer who lost his life in a mine-shaft accident and she had tried to discourage her youngest son from pursuing such a reckless occupation. Yet for Victor, the quest for gold was as exciting as the find; he devoted his life to it.

Mining underpins Australia's prosperity. Most Australians, clustered in their millions in the capital cities on the coast, spend little time pondering the source of their wealth and the cost of getting it, both environmentally and on a personal level. Yet many people's families were lured here by the glitter of gold.

On the other side of the continent, my mother's ancestors arrived virtually penniless in the fledgling colony of Victoria. They came to seek their fortunes in the goldrushes of Ballarat and Bendigo in the 1850s and 60s. Melbourne's fine bluestone buildings were funded by the goldrushes. The city was, for a time, the richest in the southern hemisphere, but wealth eluded my mother's family and they lost interest in searching for treasure. They became farmers and publicans and, in the next generation, teachers and office workers.

Only Victor and his wife Eva succeeded in the gold business and, for us, their story became the stuff of legend.

I never knew my grandfather, who died the year before my birth. But our feisty grandmother! Born in 1881, she came from London to be a teacher in Western Australia in her late twenties. After their marriage she and Victor moved to the distant outback, where goods we take for granted were in very short supply. As was English gentility and propriety, which Eva dispensed with fierce determination in lands taken only recently from peoples who had lived there successfully for 40,000 years. Within a generation, the quiet mulga rangeland of the goldfields in Western Australia's Great Victoria Desert reverberated to the sound of saws cutting wood props for the mines, the clang of machinery and the shouts of men. Displaced, the Indigenous people witnessed the destruction of their ancient hunting grounds.

Confronted with discomfort, the rough manners of miners and the degradation of the native inhabitants, perhaps Eva attempted to retain her sense of self by clinging to the notion that class hierarchy mattered. She carried this baggage to Melbourne after Victor was promoted there to head his company's Australian operations. He died there, still in harness, at the age of sixty-five.

After his sudden death, our forbidding grandmother moved into our house in Kew. 'Our house' was a misnomer. Eva soon dominated the place as though she owned it which, in fact, she did. Echoing the Cold War, value systems immediately clashed. Granny, who had brought up her four children mostly in the desert in primitive conditions, found it a challenge to live cheek by jowl with four unruly children. In the vast space of the outback, children could be seen and not heard, but in Kew we kids were both seen and heard, particularly during Melbourne's winters.

Granny, as a young woman, was a teacher of domestic science, a professional in the art of running a home. She took pride in the way a house was kept, the food it served and its nutritional value. Eva wanted to run our house like a business operation. For my mother, keeping a home got in the way of the life of the mind. She loved her children, appreciated order and beauty, but had too much to do. Eva, then in her sixties, battled with my mother over housekeeping standards and child-rearing practices. In Melbourne she was devoid of friends and an opportunity to develop outside interests. This domestic battleground dominated our lives.

Granny's mind remained sharp even after her body betrayed her. The sunlight of the goldfields had failed to halt the osteoporosis that humped her back. Blue veins stood up in her pale hands as her weak heart pulsed in vain to warm fingers whitened by Melbourne winters. Her vision had expanded from an indoor life in a restrictive English childhood to the vast skies of a desert landscape, only to be reduced again. By the time we knew her, my frustrated and despairing grandmother's empire of sand had diminished to a sitting room in a suburb. She took out her fury on her daughter-in-law, our mother, and on us, her grandchildren. For years, my brothers and I blamed her for our mother's unhappiness.

I see now my mother's sadness had a larger cause; part physical, part unresolved grief, part resentment at how society valued women so poorly. Her husband had no idea how she felt since she never dared tell him. Granny, of a previous generation, never felt devalued. A product of the British Empire at the height of its powers, she carried a colonist's disdain for the locals. And even more so for the foreigners who flocked to our shores, eager to become New Australians.

Meanwhile, this 'new Australia', tested by war and shocked to realise that Great Britain had not come to its rescue when the Japanese threatened to invade it, put feelers out into the world, inventing a new image of itself as a Pacific nation. What this nation should be, and how its values might change, obsessed my parents and their friends. My parents did not agree about these matters but remained devoted to one another. Holding contradictory ideas in one's head simultaneously is something I absorbed and have had to live by, perhaps frustrating those surer of themselves.

My necklace is a simple chain but made of pure gold. As she caressed her wedding ring on her thin, long ring finger, all those years after Victor had died, Eva might have speculated about the work taken to extract the precious metal from the earth. Work, and what it meant to my family, formed a surprising thread in my investigation of the past.

I stroke my necklace. It would break my heart to lose it. And I wonder what it means that my mother's wedding ring was not gold, but platinum, a mineral more valuable than gold. And that my father gave it to her.

Chapter 2

The World's Edge

The sun dazzled and the sand itched. My brother, John, lay asleep on the baby blanket, and my mother was talking to me, undistracted for a change. I tossed cooling handfuls of sand on her pale legs protruding from her flowered sundress. Though she'd spent her thirty years in our city on Port Phillip Bay, its public beaches never more than a tram ride away, she rarely ventured there. She hated the sun and, even sitting under the umbrella, she wore a big straw hat.

The sea looked inviting, cool and still, little wavelets lapping at the sand. I wanted to run in. The horizon stretched like a saucer's rim, far away where the sea was flat and grey as slate, and what looked like a toy ship glided silently across the world's edge.

'Mummy! What's that?'

'It's just a ship, darling, coming from overseas.'

'Can I go there?'

'No. Overseas they have had a terrible war, and lots and lots of people died. You are so lucky to live in Australia.'

Mum started to cry. I swatted flies and resented my brother's awakening wail, not understanding that Mum's tears might not be associated with her physical comfort. Tears puddled in my eyes because crying is infectious. Why was my mother sobbing so sadly on that suburban beach? I bashed my hand on the towel. Its stripes rippled. A tiny crab scuttled away and burrowed into the sand, leaving a hole.

Memories of homelands lost would surface for those aboard that ship on the horizon, wondering what awaited them as they came into shore. If you took a ship from Europe to Melbourne in 1947, you'd be six weeks older by the time you arrived. You'd lose your sense of time, and the swell of sea would make you sick.

A young child watching from the beach could think the ship a toy. I gathered up the painted metal bucket and spade, a present from Father Christmas, while Mum folded the towel and jackknifed the umbrella, tucking it all into the sagging netting at the bottom of John's pram. Impeded by our burdens, we struggled up the beach to the foreshore, our bare feet pillowing the sand so it fell like heavy slippers around our ankles.

What do we choose to remember? What do we choose to forget? I was not yet three, but I remember this day, this first tension between my mother and me. Her love of home. My horror of hurting her feelings, while wanting very much to be away, having adventures. And on that beach, so long ago, I had my first inkling of Australia as an idea. A place so far away from the rest of the world that distance offered safety. A fortress surrounded by sea. Had I been a few years older, I might have wondered if Mum was crying for all the people lost in the conflict, or for her own battles, just beginning.

Chapter 3

A Suit of Pale Blue

On 30 October 1943, my parents married; my father very thin but grinning happily, my mother, Ruth Charlholmes, in a suit of pale blue. In the photographs, her face is tilted towards the light, and her odd-looking hat, shaped like an admiral's tricorn, draws attention from her fair, beaming, upturned face.

When I was conscious of such things, after my beloved Betsy Wetsy doll was replaced by a bride doll, I asked Mum, 'Why didn't you wear a white dress and a veil like brides are supposed to?' I smoothed the doll's prickly tulle over her pink, plastic leg.

'It was wartime,' she said.

The battle raged not so far away. In the Pacific, the Australians and the Americans fought together, island by island, winning and retreating, retreating and winning. My mother had a large extended family, but my parents married with only a handful of witnesses. Most of their friends were away at war and would not return until after the final conflagration in Japan.

If it had not been for the outbreak of World War II my father would have remained in the Western Australian mining industry, like his father. Fronting up at the Army recruitment office in 1939, as soon as Prime Minister Robert Menzies declared Australia's commitment to help Britain win the war against Germany, Dad learned that his degree in chemistry could be put to better use in Maribyrnong, Victoria, making munitions for the conflict. A schoolfriend who had married my mother's best friend introduced the two.

Even from the beginning, the political and personal differences between them must have been marked. Mum had lost her mother at a young age, but the shy and intelligent young woman had persevered in getting a university education. Dad, with a logical, scientific mind, had inherited his parents' mental toughness. His outback upbringing had given him the ability to take hardship lightly and with humour. He could withstand a good deal of physical discomfort without seeming to notice. He did not spend much time dwelling on emotion.

It is said that when two people marry, there are actually four others crowding into the marriage bed: their parents. Mum, hater of injustice and a socialist at heart, came from a large warm-hearted family that had known its share of tragedy, but that, in times of adversity, drew strength from its remarkably resilient women. She felt compassion for those with hard lives and treasured those to whom she was closest.

Dad's parents had an intrinsic toughness and drive because both had left home when young and struck out on their own. They were politically conservative, unsentimental, and strong-minded.

Although conflicts in their values may have been present from the beginning, my parents, like the country as a whole, were intent on surviving the war and finding their own measure of happiness.

The grown-ups around me were in their twenties during World War II. Their bravery had saved our nation. Some of the adults talked about this adventurous time constantly, relating anecdotes. The skinny men who came back from the Japanese prisoner-of-war camps never talked about their experiences, nor did anyone who'd lost a family member.

Not only did my father lose his youngest brother, but my mother's two sisters lost fiancés. Aunt Marjie's young man died in Burma, Aunt Nan's American submarine commander disappeared in the Pacific.

Disoriented and patched-up, those who had spent the war at home and those who had been at the scene of the action covered their psychic wounds like a sleeve pulled over a bruise. Like all other couples who'd survived the war, my newlywed parents launched eagerly into the peace. They had a lucky country to celebrate, they had jobs to do, families to make, and they did it all as if to make up for lost time. Children came fast. I was born at the end of 1944, my brother John in the middle of 1946. No one worried if they could afford it; after the negativity of war children were a welcome affirmation of life. This resilient generation of young adults stitched together their lives, and the wounds from the seemingly endless war began to heal.

However, a letter Eva received from her cousin Muriel Hobbs in London in November 1943, two weeks after my parents had married, indicated difficulties ahead. Muriel, expressing her condolences on the death of Eva's RAAF pilot son, John, said, 'His loss must have been terrible,' and she hoped that Eva's daughters-in-law would have boys to replace him. She went on:

> We can't make out why you don't want any grandchildren, it seems strange to us, especially when there are such losses on the battlefield. The birthrate in England is taking a big upward move. Dick and Ruth sound as if they are the type who ought to have children. We need them from the better stocks.[1]

But in Granny's eyes, my mother was not of 'the better stocks'. Even the birth of my brother, named after his lost uncle, did not alleviate Eva's bitterness. She did not, my mother recalled, bother to visit the hospital when her firstborn son's own firstborn son made his appearance.

Chapter 4

The House on Florence Avenue

The arrival of baby John when I was a toddler was probably traumatic, as the abrupt dethronement of the eldest child has been since the beginning of time. However, it was not as traumatic for me as it was for my first friend, Anita. Anita lived in the next apartment to ours when John was born. She was jealous because I had this new baby doll called a brother. She tried to throw John down the stairs. My screams brought Mum flapping to the rescue.

Soon afterward, we moved from our cramped second floor flat to Florence Avenue, Kew. Our new house was, in my memory, the most pleasant of all we lived in. Here we had a house to ourselves, with a lovely verandah to play on, and a green lawn upon which my mother set up my easel and butcher's paper so I could paint. I was happy. I even had a new bestie to replace the naughty Anita. A little girl with the same name as me, Margaret Ann, known as Margie, lived in the next street over and we became fast friends.

The idyll of an intact household must have lasted only a few months. In October 1946, my father embarked on a long sea voyage to his company's headquarters in cold, hungry England. He would be away for nine months. A chemical engineer, during the war he had been one of the highly trained technicians at the No. 5 Explosives Factory outside

Melbourne. This munitions-making factory was owned by ICI (Imperial Chemical Industries), which also jointly owned the phosphoric acid and phosphate manufacturer, Albright & Wilson. The British-based company had set up in Melbourne in 1939, and now, in peacetime, wanted to expand. Our country's geographic position offered the promise of new markets in Asia.

Before the war, Australia had based its economy primarily on the export of raw minerals and on agriculture. Looking to the future, the Labor government's agenda included big plans to invest in infrastructure, immigration, and irrigation schemes to tame the arid continent and lay the foundation for a homegrown manufacturing economy. This was a siren's call to my father. All his life he lamented Australians' lack of commitment to economic independence, and he welcomed the chance to go to England to be trained in the management of Albright & Wilson in Melbourne. His wife and children did not go with him.

England in the winter of 1946 and '47 was grim and bitterly cold. In the cratered cities, scarred by gritty bomb sites, people lived by the ration coupon, eating very little meat and few vegetables. In Australia, while butter, meat, tea, clothing, and petrol were still rationed, deprivation was not nearly as severe as in England. No doubt John and I, left behind in Melbourne, were better fed, and much warmer.

Dad left in October and spent his first Christmas abroad in what to him, brought up in the desert, must have been unimaginable cold. Mum showed me a picture of my father in England. He stood next to a car, ankle-deep in a white blanket. He held a shovel. In front of the car a man bent with a spade, heaving it under the wheels.

I ran my hand over the black-and-white photo, outlining my father's dark coat, pushing at the strange stuff on the ground with a pink finger. My mother tried to describe it to me, but she'd never seen it either. Snow. So white, so pervasive, crystalline and frozen. Whether she regretted not hauling us all off to England (or accepted that this offer was never made), I absorbed, sitting on her lap, warm and safe, that home was better than being away.

My father's absence brought little change in our routine. At first, when our father went away, Mum put reins on the back of my coat so I couldn't stray, and she hoisted me and John's stroller up the steps of the tram to shop at Kew Junction. The net shopping bags sagged low with their catch of white-wrapped meat from the butcher's and fruit and vegetables from the greengrocer's.

Mum realised that the black Vauxhall, sitting in the driveway in Dad's absence, could make life easier. She learned to drive. She got out and about, taking advantage of an offer by our neighbour, Mrs Wadsworth, to care for John and me. I greatly enjoyed these excursions because there were other children to play with.

I sat on the lawn at Florence Avenue with the big girls. On this warm day tiny white flowers spotted the grass. I picked up a dandelion and its wisps floated off in the light breeze. It must have been late spring—just before my birthday.

The other girls were talking about their dolls. Older than me, they clutched their superior dolls.

'I'm getting a sleepy-eyed doll. For my birthday,' I announced.

'I already have one who closes her eyes,' said one of the big girls, deflating me.

'I've got a bride doll!' proclaimed another, trumping us both.

'I have a doll who wees,' said the third.

I found this hard to believe.

'Do so,' said the doll's owner, pulling up her doll's pink gingham dress. The doll had no hair—thus missing a status symbol among dolls—but she closed and shut her eyes. She had clothes, but no underwear, which turned out to be very sensible. This was the best part. The doll's mother whipped out from her carry bag a little plastic bottle and filled it from the garden hose. She then stuck it in dolly's mouth, and whoosh! Water flowed out at the other end.

'She's called Betsy Wetsy!' her owner announced proudly. I rushed inside to tell my mother. My Teddy Bear seemed suddenly inadequate. I ordered my mother to make him dinner—a routine we ordinarily enjoyed together. Mum mixed cornstarch and water and food colouring and cooked up a mess on the stove. I grabbed it from her in a great hurry and smooshed it all over Teddy's face. His black bead eyes did not reproach me even when his fur became completely matted with pudding. I wailed in rage. Teddy's little stuffed body was without entrances or exits and he had failed the elimination test. Mum looked perplexed. Our routine of feeding Teddy was something she'd patiently put up with for months. I told her about Betsy Wetsy. She smiled.

On the day of my birthday party, the table sported a long tablecloth made from a white sheet and was crowded with chairs, some borrowed from the neighbours. Balloons wafted above and children arrived with presents and were awarded paper hats. My chest expanded with pride at being the centre of attention. Beside me on the telephone book that boosted my seat of honour was my brand-new Betsy Wetsy. To the sound of *Happy Birthday*, I reached out for my cup of lemonade. I perched Betsy on my lap, and hardly spilling, I poured her tiny bottle full. I tipped it into her mouth. My party dress soaked through. I felt wonderful. I was a proper doll mother at last.

My grandmother did not attend my third birthday party. Although she lived in South Yarra, only a few miles away, I do not remember her ever visiting us, nor we her, while my mother was left alone with two small children. By the time Dad came back from England, John had learned to crawl, then walk, and did not remember his father.

Chapter 5

Phosphorus and Father Christmas

Dad had returned from England to resume his job manufacturing phosphoric acid and phosphates, the ingredients for fertiliser. I ran to the door every evening to greet him, his day's absence seeming almost as long as his lengthy disappearance earlier in my life. As December approached, he came home later and later.

In the wobbly return to normalcy after the war, there were no toy stores pushing out a plethora of plastic. However, the fathers who worked at Albright & Wilson saw to it their darlings would not be without toys at Christmas time. The company set up a wood workshop, and during their lunch hours and after work, the men devoted themselves to the bandsaw and the lathe, making toys for their children.

The factory seemed a funny place for Father Christmas to live. Yet that was where we were going to greet him on a cool, breezy December day, miles and miles away in the smelly industrial wasteland of Yarraville. Huge pillars blew white smoke into the sky there, and great stone pipes littered the area near the parking lot. We sat in a big room and waited excitedly for Father Christmas to announce our names. That year, Christmas 1947, he gave me a beautiful big, wooden dollhouse. Seventeen-month-old John got a wooden pull-along toy in the shape of a duck. He wailed in rage at his age-appropriate present and Mum had to take us outside.

Even from my earliest visits to the factory, I knew that its business was dirty, hot, stinking, and sometimes dangerous. Phosphate rock is mined, crushed, then reacted with sulphuric acid to make phosphoric acid. Mixed with finely crushed rock, it creates superphosphate fertiliser or, in another process, sodium tripolyphosphate (STPP), used in detergents. The sulphuric acid itself is made using molten sulphur.

Some years after the man in the red suit and white beard gave us our toys in the factory cafeteria, perhaps when Mum was in the hospital recovering from giving birth to one of my younger brothers, Dad took John and me to work. Looking down from a gallery, we saw workers stripped to the waist, sweating near a fiery furnace as it disgorged molten slag. I was frightened by the noise and the heat as we watched, silenced by my father's intense concentration and concern.

Phosphorus fires happened from time to time, resulting in fatalities. My father's immediate predecessor at Albright & Wilson, Joseph Henshall, died in a fire at the phosphate furnace in 1945, only ten days after starting the job. Henshall had been manager of the No. 5 Explosives Factory, where my father had also worked during the war, so my father well knew the dangers. Henshall was one of two men burned to death when, according to a news report, a steam jet was put on a vacuum filter to clear away a residue of phosphorus, causing an explosion.[1] The horrifying account related:

> The lid of the furnace was blown open and Gorrie and Henshall were showered with molten phosphorus, 50 lb. of which was flung in particles all over the building, part of the plant of Albright & Wilson Pty Ltd, a subsidiary of Imperial Chemical Industries.

The inquest noted that John George Matthews, leading hand at the works of Albright & Wilson (Aust) Pty Ltd of Yarraville, said he saw Henshall 'fly' down the steps from a landing near the pump in a 'mass of flames'. He was screaming to his rescuers to get Dave who was 'still up there'.

The news story sheds light on worker–management relations at Albright & Wilson. Joseph Henshall, 'industrial chemist', according to the inquest, was right there with 'chemical worker' David Gorrie doing the same filthy job. To my knowledge, workers did not go on strike at the company at any time during my father's tenure, but the job itself provided sufficient pressure. The workers endured difficult working conditions day after day, and the managers, responsible for safety and training, had to meet production targets.

While my father was busy at the factory, Mum's time was also productive. My father left the education of his children to his wife. He probably listened with only half an ear when she told him that while he was away, she'd heard of a progressive school, Preshil. She had, she told him, enrolled me for February, the beginning of the next school year.

Chapter 6

A Bookie's Daughter

Preshil was a non-denominational, coeducational school founded on ideas espoused by Maria Montessori and Rudolf Steiner, and its educational philosophy embodied Mum's principles of kindness while instilling a love of learning.

I hung on Mum's skirts as she sewed my school dresses. At three years old, I could not wait to go to school. On a February day in 1948, we walked up the gravel driveway from Barkers Road, my mother carrying John. When I spied the green wooden tram in the playground, I raced ahead. Children swarmed, climbing the roof, clambering over seats, pretending to be passengers and conductors. In the infants' section of the schoolyard a sandpit, spilling with buckets and spades, angled itself invitingly.

'You go now, Mummy,' I said, jumping into the chaos.

Mum looked crushed, absorbing, as mothers do, her first baby's first day of school, a milestone tinged with sadness.

Our rented house on Florence Avenue was two tram rides and a bus ride from the school. Driving the car, new to Mum, was still a luxury. She had to use ration cards at the petrol pump, so she arranged for me to go to school in a carpool. Each morning, she walked me, with John in the stroller, around the block from Florence Avenue to the Whitelaw's house. My friend Margie lived there with her parents and her mysterious, seven-year-old sister Elizabeth.

A timid little flaxen-haired boy, Ivan Ralph, clutching his lunch box, joined us in the carpool.[1] Ivan, at three, was the same age and size as the Whitelaw's enormous teddy bear. Teddy was one of the gang. Each morning we said goodbye to him, and we three younger children crushed into the back seat of a seat-belt-less black car. Elizabeth sat proudly up front next to the driver, a thin, nervous woman with a bun—Miss Wren.

While I loved going to nursery school, Margie seemed more ambivalent. At only two and a half to my three years of age, her infantile behavior annoyed me. She sniffled as we piled into the vehicle. 'Goodbye, Mummy, goodbye, Mummy,' Margie crooned all the way to school, scrunched up on her knees on the back seat. Waving, and kissing the back window, she mourned her mother and made white smears on the glass.

'Don't be a baby,' I said to Margie, then, guilty, put my arm around her.

Elizabeth stared forward resolutely, ignoring her little sister. Miss Wren's brown bun wobbled slightly as she gripped the steering wheel, but she didn't turn around to tell us not to squabble as she motored the Humber with careful precision to school.

How Miss Wren came to drive us is a mystery. I presume it was a paid job. The Wrens had petrol to spare. But since no one else had petrol to spare, it seems my painfully honest mother had not enquired too closely into the provenance of the fuel, almost certainly bought on the black market.

I cannot prove this, but from some deep recess of memory, I knew that Miss Wren was the daughter of the notorious bookmaker John Wren and, possibly, a member of the Communist Party. John Wren[2] has been the subject of several books. Born into poverty in Collingwood, he rose to political—if not social—prominence through business acumen, shrewd investing, and widely presumed criminal activity, although he was never charged. When he made his money, through the so-called 'Collingwood Tote', Wren and his wife moved to a mansion in Studley Park, Kew. His close friend, the Catholic Archbishop Dr Daniel Mannix, lived nearby. Wren became politically active in Labor Party circles as an avid anti-communist.

Poor Miss Wren! Several years later, her life would be torn apart when Frank Hardy's book, *Power Without Glory*, became a sensation. The novel, about a man called John West, paralleled Wren's story, revealing him to be a gangster. Hardy wrote the novel to show the desperation of working-class life and how the accumulation of great power is corrupting. In the novel, West exerts influence and sows fear wherever he goes, becoming close to the archbishop and politicians.

Written in a wooden, social-realist style, the book would have sunk into oblivion were it not for the fact that its author was sued for criminal libel. Frank Hardy was a known member of the Communist Party. Wren's sons no doubt thought that a judge would side with them when they sued Hardy for his depiction of 'Nellie West', based on their mother. The sons were outraged that in the novel Nellie had an affair. A debacle ensued, as Wren as West became cemented in the public's mind, and Frank Hardy was acquitted.

Wren's biographer, Niall Brennan, says one of Wren's four daughters, a product of the elite Sacré Cœur Convent, became a communist. *Power Without Glory* has this daughter—'Mary'—married to another communist. One of Wren's daughters was in fact a communist.[3]

That one of John Wren's daughters became a communist shocked some people. But she would have been much closer to the proletariat than the doctors and lawyers in the Kew

Branch of the Communist Party of Australia, of which, living nearby, she may have been a member, along with Ivan Ralph's parents. Presumably she had many relatives living on the wrong side of the Yarra River[4] who dreamed of a better life for the masses.

John Wren had grown up in destitution in Collingwood, just outside the inner city, and his brother (like West's brother in the novel) had been flogged in prison, leaving outer and inner scars and a hatred of the Establishment.

* * *

My family lived in relative comfort, but poverty and how society should alleviate it worked its way into my childhood subconscious. Two-and-a-half years after the war had been won, the country still struggled. The federal Labor government had asked Australians to make personal and financial sacrifices during the war. Without anticipating the pent-up demand for physical comfort, the government maintained strict rationing of goods, some even up to 1950. These moves to maintain stability may have been well intentioned, but they were unpopular with the very people they were supposed to help.

At the beginning of 1948, when petrol rationing made driving a luxury, Melbourne tramways employees struck for more wages, despite the fact that the Commonwealth Arbitration Court had just mandated the forty-hour working week, a major victory for unions. Alarmed about the rocketing inflation rate, the Labor government wanted to maintain control over prices and rents. It put the question of price controls to the people in a May 1948 referendum. The people rejected it.

The federal government tried to nationalise the banks, but this move, too, proved unpopular with the conservatives, and unsatisfactory for the left. Labour unions, sixty-three per cent of the workforce, were rumoured to be controlled by communists. Disruption was their weapon of choice. Even a Labor government, traditionally friendly to workers' rights, lost patience.

In Queensland, railway workers struck for nine long weeks from February to April, 1948.[5] A severe drought had caused milk and meat shortages, which exacerbated nutritional challenges caused by rationing. When unions struck for more wages, the Queensland government responded with restrictive measures, including warrantless arrests. The only Communist Party member ever to be elected to parliament, state or federal, was hospitalised after being beaten by police. As soon as the strike was over, Prime Minister Ben Chifley, a Labor leader in general supportive of workers' rights, instituted the Australian Security Intelligence Organisation (ASIO), the country's first secret service, to investigate suspected communists.

In our geographically enormous country, essential services such as transport, electricity, and coal production were state run. When workers in these crucial industries struck, chaos ensued, and anger grew. Industrial disruption became a way of life for a large part of my childhood, with rippling effects into our own family.

Bubbles of dissatisfaction had begun to boil around us. We children lived right in the middle of it, unaware, but affected nonetheless.

Chapter 7

A Haven in Hampton

My daily delight at Preshil soon came to an end. Perhaps our landlords had taken advantage of their new ability to raise the rent and pushed it beyond my parents' ability to pay. In any case, as the first blossoms of late August opened to the cold southern winds, we lost the lease on our house on Florence Avenue.

Melbourne was in the grip of a severe housing shortage. Soldiers had returned to pluck wives and perplexed babies—all those babies—from makeshift quarters in cramped spare rooms. Shiploads of refugees from Europe found their new homes to be communal tin huts. Suddenly, there were no houses to buy or even rent.

'What's a *maisonette*?' I asked as we drove for miles at night, way past my bedtime. Dad had packed up our car with our suitcases—we owned no furniture—after he came home from work. It seemed a hurried departure. Possibly my mother had seen an advertisement in the morning paper and resolved to take the place sight unseen.

'It's a house, divided into two,' my father explained.

The move was a step down in our living conditions. Ominously, the landlady lived on the other side of the paper-thin walls.

The next morning, Dad had just gone to work, and a shadow fell across the door. The landlady had come to call.

As two-year-old John caught sight of this strange woman staring at him unsympathetically, a stream of urine trickled from the hem of his overalls onto the floor.

'No!' the woman yelled. 'No, no. No, I will not have it!'

Mother made light of it and offered tea. To no avail. The outraged termagant told her to pack our things immediately and leave. Less than twenty-four hours after we had moved to our new house, we were homeless.

Mum's first thought was to ring Aunt Kitty, the youngest of her own deceased mother's siblings, and only sixteen years older than my mother. Great-aunt Kitty told us to come right over to her two-bedroomed bungalow in seaside Hampton, with our suitcases.

Kitty, also known as Kit, was not a kisser. She was over six feet tall and her spinal curvature, which in her last years confined her often to the couch, limited her ability to bend to kiss a small child. Oh, but Kitty positively spilled love. Laughter, too. Great gales of it. She made a game of our presence. That night, I slept on the sofa and John on two club chairs pushed together. Our parents took the spare room.

Kit's husband, Bill Rudd, was in poor health, caused by injuries he'd received fighting in Gallipoli.

'It's his stomach, shot up in the First War,' Auntie Kit explained. 'Ruined him. Shrapnel in the belly,' she said. 'Never got it all out, and it gives him nerves.'

In spite of his problems, Uncle Bill and Auntie Kit were generous in the extreme. With their only son grown and out of the house, Kit found us an outlet for her prodigious energy. While our father went to work, Mother combed the classifieds and bravely tested her new driving skills in the battered black Vauxhall as she roved far and wide looking for a rental. Kitty made a suggestion to get us out of her way while she did the housework. Bill would take us crabbing off the breakwater in the Bay.

Bill marched us down to the windy pier, where we settled on rocks, water slapping at our feet. We dangled rods made of sticks and string on which we hung little parcels of rotting meat obtained for a few pennies from the butcher. The greedy crabs extended their claws around the bait and we hauled them up. John picked up the tiny crustaceans and stroked their soft bellies as their claws helplessly waved in the air.

'Throw back the littlies so they'll grow big,' Bill said.

But the pier was so busy with anglers the crabs never had a chance to grow bigger than a shilling. Bill often caught a fish for dinner, and we carried it home in a bucket to Kit's kitchen. We learned to look forward to her strange cooking: steamed cauliflower with tomato sauce!

With rationing still in place, feeding an extra family of four must have challenged Kitty and Mum. A weeklong bakers' strike in Victoria in October 1948 did not help. John remembers the women's trepidation about 'borrowing' one of Bill's beloved bottles of beer to use its yeast to make bread.

Nevertheless, they put on a spread for my fourth birthday, celebrated in Hampton. A table had been laid in the sunroom and the neighbours invited. I filched a pre-party sandwich and was reprimanded. I cried, but the tears stopped when I saw the cake. Perhaps Mum and Kit shared their ration cards to make the bright yellow cake, rich with butter. Until 1950, each adult received a ration of only 454 grams of butter every two weeks. Fortunately, Kit and Bill kept hens, so eggs were freely available.

I remember this as a happy time, my parents handsome and loving and reunited after Dad's absence. As winter turned to spring, miles and miles of bushland outside the city lay waiting for the word 'developer' to be invented. The opportunity had arrived for my parents to be free of landlords and living with relatives.

'We'll build a house,' Dad said. 'Just for our family.'

My parents put a deposit on a block of land, hopeful for a brighter future, certain it would come, even if they'd have to wait.

Meanwhile, John and I lived in the present that spring, as we clambered over rocks to investigate the precarious life of the crab, held in the bosom of love by an older couple (as it seemed to me, though they were only middle-aged) whose lives had been far from easy. As always, in times of trouble, Mum had turned for emotional sustenance to her mother's family, the Lords. The sense of security this beloved great-aunt, this vast family, bestowed took me through my childhood and beyond.

Chapter 8

Lords and Ladies

The Lord family included a vast panoply of first, second and third cousins, all known by name, age and location. Mum's matriarch was her maternal grandmother Ruth Lord, a woman of great energy and determination. In 1948, Ruth Lord had only been deceased for eight years, and her influence was still felt in the family. My mother's mother, Estelle (called Stell or Stella), had been the fourth of Ruth's ten children. Kitty and her twin Jack were the youngest.

My mother's family had settled by the 1850s in the cool, south-eastern portion of Australia. Like many who came to its shores, the family had many unhappy migrants in its ranks: orphans, juvenile delinquents, absconded sailors, and adventurers. They were English, Irish, or Swedish by birth. The women found themselves (as so often happened) unwilling partners in the dreams of others, a common story among pioneers. Every one of my immigrant forebears to Australia came to the goldfields. But they found more gold in supplying the diggers than in the digging, and so became grocers, farmers and publicans.

Great-aunt Kitty was the keeper of the family lore. My youngest brother Chris remembers Kitty's stories well.

> Kit was a great talker. From the perspective of six decades, I can see she was more than that. She was a storyteller. I

remember countless evenings in the kitchen, my mother at the stove in the corner and Kit and I shelling peas at the table as she peeled off the legends. How Jane Leary from Skibbereen in County Cork had set out for America with her brothers, but had been separated from them on the docks and come to Australia by mistake. She never saw her siblings again. How Jane married Thomas Constable at Geelong and went to the goldfields at Ballarat. How their daughter Ruth had married Sam Lord II, and bore five girls and five boys. How, when the war came, the older boys enlisted in the Lighthorse and took all the farm horses with them.[1] How Kit's third brother (yet another Sam), had been trampled beneath hooves and never really recovered, but first and second brothers Arthur and Frank had been heroes and won medals. And how Kit's dear husband Bill had been shelled at Gallipoli, shipped back to Australia, patched up, and sent back to the Western Front only to be wounded again at Ypres. Kit taught me that my family's past is a real part of my life, just a part I wasn't there to experience.

Kitty inherited her great height from the Lord side of the family, and their destiny captured her imagination. Kitty's grandfather, Devon-born Samuel Burgess Lord, arrived in Australia in 1845. He returned to England, but found he missed the young colony so much he wangled a job as a steward on a passenger ship bound for Australia. The ship sailed from Ireland, and Ann Williams, the daughter of an English army officer stationed there, heard that groups of impoverished girls from the workhouses were being sent to Australia to populate the colony. This scheme, initiated by Lord Grey, Secretary of State for the Colonies, helped alleviate the effects of the famine then depleting Ireland and provided domestic servants and future wives for the distant land, where men outnumbered women. It is not clear how Ann came to be recorded as 'an orphan from the Clonmel Workhouse', since her mother was still living in Ireland, taking care of Ann's two younger brothers. In any event, Ann was one of the shipload of Irish teenagers on the *Elgin*, which docked at Adelaide in September 1849.[2] Doris Draffen, her granddaughter, wrote, 'Grandma must have been a very attractive lass at seventeen. Dark curly hair, and Irish blue eyes, she was very nice looking. Grandfather fell in love with her and they were married when the boat reached Adelaide'.[3]

After their marriage Ann moved to Geelong to join her married sisters, and Sam rejoined his ship. After two more years, he resigned or deserted from the merchant navy, and the Lords set off for to try their luck in Ballarat at the height of the goldrush. Ann was pregnant with a baby girl, who died soon after birth. At some point, Sam had a leg amputated in Geelong Hospital—presumably the result of an accident— and, without anesthetics and antibiotics, he is lucky to have survived. After his venture at the Ballarat goldfields, Sam took his profits, and in 1865, he and Ann settled on land in a district with an unpromising name: The Stony Rises.

By then the first easy finds of the goldrushes had begun to diminish and some of the former miners 'selected' land, which the government insisted the squatters relinquish to others. Samuel Charles Burgess Lord was one of these selectors. He ended up owning hundreds of hectares of dairy land at Pomborneit in a beautiful fertile region of the Western District of Victoria near Camperdown.[4]

My aunt, Nan Hutton, imagined Sam and Ann Lord's journey to their selection:[5]

> My great-grandmother set off to found her first home walking with her young husband behind the bullock wagons they were pushing through the Otway Ranges.

She was travelling light. There were no fine dresses packed among the stores and farm machinery. Flour, salt, the crates of hens and the few sheep to found their flock were more important. In time, she did enlarge her first slab hut, and there was space for new furniture and English carpets bought in Geelong. She achieved her heart's desire, a good solid house furnished in the 1860 mode.

Sam Lord also selected 200 grazing hectares at Princetown, about sixty-five kilometres away near Warrnambool. These were the years of Australia's newfound prosperity, brought on by gold, but also by abundant rain and good harvests. In the 1870s, the Lords found themselves in an agrarian paradise, with enough for all, each (white) man equal to any other, workers and owners alike. Meanwhile, Ann kept on bearing children, eleven after the death of baby Sarah.

Sam and Ann had eight sons. In their adolescence, these boys must have helped Sam manage the farm. As they grew older and married, the farm could not support them all. They moved, seeking work, returning with their families when their father aged. In 1898 the land was subdivided, part of it bought by Sam Jr, the eldest son.

Sam Lord II and his wife, Ruth (*nee* Constable), moved with their ten children to 'Colantet', the house on the dairy farm at Pomborneit. A devastating drought followed, along with an explosion in the rabbit population and possible mismanagement. With the dairy farm no longer profitable, Ruth Lord saw a life of unpaid drudgery ahead for her older children. In 1908, she abandoned Colantet, and her husband.[6]

Ruth, using a small sum she had obtained from her brother, acquired a house in a fashionable terrace in the city and ran a boarding house. Ruth Lord almost certainly had other reasons for leaving Sam Lord—reportedly, he loved to gamble more than he liked to work—but the move meant the youngest five children, three of whom were teenagers, could be educated to the secondary level.[7] At the time, public high schools did not exist in country districts, and at Pomborneit, children were educated only to eighth grade in a one-room schoolhouse.

By the time Ruth Lord made the move, Stella, my mother's mother—apprenticed as a 'junior teacher' in this rural school—was working toward her formal teaching qualification in Geelong. Stella met Bertrand Charlholmes when she was teaching at a country school in the Wimmera with the unfortunate name of Carapooee West. Bert was visiting his aunt Eliza nearby. They married while World War I raged a world away, and had three daughters, Ruth (our mother), Nancy, known as Nan, and Marjorie.

Chapter 9

Shaped by Early Grief

Bert supported his family, modestly, on his salary as a clerk for the Victorian Railways.

'My father was very good with sums,' my mother said. 'But, as a country boy, he had no chance of secondary school education.' He left school after eighth grade, possibly even sixth. Obtaining a job at the Railways gave him job security, but not much chance of advancement. Stella helped with family finances by going back to teaching, even while the girls were young.

Then disaster struck. Stella was diagnosed with Hodgkins lymphoma. The expense of Stella's radiation treatments threw the family into a financial crisis. My mother's memoir[1] tells of the terrible year of 1928.

> It was obvious that the disease had returned and she [Estelle] was put into a nursing home close to our house, where our father and Nan and I were able to visit her every night. Little Marjie, our mother's darling baby, had been sent to Aunt Jean and Uncle Stan in the country for the school holidays, but in fact she did not return from there once the illness became rapidly more serious.
>
> For the rest of the year, Dad, Nan and I remained in the house, we two girls got the meals after school while Gran [Ruth Lord] used to come to do the washing and clean the

house once a week. By January 1929 mother was so ill that she had to be taken to a different hospital, and Dad, Nan and I went to live with Uncle Ern and his wife, Aunt Nell, who at that time had one child, Shirley . . . Nan and I saw her [their mother] only once during that year—probably also because it was felt that it would be too upsetting to see the change in her, as it was. Our father continued to visit her regularly, despite the long journey, until she died on 2 September 1929. He was most devoted to her always and never married again, although I am sure he could have.

An alderman at his church and a Mason, Bert was said to be a gentle, kind man, but he was not about to shake up the world. When Stella died at the age of thirty-six, she left her husband with three daughters, aged thirteen, twelve, and eight. Her unsuccessful X-ray therapy for Hodgkin's Disease had cost more than her husband's weekly wage. This was now cut by two-thirds because Stella's death coincided with the start of the Great Depression. Eight-year-old Marjie continued to live with the relatives who had taken her in, while the older girls lived in a succession of temporary placements until they moved in with their grandmother, Ruth Lord, in Melbourne. My mother's memoir dwells lovingly on the way their grandmother, trying to make up for their loss, 'woke us each morning with a glass of lemon juice' and prepared a breakfast of boiled eggs. She continued this practice until they were well into their late adolescence.

Both bright, Ruth and Nan each gained entrance to the MacRobertson Girls' High School, the most academically competitive state high school in the city. Their differing personalities became evident as they became teenagers. Mum was diffident, and uninterested in clothes. Nan loved a bit of bling. She wanted money to buy clothes and go out. Bert wanted his daughters to have an education, but Nan insisted on leaving school at sixteen to become a typist. Mum wrote:

> Our father was not happy with this. Nan had disappointed our father by refusing to stay on at school after the Intermediate year; she wanted to get out into the world and had insisted on going into the Commercial forms, where typing and shorthand were taught, although she would no doubt have gained a scholarship if she had stayed the extra two years. So, by the time I started at the university, she had been working for one year, in the Repatriation Department. She was always so pretty and popular, full of life as she was, with so many suitors.

Shy and serious, Ruth wanted to go to university. Evidently her teachers had told her she had the talent to do so. But as the Depression deepened, there was no money for it. Moreover, she felt guilty that, unlike Nan, she could not contribute to the family's finances. At the very least, she would have to earn a scholarship, but in 1932, the Depression's nadir, very few girls completed their full secondary education. Stella's brother, the brilliant Uncle Frank, a teacher, persuaded my mother that if she were to study extra hard under his coaching, she might take the two final years of school in one and thus qualify to matriculate. They did not tell her father.

While Bert had apparently wanted his daughters to get an education, he probably imagined them finishing high school or, like most girls of the time, leaving before the final year. His mindset is implied by my mother's secret plan. Was Mum afraid that Bert would mock her ambition, be jealous of it? Perhaps she did not want to make him anxious about her lofty goal and the great possibility of failure.

The matriculation exams were very difficult and remain so. When I was a teenager, only eight per cent of Australian students went on to university. Ruth's chances of admission were slim. She was trying to cram two years of study into one. Despite the hardships, she persisted.

My mother recalled that her grandmother Ruth Lord would try and get her to go to bed; Mum wanted to burn the midnight oil. Nan was in on the scheme, saving from her typist's salary so that Mum could pay the university fees and buy books.

To her surprise, my mother not only passed the matriculation exams and was accepted at Melbourne University, she was awarded a Free Place, a scholarship on condition that she undertake teacher training while working toward her BA. As indicated in the announcement of this achievement in the *Argus* on 3 February 1934, only forty of these university scholarships were awarded among high schoolers across the state.

But teaching was not in her future. Unlike her apparently more outgoing mother, my mother hated the profession. She wrote in her memoir:

> I had applied for a place in the Education Department before leaving school, and in the August term break a notice came from the Department appointing me to a position at the State School in Cremorne St, Richmond (a Melbourne inner suburb). Because of the Depression I was among the first group to be appointed in that year and was considered very lucky to have been given a place in the city and directly on the railway line which was closest to us. I started as a junior teacher ... Going in with such high hopes, after the happy picture I had gained from my mother and Uncle Frank, who both loved teaching, I found that I hated it. I was far too shy, and although my pupils were very young, it was incredibly hard for me to control them. Richmond at that time was a slum area and the poor children were

already accustomed to being disciplined violently, quite differently from the way we had been brought up. Each morning I got off the train feeling sick in the stomach at the thought of the day before me. At the end of the year, I applied to the Education Department again, to allow me to finish the final two years of my BA, to which they agreed. How happy I was to return to the university in 1936.

My mother hated teaching, but she craved learning. If she was not going to teach, she needed another way to support herself. After graduation she worked as a secretary, and later applied for a job in the music department of the ABC, the Australian Broadcasting Commission. Within three months she was transferred to the Talks Department. Soon her role changed again when, following Britain's lead, Australia entered World War II in September 1939. She wrote:

> The university released Macmahon Ball to take over the position (leading the Talks Department) . . . and my favourite lecturer became my boss. He was there for about fifteen months, until he was asked to head the newly established Radio Australia, which was set up as a counter-propaganda agency against enemy broadcasts.

Here my future mother found a job that not only suited her temperament, but profoundly influenced the rest of her life.

> It was a very interesting job, with several departments, a news service with a number of journalists, 'talks' writers to counter the Japanese propaganda in the Pacific area, and linguists in the Listening Post who translated the incoming enemy broadcasts.

As the war wore on, she composed and edited propaganda aimed to counteract the Japanese offensive. She felt, she told me years later, that she was fighting for her country no less than any soldier. She was grateful to be doing something useful in a way that burnished her skills of analysis and writing instead of trying to keep order in a classroom.

My mother had fought for her education and seen its transforming power. Yet, this lesson seemed lost on most of the population, obsessed as it was with football and horseracing, gambling and alcohol. Her experience teaching in the violent slums led her to challenge the idea of conventional education for her children. And her job—its international outlook contrasting sharply with the small-minded provincialism of Melbourne suburbia—gave our mother progressive ideas.

Education had given my mother a job she loved and access to an intellectual milieu. Quite possibly her mind-expanding job made my father—highly intelligent, handsome, but from a background vastly different from her own—attractive to her. My parents both loved books and hated most spectator sports, which made them unusual in their environment, allowing my mother, when she first met him, to feel 'as if I had come home'.

That was an ironic statement, considering what home was to mean to them both later. But for now, living with his wife's relatives in cramped quarters in Hampton, my father made the best of the situation. Soon things changed for the better. My mother had found us a house.

Chapter 10

Charlie and the Cherry Cake

Although cheerful and uncomplaining for the ten long weeks we crammed into Kitty and Bill's modest two-bedroom home, my father must have been relieved when we moved to a rental at 42 Fairfield Avenue, Camberwell. The house had been part of a deceased estate, with filthy floors and old furniture that John remembers 'a fat man took away'.

In their delight to have their own home again, my parents made moving an adventure. Behind the simple, one-storey bungalow was a backyard of grass higher than my head. That disappeared quickly. I remember a scythe, forbidden even to look at, let alone touch. The bedroom walls soon bloomed with the pastel calcimine paint my parents sloshed on together, singing. Their bedroom became pink and remained so, no matter where they lived. They painted the children's room yellow, so neither gender could claim it.

John Edquist recalled: 'There was tremendous excitement when an instant hot water heater was installed above the kitchen sink. Until that time, the only hot water available was in the bathroom, and to wash dishes Mum had to boil water in the kettle.'

Every day, Mum piled the clothes, sheets and pillowcases into a huge, dangerous copper washing tub to boil them. In an age of cloth nappies, it boiled and boiled, heated from below the copper by a gas-fired burner. After the wash,

Mum fished out the steaming laundry with a hook, wrung it through an enormous wringer till the water ran out in a flood, and hung it out on the clothesline with wooden pegs.

In the kitchen, an icebox cooled our food. Every few days, a man with a horse and cart came with huge blocks of ice, hoisting them in canvas sacks from a dolly into the cavern of the ice chest. In hot weather, the ice drooled down the door when it opened, and condensation formed mist on the front.

Horse-powered deliveries of ice, bread, and milk greatly assisted homemakers. At that time everyone had vegetable gardens to supplement rationed food supplies. A Chinese market gardener drove his horse-drawn cart through Camberwell, selling fresh fruit and vegetables. Any horse manure left on the road was immediately shoveled up and put on the vegetable garden.

Soon after our arrival, a little boy appeared at the door with a plate of cupcakes.

'Mum says these are for you,' he said.

'Thank you, little boy,' said Mum. 'What's your name?'

'I'm Stephen. Can you,' he said, peering past our mother to John and me hovering behind her in the hallway, 'come and play?'

At Auntie Kit's and Uncle Bill's, John and I had spent playtime with the older couple, but here at our front door, to our shy delight, stood a boy our own age. So began a friendship between the Wilkins and Edquist children and their mothers. Mum and 'Charlie' Wilkins, mother of Steve, his baby brother Peter, and yet-to-be-born Suzette, became lifelong friends. Years later, Steve, a physicist and friend of my husband John Spence, delighted in telling people he and I had known each other since we were three and four.

Each morning we'd race down the hill to greet Stephen, who'd bolt his cereal in his haste to get on with the action. We were cowboys and Indians, cops and robbers, tricycle experts, and paint aficionados. Children in those days had little supervision. John and Stephen took turns in bashing each other on the head with a rake. Whoever had his revenge on the other proudly remembered the event for years afterwards.

Mum had so much to do in the house she could not watch over us the way mothers watch over their kids today. We children played on the verandah, often out of sight. This was how, one day, I served the neighbourhood kids 'tea' in the tiny cups of my toy set. We had no real tea, so I substituted. I'd often hosted pretend tea parties with my dolls and my imaginary friend, Lady Jane. When I poured the kerosene, I didn't mean for anyone to drink it. But John put the cup to his lips, about to take a sip. I screamed, and Mum came running. I was spanked for this infraction, and John was made to vomit.

Tea parties soon became too tame for our gang. As the oldest, I was the ringleader in naughtiness. It was my idea to paint ourselves red to make ourselves look more authentically 'Red Indian'. We found crimson paint in the Wilkins' garage and emerged, fierce and scarlet from eyebrow to kneecap, from a garage now decorated in Jackson Pollock fashion. The tribes were just getting going in a wonderful battle, whooping and hollering, when Mrs Wilkins—Charlie— emerged from the kitchen.

Charlie had the mildest manner. I had never heard her raise her voice to her children. Now, she stood there, completely silent. We froze. Her lips thinned and tightened.

'Hand me that turpentine,' she said, finally.

'Ow!' we squealed as she applied the smarting liquid with a coarse cloth. 'It hurts!'

'Good!' said Charlie. She scrubbed and scrubbed till our skins were shiny as lemons and we were sent home in disgrace.

The Wilkins family had escaped from Czechoslovakia just as the Germans invaded. The war had ended four years earlier, before John and Stephen were even born, but images of war still intruded into our consciousness, and into our games. John remembered:

> Sometime in 1949, I was at the Wilkins' house. We heard a low flying plane approaching. Stephen insisted we had to go outside, so I ran out with him. He instructed me in the appropriate behaviour for such a situation. You had to examine the plane's wing markings. If it had British roundels (red, white and blue concentric circles) or American stars, you had to cheer, jump up and down, and wave your arms. If, however it had black crosses (German) or rising suns (Japan) you had to run down into the vegetable patch and lie down in the ditch between the cabbage rows. We jumped up and down, waving our arms and cheering the British (Australian?) plane. Somehow, we never saw a German or Japanese plane.

Steve also told John that, unlike us, he had no cousins. 'They were put in trucks and gassed,' he said. John could not believe this preposterous tale.

> This clearly untrue story of Stephen's worried me. Why would people do such a terrible thing? I feared he would get into trouble saying crazy things like this. I worried how I could warn him about this without upsetting him. I never did get to talk to him about it.

But Stephen's tale was true. Around the window frame in the kitchen of the Wilkins' warm and happy home hung black-and-white photographs of dark-haired people, their heads tilted towards each other. In the backdrop of these posed pictures rose tall mountains Charlie called 'Alps'. I asked about the photos.

'They left too late,' Charlie said.

I stared at her, bewildered. 'Why are you crying, Charlie?'

'Because they couldn't come with us. They died in the camps.'

How could camps, which I associated with tents and cozy campfires and picnics with the billy boiling on its stick over the flames, be a problem? But the people in the photos were, indeed, gone, lost in the concentration camps of Europe.

How could this wonderful Wilkins family, so filled with love and living in a house wafting with the tempting aromas of cooking, walls of books, and a swing in the backyard, pose such a threat that police would come, herd them into trains, throw them into prison camps, and then . . . I asked Mum about it, and she tried to explain the Holocaust. I couldn't understand it. Who can?

Over the next few years, my parents would befriend a number of Jewish refugees and their families, and they added great *joie de vivre* to our lives. Charlie made the best cherry cake I've ever tasted. The recipe was Czech, a word I learned to spell early, thanks to her.

After being squeezed in with relatives, we were finally living like the families in picture books—a mother, a father, a daughter, and a son.

Chapter 11

Cherry Blossoms

Sometimes on Sundays we packed the car and drove to Eltham. At that time, Eltham—muddy in winter, euphoric with the scent of eucalyptus, the peal of bellbirds, and sudden spills of pink as galahs cascaded through the trees—was a settlement on the fringes of Melbourne. Carved out of the scrub on a hilltop, our destination had earned a bohemian reputation through its artists' 'colony' of Montsalvat, a small medieval-style village with cobbled courtyards, mud-brick art studios, cottages, church, great hall and refectory. Sprawled under the gum trees, its chickens pecking at the pebbles, Monsalvat looked like Tuscany in the Antipodes. A little higher on the hill, a productive farm with several mud-brick adobe houses was just as charming.

My godfather, W. Macmahon Ball,[1] lived here with his wife Katrine and their daughter Jenny. Mac, professor of political science at Melbourne University, had become fond of my mother when she worked for him at the Australian Broadcasting Commission during the war.

Blue-flowered plumbago spilled exuberantly over the adobe walls at Mac and Katrine's farmhouse. Jenny, then aged eighteen, had her own separate dwelling on the property, which she showed us if we were good. Her unmade bed and the university books littering the studio room made her life seem audaciously free. The fruit from apricot, peach

and apple trees was used in Katrine's scrumptious jams
and pies. Ponies, a cow and its dairy, chickens, ducks and a
large vegetable garden—which included maize, a vegetable
I hated and had to eat politely when we were there in late
summer—added to the country atmosphere.

Inside the mud-brick house, a flagstone-floored kitchen
with an old cast-iron stove and one big open living/dining
room seemed to me to contain everything needed for the
art of living. Oriental carpets overlaid the polished floors.
Books lined the walls and spilled over every available
desk and table. Around the room, with its gleaming long
table and dark ceiling beams, oil paintings glowed softly,
their traditional themes of landscape and still life evoking
tranquility. One artwork in particular drew me, of a table,
a small jade bowl, and a tall blue-green vase overhung with
pink cherry blossoms, one or two of which dropped to the
table. How could an artist create another reality, I wondered,
so static, yet so true?

Along the shelves, Katrine displayed Japanese porcelain.
Mac had collected the delicate, almost transparent
china when he was a member of the Allied Council for
Japan immediately after the war. This appointment is
an extraordinary footnote to history. Mac Ball not only
represented Australia's interests in the reconstruction of
Japan, he represented all the Allies. The appointment did not
go down well with the British Foreign Office, nor General
MacArthur, who knew that Australia's Labor government,
which had chosen the liberal-minded academic, was not pro-
American. Inevitably, Mac Ball had sparred with General
MacArthur and been recalled. He'd only recently returned
from Japan.[2]

Mac was a towering man. Even a child could see he was
handsome, with thick wavy hair and a dimple so deep on
his chin you could stick a finger in it. His voice, whether

offering an opinion or suggestion, resonated with the deep, vibrating tones of a double bass.

'Here, just touch this. See how smooth it is.' He took my hand. A child who still played at tea parties with my imaginary friends, I stroked the surface of a tray as black as licorice. On the lacquer, a delicate peachy-brown twig flared to a blossom. Gold paint trimmed the tray and glowed inside the cups. 'I'm giving this to your mother,' he whispered to me. 'A present from Japan.'

Katrine smiled. Small, pale and powdery, with snowy hair piled on top of her head, she reminded me of a meringue. 'It's good to have him home,' she said, taking my mother's arm.

'Let's see what's in the cellar, shall we?' Mac led us away from the women. Dad grinned—wine at lunch!—and from a trapdoor in the kitchen we scrambled down the rickety steps to the cobwebbed cellar. Dark and spooky and smelling of the ripe apples stored there, the cellar was lined with shelves, where, in the dim light, row upon row of fruit-filled jars shone in muted colours.

'I bottled this myself from a local vineyard,' said Mac, selecting a dark wine bottle from its recessed cubby. He brought it upstairs to the lunch table.

With the dark-red plonk enlivening the conversation, my father would be in no condition to drive home for hours. So, after lunch, we children went exploring, creeping over the cobblestones. Just as in fairy stories, a wishing well tempted our fate. John and I struggled to move its splintery wooden cover to look into its depths. Curious ducks from the fowl yard waddled over to get a look-in, as did the dog.

'Let me put the bucket down the well! Please!'

'No, I want to!' We squabbled, then took turns.

Soon we moved to climbing the trees in the orchard, swinging from their wide low arms till the grown-ups called us in. For afternoon tea, Katrine boiled up an enormous kettle, and produced scones light as goose down, laden with cream from the cow and homemade jam.

Katrine, with her bun of fine white hair, blue, kind eyes and below-calf-length flowery dresses, would have been called an 'earth mother' in the 1970s. Her huge canning pot was always on the boil with the season's apricots, tomatoes, or beans. Mum always said John would have been named Katrine, had he been a girl, so beloved was the older woman. Mum pronounced the name 'Katrin', but to Mac his wife was always 'Kay'.

Kay's serenity provided the rock on which the busy life of Mac Ball depended. In addition to teaching at Melbourne University, he also wrote books and newspaper articles, opined on international affairs on radio each Sunday, hosted convivial parties and, in his role in Japan, had ridden the bucking horse of diplomacy.

Mac was able to see both sides of a question. At the start of the war, then Prime Minister Robert Menzies had asked him to become controller of short-wave broadcasting, later called Radio Australia. As leader of the conservative Liberal Party, Menzies must have disagreed with Mac's more progressive views, but the emergency of wartime made him overlook petty concerns in the cause of national salvation. In fact, though they disagreed politically, Mac Ball and Robert Menzies had been friends since youth. In that spirit of broadmindedness, Mac picked people of widely divergent backgrounds to work at Radio Australia. Besides journalists and academics, some of them were immigrants who could be described as 'enemy aliens'. Presumably Mac believed brainstorming with people who'd experienced a wider life could help Radio Australia inspire those trapped by the conflict.

As she helped Mac Ball write the copy for the airwaves that beamed out over the Pacific, my mother must have considered the values of the country she promoted. She believed in the Australian version of democracy as deeply as any soldier in the field. In this heady, fair-minded atmosphere my mother had thrived in a job she loved. And now she relished the lively conversation over lunch and bottles of wine at the home of her former boss and his wife, who had become a mentor. While Katrine did not work at an outside job, her productivity was tremendous, and she enjoyed— apparently—the frequent parties at the farm. These often resulted in guests staying the night after they had imbibed too much to risk driving down the steep, potholed hill to town.

My parents' block of land was in Heidelberg, not so far from the earthly paradise of Eltham, its natural beauty captured by the Australian Impressionist painters Tom Roberts, Arthur Streeton, Charles Condor and Walter Withers.[3] At that time, the houses petered out at the edge of the foothills, and eucalypts outnumbered the telegraph poles, rising as high into the sky, giving the hills from a distance their distinctive dusky blue. The developers had just begun to invade the orchards that thrived by the river below the hills, and in spring the apple, peach, pear and cherry branches hung in a haze of pink and white spring blossom. My parents were saving to build a house there.

But during the spring of 1948, just after we'd moved to Fairfield Avenue, and our old-fashioned house had been cleaned and painted and we'd made friends with our neighbours, we were in for a surprise.

Chapter 12

The Family Grows Sideways

'Daddy's going to bring us a baby this weekend,' my mother said. I did not believe her.

'But Daddies can't have babies!' I protested. My favourite game was to play having babies with my numerous dolls, including my favourite, Betsy Wetsy.

'Dad's going down to Tasmania to bring back your baby cousin Kristin and your Aunt Nan,' Mum explained. Or, rather, didn't explain at all.

White-bundled, Kristy arrived in a pram. The spring sun shone on her tiny, curious face as she took us in. John and I stared down at her. Suddenly, she smiled. I was enchanted. This was not a scrawny newborn, nor a plastic doll, but a baby five months old, already pretty, with blue eyes and vanilla hair beginning to curl. John and I adored her as if she were a little sister. For the first four years of her life, she lived with us as a sibling.

My mother was quiet, serious, placid and patient; her sister Nan, just fourteen months younger, was pretty, impulsive, passionate and vivacious. Nan was a blonde foil to Ruth's dark hair and hidden nature. My mother, five foot three, with blue eyes and Scandinavian skin so fair she broke out in hives when she went in the sun, was a non-favoured brunette. Or so she thought.

'Gentlemen prefer blondes,' she would say to me, who compounded the apparent unattractiveness of brown hair with brown eyes as well.

My mother always thought Nan's flair came from being blonde and, thus, more popular. But in the genetic lottery, my mother had also inherited beauty. With her high cheekbones, she looked a little like Ingrid Bergman, and with her dark hair flipped at the end, a little like Jane Russell. From her Irish ancestors, she had inherited skin as creamy as a bar of Ivory soap. The sisters had lovely figures and legs that curved as neatly as violins.

Soon after the war, and a three-week engagement, Nan had married Dick Nicholls, a handsome, fair-haired Tasmanian. His late father, Sir Herbert Nicholls, a judge, had also been a politician and had served as Tasmania's lieutenant governor. His mother, using the name 'Lady Nicholls', which her husband's knighthood conferred, was intimidating.

Perhaps the family's local fame had dazzled Nan's normally perceptive eye. Dick and Nan had little in common, but the marriage started with high hopes and a sense of adventure. On their honeymoon, they'd driven through the Victorian countryside with horse and gypsy cart. Nan and Dick, both aspiring writers, planned to write a book about the experience. But, as the weather cooled, cooking over an open fire and sleeping under the stars lost its appeal.

In her autobiography, my mother wrote about the couple. 'On their return they went to Tasmania, where he had been given a position as a (farming) trainee on a property in the midlands. It was not a happy marriage.'

Mum was prone to understatement. Tasmania is colder by far than Victoria, let alone tropical Queensland. Nan, one generation removed from the farm, had never before lived on one. By August of their second year together, when the frost and snow had melted and the apple blossoms again scented the air, a pregnant Nan wanted her husband's farm life to end.

Worrying letters came from Tasmania. Dick Nicholls showed little interest in the farm and was not taking responsibility as he should.

'I had to calm a horse bucking in its stall, by myself, when I was seven months pregnant,' Nan reported.

In fact, Nan faced a much bigger challenge. Her husband was caught in the vicious, hopeless grip of mental illness.

'After her baby girl was born, Nan couldn't pretend any longer,' Mum said. 'She couldn't stay there without any family to protect her. She was not safe.' She did not explain further.

Nan had called my mother for help. My father took only a few minutes to decide. 'I'll go and get her,' he said, thus earning my mother's eternal gratitude. He, with Aunt Kitty in tow to help, brought Nan back with her little girl Kristy to live with us at Fairfield Avenue.

It all seemed perfectly normal to us at the time. Only as adults did we—John, Kristy and I—consider the implications of what Nan had done. Her departure horrified her mother-in-law. Nan had snatched her son's baby away, fleeing without custody arrangements in place.

My father nearly lost his job over his intervention into Nan's domestic affairs. Lady Nicholls knew the chairman of my father's company. Indeed, she was his sister-in-law. She tried to have my father fired. After he'd flown to Tasmania over the weekend to rescue his wife's sister and her baby, my father was called before his boss. One can imagine the scene.

Awkward to the point of inarticulateness about this intensely personal matter, the director and my father drew on vast reserves of Anglo-Saxon restraint to beat about the bush.

'Called you in to tell you I married my wife, not my wife's family,' my father's boss croaked, finally. Dad went back to work.

Somehow, we all squeezed into the little house on Fairfield Avenue. We three kids shared the lemon-walled room crammed with two single beds, a cot, a big yellow chest of drawers, and a changing table. Nan took what had been the dining room for her own. One bathroom, our parents' room, a 'sitting room', a washhouse where the cat lived, and a kitchen completed the house.

I loved Kristy like a large doll. On cold July days when rain kept us indoors, I clomped through the house wheeling Kristy in her pram, talking to my imaginary friends and tottering in Mum's dusty high heels and one of Nan's tilted hats, its veil obscuring my vision as I knocked into the walls.

Mum looked after the kids, while Dad and Nan, to whom Mum felt a blood-loyalty, went to work. Dad worked on the other side of the city, a tedious commute, and he left early. Nan always got into a lather about being late as she dressed Kristy in the mornings, then cursed a laddered stocking. She expertly applied her lipstick without a mirror and grabbed her purse to clatter down the street in the near dark. As we were eating breakfast, she was catching the tram, then the train, into town.

Nan, a typist, had found work as a journalist on the *Argus*, Melbourne's oldest newspaper. Her prose flowed, as witty and lively as her conversation. By the time she came to live with us, she was already a published writer, thanks in large part to Mum. During the war, when Nan had been working with the American forces in Queensland,[1] my mother had sent in a few of her entertaining letters to the *Argus*. The editor published them. So, when Nan arrived in Melbourne in late 1948, as a single mother in urgent need of a job, the newspaper took her on. Later, she wrote her own newspaper column and dished out advice as the lonely-hearts expert for the Australian magazine *Woman's Day*.

Mum never mentioned her own days in the paid workforce, of lunch with friends and her own spending money. Our family had grown sideways, as it were. And now we were to grow again. John and I were sent to Auntie Kit's for a few days because my mother 'had to go to the hospital'. When she came home again she was still large of belly.

'You're a fibber!' said one of Kitty's more tactless friends. 'I thought your mother was having a baby!'

John and I were confused and embarrassed our mother's failure to produce a brother or sister. In fact, our mother had been rushed to the hospital in premature labor, and after a few days of rest in the heat of early summer, came home. Her asthma, which always flared up under duress, returned.

Chapter 13

The Move to Grange Road

In January 1950, the summer burned so hot that leaves turned brown, shrivelled, and fell to the ground. As we slid out of our cramped car, legs sticky from sitting on the back seat, our sandaled feet felt the stab of gravel as they dropped onto a curving driveway. An old, wide, two-storey brick house with a dark, cool porch stood in front of us at 5 Grange Road, Kew. Built in 1904, the house had all the latest features of the Arts and Crafts style: pretty stained-glass windows, large rooms, and window insets in the front door. It was, I learned later, the kind of house real estate agents advertised as a 'Gentleman's Villa'. Even my childish eye could see that this house was much bigger than any house we'd ever seen.

Our father and his mother, Eva, our Granny, had gone inside. Outside, my mother remained with John and me, perspiring in the heat.

'This is our new house,' Mum told us. 'We're moving soon.'

'Tomorrow?' John and I asked.

'Soon,' she said. 'Stay in the shade.' A huge yew hedge, soaring to meet the jacaranda swaying purple in the corner, separated the garden from the street. White oleanders hid the side fence. Pink lady lilies nodded their heads in the flowerbeds, along with fuchsia bushes, whose buds I was dying to pop. Mum, in a white sleeveless shift, sat in a canvas chair in the dappled shade of a liquid amber tree, her dress spread wide over her pregnant belly.

The pink, purple, and white-flowered garden, washed in searing light, contrasted with the cool, dark interior, we were to find out later. The interior, however, was forbidden territory. Neither we children nor our mother were invited inside.

Mum sat in her sagging chair that hot afternoon, while John and I sprawled around her feet. I looked up from her white ankles to her swollen maternity shift and into her face. It wore a look I would come to recognise. I can only describe it as 'stricken'. Why were we waiting so long for Dad and this Granny we barely knew to rejoin us?

In January, faced with her doctor's belief that she could no longer live alone, Eva Edquist, our paternal grandmother but a virtual stranger to us, bought the house at 5 Grange Road. About ten kilometres from downtown, Kew even then was an older, desirable suburb. Houses dated from the early twentieth century, and the streets were wide and leafy. Grange Road ran from its top at Cotham Road—on the tramline to town, opposite the Genazzano Convent—then alongside the Kew Reservoir and its green 'oval', or park, down to stately Sackville Street, lined with large old houses. Sackville Street ran perpendicular to Grange Road and intersected with another tramline on Burke Road.

'Private School Mile' it was called. A slight exaggeration, but no less than six well-known private schools stood within a walk or a short tram-ride from our house. With a great address, a dozen rooms, and a mature and lovely garden planted by a botanist, 5 Grange Road had the potential for gracious beauty. A well-to-do widow by then, Granny must have wanted to help her son achieve the social status she and her husband had once enjoyed. At the time, the bargain my father struck with his mother must have seemed like a good deal to him, too. She would buy the house, and he and his family could live there as her tenants. What my mother thought of this arrangement no one seems to have asked.

As my brother Chris put it, 'For reasons best understood by my father, he had allowed himself to be persuaded to forego building a new house near the river and, instead, move his family in with his mother. Convenient for her. A sort of low-level marathon in hell for my mother.'

Granny bought the house and, in March, she moved in—with my father, my very pregnant mother, Nan, and three children. Our grandmother took the two front rooms with their view of the gracious front garden. One of the first things she did on settling in was to fill two glass-fronted cabinets with her treasures. She carefully placed her vibrantly coloured Royal Doulton china, her collection of ruby glass, and a big block of quartz in two glass-fronted, white-painted cabinets. The quartz glowed, shimmering and mysterious, seamed with gold. It came from the mine Victor had owned when they met. We scarcely knew Granny Eva. But now, as we gazed at the large, white rock with its ribbon of gold, we wondered about it. This rock, and what it represented, remained a mystery for us Edquist children, because despite the fact that Western Australia was our father's birthplace, he rarely talked about it and never took us to see it. Nor could we imagine that Granny could ever have lived in a place so far away.

While Granny inhabited the front rooms, the rest of us—including Nan and Kristy—lived upstairs and in the back of the house. There was no upstairs bathroom. Strings dangled from light fixtures. On the windows of the upstairs 'sleepouts', or sleeping porches, hung the remains of brown blackout curtains from the war. What later became my parents' bedroom served as our living room downstairs, and we also used the dining room with its long slim windows opening onto the verandah.

Between the kitchen and dining room, a 'pass through' provided great delight. A set of drawers held everyday cutlery on one side, good silverware and table napkins on the other. If a child, in the kitchen, pulled hard on the cutlery drawer, it could be forced from the grip of the person holding on to its knob in the dining room, leading to many satisfying tugs of war.

The kitchen, at the centre of the house, was poorly designed and hard to keep clean. On one wall a cabinet rose from floor to ceiling. This 'cool cupboard' held bags of onions and potatoes on its floor. Above them, on slatted wooden shelves, we kept the fruit and vegetables and, above those, brightly labelled jam and canned goods. The one-doored refrigerator burst with butter, milk, cheese, meat and, occasionally, ice cream in its minuscule freezer. Next to this, a tall, narrow wooden cupboard held spices, oil and vinegar, packets of tea, and what was charitably known as 'coffee essence'. To its left, nestled in a corner, a gas cooktop and grill sat next to an oven, its cream door edged in apple green. Battered saucepans competed for space under it and spread their way across a corner, then to cabinets beneath the sink. The sink sat under a tall window looking onto a bottlebrush tree next door. Its slightly dented sill always held a couple of water glasses holding parsley, or a child's science project, with sprouts growing in damp cotton wool.

Across the kitchen, on the other side of the wooden table and chairs, drawers held scissors and string, shopping lists and bottle openers; while, underneath, cupboards held cereals, flour and baby foods. On a counter above, crowded with the toaster and the bread bin and its board, my mother and grandmother carved bread into slices with a serrated knife. There, too, stood the Vitamiser in which Mum blended milkshakes and juiced our oranges.

The back door from the kitchen opened to a little room

filled with the water heater and tall cupboards holding brooms and cleaners. To get outside, you had to open yet another door. This tiny vestibule functioned as an airlock, keeping the house warmer in winter. We did not have central heating till I reached high school.

The main bathroom we shared with our grandmother.

'I'm not sure if "shared the bathroom" is a fair description,' my brother John said.

> I recall having baths and, later, showers there, but we boys, at least, were forbidden to use the toilet. We had to use the servants' and tradesmen's toilet that opened to the outside between the kitchen and the laundry. It was always cold out there, which I guess is why Granny insisted on it— along with the pleasure of humiliating our mother. Mum put up with this sort of petty tyranny all the time, but seemed to feel she could not complain to Dad, who must have had an amazingly large and well-developed blind spot not to notice anything.

Never warm, the relationship between my mother and her mother-in-law soon iced over like the Antarctic. My grandmother's constant, disapproving presence in what should have been my mother's domain—her own household—drained Mum's emotional and physical energy. It sucked the joy out of her. The move to this house in 1950 marks for me a dividing line between the happy mother I remember as a very young child, and the harried and anxious one I knew afterwards.

Chapter 14

From Spinifex to Suburbia

Before moving in with us, Granny had been living alone, surrounded by her antiques, in the upscale suburb of South Yarra. Despite its address, her 'English style period brick building', in the words of a real estate advertisement, must have seemed to her a mockery of the living quarters she had come to expect.

In 1935, her husband—our grandfather Victor—had received a promotion, from manager of the Sons of Gwalia mine in Western Australia, to be Bewick Moreing's[1] senior operating officer in Australia, and to serve on its Board of Directors.

My father wrote, referring to his parents by their initials, VTE and ELE, 'They looked for fully-serviced apartments to save housework, since ELE [Eva] suffered from asthma, and settled on "Myoora", Irving Road, Toorak.' Toorak was Melbourne's wealthiest suburb. Not only that, but my grandparents chose to live in a house with servants. Even in Toorak this was unusual, particularly then, given the extent of the Depression. In 1936, as today, home foreclosures must have haunted some of Toorak's nouveau and not-so-nouveau riche.

My father goes on to reflect—with some pride and embarrassment—on what this move, with its prestigious address, meant to his parents.

They were quite unconscious, of course, of the social implications that many Melbourne people read into such an address. It was well within VTE's means; his income, which included a share in BM & Co's profits in Australia and some consulting fees in addition to salary and director's fees, was higher than most in a Melbourne that was just emerging from the Depression. The life style was not entirely unfamiliar; they had had domestic staff at the manager's house in Gwalia, and distinguished visitors to the goldfields invariably stayed there, in the days it was a full day's travel from Kalgoorlie. VTE was well known and respected in the mining world, whose headquarters were in Melbourne, and his circle of acquaintances had included pastoralists since the days at Gundagai. ELE, as an educated Londoner whose sisters and cousins were university graduates when this was a rare distinction for a woman in England, was not likely to be overwhelmed by the cultural weight of Toorak socialites. The chief trouble was the climate. After so many years on the goldfields, they needed a fire in their rooms right through their first year in Melbourne. They stayed at Myoora until after VTE's death in 1944.

Granny had not just been the wife of a man who had risen from humble beginnings to one who had a 'seat at the table'. She saw herself as his full partner in every way. However, in spite of Victor's upward mobility, one can see that, given Dad's implied attitudes to their new neighbours, their move to Melbourne must have been a two-edged sword: good for them financially, but challenging on the social front. If my father thought pastoralists were at the top of the social tree, there were none to be found in Toorak.

At the time of Victor and Eva's move to Melbourne, their daughter Mary was seventeen. After the family moved east, Mary earned a bachelor of commerce degree from Melbourne University. Few women chose this course of study. However, the university experience, far from encouraging her social life, probably reinforced Mary's isolation. And her mother could not help her.

Eva, who'd never had a social life as a young girl, did not know how to launch Mary, dressed in the plain and proper clothes of a provincial town, in fashions already out of date. Upon graduating, Mary took a job as a bursar at Invergowrie, the finishing school for housewifery, and remained living at home.

Then Victor died of colon cancer. Only ten months earlier, Eva and Victor had learned of the death of their beloved youngest son, my father's brother John. My father wrote:

> John, Flight-Lieut. RAAF, died in an aircraft accident at Wagga, 30 July 1943. He had joined the RAAF in 1940, and had logged 1089 flying hours. VTE was deeply affected. A few months later he was operated on for cancer, and he died on 4 May 1944.

Only sixty-two when her beloved husband died, Eva was completely devastated. She often said, 'I married the best man in Western Australia.' Without Victor, Eva was left virtually friendless. She had said goodbye to her mother and sisters in London in 1908 and had returned only once to see them. Eva relied on Mary for companionship. The two moved to a flat on Kensington Road in South Yarra. This address, too, was upmarket. Presumably, the apartment was less expensive than the one they'd left, but it had several flights of stairs.

My parents by this stage had two children, myself and John. Yet, we were rarely invited to visit our Granny and our Aunt Mary in their aerie. Seemingly looking down on us from their nest, they lived quietly among their English antiques and faded Oriental rugs, virtual strangers.

Mary remained unmarried and lived with her widowed mother until she was well over thirty. Then she received a letter from Western Australia. Mining engineer Peter Wreford's wife had died, leaving him with boys now four and two years old. He looked through his little black book for candidates for wifehood, he recalled, and remembered Mary Edquist. No one could be more suitable. She knew the hard life of a mine manager's wife, was clearly capable, intelligent, and unattached.

After Peter Wreford travelled the width of the continent to Melbourne and took Mary to dinner, the deal was struck. As they parted at Granny's front door after this date/proposal, Mary raised her face to her future husband's and said, 'It is customary for engaged couples to kiss.'[2]

They married in 1948. Mary moved back to Western Australia to raise Peter's boys, to have three children of her own, and to follow the itinerant lifestyle of a mining executive's wife. It was a life much like her mother's, albeit, thirty years later, more comfortable.

After Mary's departure, Eva was left completely alone for the first time since she'd met Victor. She was not well. Grief-stricken by the compounding losses, in less than six years, of her son, her husband, and her daughter's companionship, she turned to her eldest son, Dick, for support.

There was much more to learn about my grandparents' life in Western Australia and the mystery of why my grandmother behaved the way she did, but it's clear that the move to Melbourne had plunged my grandmother Eva into a far different social situation than the one she had known in Western Australia. And now, she had to enter the household of a woman with whom she had absolutely nothing in common: our mother. For our mother, the situation must have seemed reversed. A battle for control of the household began.

Chapter 15

Seen But Not Heard

For Granny, downsizing from a flat in exclusive South Yarra must have been galling. Even though she took the two best rooms in the house, the living arrangements would have been uncomfortable for an arthritic old woman. She slept on a chintz sofa made up as a bed in one of the rooms each evening. In a more formal room, beyond a maroon velvet curtain, she entertained other elderly ladies at bridge from time to time, using the precious Royal Crown Derby china she kept under lock and key in glass-fronted cupboards. In her bed-sitting room, she warmed herself by a porcelain stove, which John filled with coal every day in winter.

> I still clearly remember how hard it was to fill a coal scuttle about half my height with coke and then carry it inside to Granny's room on freezing cold mornings. After that, I had to take the saucepan of boiled vegetable scraps, stir in bran stored in the garage, and feed the resulting hot porridge to the chooks in their pen behind the woodshed.

Near the stove, Granny had her writing desk. A coloured plaster bust of Winston Churchill, cigar in mouth, sat in watch over the room from the fireplace mantel. The firescreen was embroidered with images of Windsor Castle. Under the window seat was a trove of English magazines from the 1930s, many featuring covers of the two little princesses, Elizabeth and Margaret. John remembered:

> Next to Winston Churchill, and taking pride of place on Granny's mantelpiece, was the framed letter from the Governor-General regretting to tell her and Victor that their son had given his life for King and Country. Losing a brother in one war, and a son in the next, must have been hard.

Granny was nearly blind and extremely irritable. Stooped with osteoporosis, her fragile frame was held together by an iron will, her skin so paper thin that her cheekbones nearly erupted from her cheeks. She tied her grey hair in a bun, wore dark dresses, thick beige stockings, and clunky black shoes. Whatever the occasion, she dressed as unassumingly as a sparrow.

To the end of her life she maintained her British formality. After fifty years of acquaintance, she still called her closest friend 'Mrs Adam'. At first, Mrs Adam and a few other old friends came to play bridge, but as they gradually died off, Granny became more and more isolated. I'm not clear how she spent her days, since she and my mother avoided talking to one another as much as possible.

Both part of and separate from family life, Granny never sat down to a meal with us. Finding us too noisy, she ate from a tray in her room and listened to the radio. My brother Chris remembers 'my grandmother sitting in a dim room, untroubled by the gloom as her eyesight had failed, listening to what we called "the wireless". She seemed always to be listening to the stock report'.

Perhaps to avoid her, we spent time in good weather on the verandah. Screened against the swarming flies, it opened to a large backyard. My father worked in the garden and we tore through it playing cops and robbers, but the adults did not relish the idea of living outdoors. Mum was allergic to the sun, and Dad had grown up in a climate where people sought shade. Those living in Melbourne in the fifties had yet to catch on to the notion that they lived in a quasi-Mediterranean climate instead of a transplanted British one in which, frustratingly, rain did not fall enough to nourish the imported plants. Our culture would be transformed by what was then regarded as the dubious influence of Southern Europeans, but that was in the future. Melbourne's Italian and Greek immigrants had yet to teach Australians to enjoy the outdoors and dine at tables on the terrace.

Still, the back garden filled all our needs. Mum pinned the laundry on the Hills hoist, that unique Australian clothes-drying contraption of spokes and wires, its centre hoist cranked up by a handle. To help carry the laundry down the long lavender path from the washhouse, Dad engineered a cart from an old baby stroller, with a lift-out basket so our mother could hang the wash alongside the rosemary bushes.

Next to the rosemary, Dad laid rows of vegetables and turned a big compost heap. We kept chickens beyond the woodshed. Plum and apple trees lined the back fence, and we planted an orange and lemon tree. All fruited prolifically. Melbourne can be very cold in winter. On frosty July mornings, the lemons hung low on the tree, sometimes falling with a squish on the icy dew. In the middle of the garden, an old *prunus* tree burst into pinky-white blossoms in August to announce the end of our sharp, but short, southern winter. Later, it settled into soothing, dark-purple-brown leaves.

John recalled:

> The *prunus* was our play tree, conveniently located over the sandpit as it was. Dad had built a small platform in it, slung between several branches. It was just big enough to hold two or three children, and many a time I and my

70

brothers, and or a friend or a boy from a neighbouring house, landed our rocket on Venus, or struggled to fly our badly damaged bomber back from Germany. Often, when flying back on a wing and a prayer, we would have to abandon the plane before it ditched into the North Sea, climbing out from the burning aircraft onto the wing (a convenient branch) before leaping into the water below (the sandpit).

In my memory it is usually summer at 5 Grange Road. Sometimes a scorching drought sent the birds toppling dead from the trees. But mostly it was somnolent in its suburbia. There were noises, of course, mostly on weekends when people were home. The hens clucked and scratched. A clop of tennis balls preceded shouts of 'love fifteen' from the tennis court nearby. The boy next door wailed as his father walloped him. My father chopped wood. Bicycles crunched the gravel drive. Children shrieked as they dashed under the hose to get cool. On summer mornings the bees buzzed in the nasturtiums. It was peaceful, safe.

If my mother had enjoyed the outdoors and my grandmother had not been so frail, perhaps the pleasure of enjoying tea in the garden could have compensated for the friction in their indoor lives. The garden was certainly my refuge. A few years ago, I took a class in gardening. The instructor asked us to remember a garden we loved, and I found myself writing, for the first time, about my father's garden. I realised it had everything in it that a gardener needed: a vegetable patch, a compost heap, a woodshed, chickens roving free in a large wire enclosure, fruit trees and, in the front, exotic plants and the beautiful jacaranda and oleanders.

For me the garden was a place of serenity. No wonder Dad spent as much of his weekend there as he could. Inside the house—my mother and grandmother's domain—the kitchen was a place of awkward interaction and emotional discomfort. Who was in charge here?

Perhaps my mother's advanced state of pregnancy enabled Granny's habitual dominance. When we arrived, my mother's main discomfort must have been physical. A month after we moved to Grange Road, our brother Andrew made his appearance. But instead of joy at his safe delivery, our mother seemed to wilt, like a head of lettuce left too long on the counter.

I wasn't the only one to notice this alteration. It was so pronounced, John said, 'I thought the nurses at the hospital where Andrew was born had switched my mother.'

When he told me this, only recently, I was amazed, because I, too, thought there had been a switch at the hospital. But I, five at the time to John's three and a half, had projected this onto our dear little brother. I believed for years that my mother brought home a baby who was not our own. Rationally, I knew that could not be true, but I could not shake the idea that a profound change had riven our family, and our mother would never be the same.

And she needed to regain her energy. She had three young children to look after, plus Kristy, and all of us were vulnerable to a polio epidemic sweeping through Melbourne. One of my classmates woke up with a headache and came back to school months later with irons on his legs. The son of Mrs Jones, the nursery-school teacher, died within a day.

Aunt Nan wore gloves to work, and she bought me little white cotton gloves, too, to board the tram, explaining how we needed to be careful about germs. Just beginning to read, I studied the Dettol ads on the tram, picturing an army of germs being slain by antiseptic.

We did not get polio, but the next raw winter whooping cough kept us home from school. One day, Mum shouted and I ran into the room where she was holding Andrew, a horrified look on her face. Andrew, about fifteen months old, had been coughing and whooping, a terrible rasping for breath. Suddenly, he went stiff and his eyes rolled up into his head in a febrile convulsion.

'Help me!' Mum cried, and I ran to Granny to call the ambulance. We were allowed to visit him in the hospital isolation ward once to bring him Precious, his grey velvet elephant. But a strict matron with a white triangle around her face shooed us out, and we had to go home with the sound of Andrew's anguished, despairing screams fading as we bundled into the car. When he came home, Andrew, already a quiet child, no longer tried to say new words. He joined our mother in an emotional space away from us all. He did not talk till he was almost four, when he suddenly broke out in full sentences.

Mother always said he'd been traumatised by his hospital experience. But then, he was born, unlike his older brother and sister, into a house in which our grandmother insisted, 'Children should be seen and not heard.' This dictum apparently applied to my mother as well. She left unspoken all the retorts that must have risen like gall in her throat. And this led to her buttoning up her feelings in front of us. The mother who used to sing as she dandled me on her knee was silent. I recognised her always-busyness. In a house with no modern conveniences, her constant work was a necessity. But this was different. Her spirit seemed to slip and sift till it sat puddled like flour on a plate. Whether Mum suffered from severe postpartum depression or whether she just collapsed under the strain of living under the thumb of her mother-in-law, I don't know.

However, my childhood expectation for the future changed. I had once believed that mothers were powerful and made decisions. Now, I saw that they could not protect their children, and they were powerless to act in their own defence. That could, of course, have been in keeping with the times, for the fifties had arrived.

Chapter 16

Battle of Ideas

Mid-century. The generation that had survived the Depression and World War II should have been celebrating. Yet anxiety grew. Not only in our home but outside as well. Public anxiety reflected events happening due to political changes to the north. During the war, the Dutch East Indies, which had been under Dutch control for more than 300 years, fell to the Japanese. After the Japanese surrendered, the people of the area now called Indonesia saw no need to return their home to colonial masters. Rebels gained support against the Dutch, with significant bloodshed on both sides.

Dr Herbert Vere Evatt, Australia's Minister for External Affairs from 1940 to 1949, had played a role in the formation of the United Nations, and was on its first Security Council. Recognising that our country's security relied on peace in the region, in November 1945 he sent Mac Ball to Jakarta to find out what was going on. His report persuaded the government to urge the United Nations to negotiate the dispute between the Dutch and the rebels.

While the issue for the people of Indonesia was nationalism rather than communism, the Indonesians' fight for their independence from the Dutch was aided by communist agitators, including Australians. The Waterside Workers' Federation openly supported the independence movement, despite the fact that leaders of both Australian major political parties gave shelter to the Dutch NEI (Netherlands East Indies) forces and government-in-exile.[1] Supported by the majority of other trade unions in the country, the Australian 'wharfies' refused to load or unload Dutch ships for the next four years.[2]

Holland had been occupied by Germany during the war, but despite their suffering the Dutch did not, apparently, empathise with Indonesians who wanted to throw off centuries of colonial occupation. A bloody Dutch operation to secure the resource rich areas of Sumatra and East and West Java in July 1947 finally led to United Nations Security Council intervention. Louis Spence, father of then-infant John Spence, who later became my husband, was attached to a United Nations military mission to Java to help supervise the ceasefire in Indonesia. In September, he spent two weeks interviewing local commanders and officials of the Republican-held areas and reported back on the difficulty of communication and finding common ground with the enemy, not to speak of danger to the peacekeepers themselves.[3] A cessation of hostilities enabled that country to move forward with independence. Dutch sovereignty was transferred to the United States of Indonesia in November 1949, a month before the federal election in Australia.

At the same time this was going on, communist and nationalist forces battled against British imperial interests in Malaya. Australian air, naval and army forces were involved in the conflict on the side of Britain. While Australia had remained neutral in the Indonesian independence wars, urging peace, the Liberal Party, which came to power in Australia at the end of 1949, took the threat of a communist victory much more seriously. The so-called Malayan Emergency lasted from 1948 until an independent Malaya was formed in 1957. Australia's military involvement lasted from 1950 to 1963, its longest military commitment anywhere. On 16 September

1963, Malaya united with North Borneo, Sarawak, and Singapore to become Malaysia.[4] The turmoil in the regional geopolitics meant that, no matter which party came to power in the 1949 Australian election, the new government would have to deal with a government immediately to the north not run by European-based white people.

Since Federation in 1901, Australians' desire to be a Caucasian island-continent in an Asian archipelago had been codified into legislation. The *Immigration Restriction Act* effectively blocked all non-European incomers by requiring applicants to take a written test. This test could be in any language. Thus 'undesirable' immigrants could face a test in Gaelic or Lithuanian, with no appeal possible when they inevitably failed. I am no historian, but in reading of these long-ago events as they affected Australia, a clear pattern of fear of Asia emerges. The dread was driven by the country's geographical position. The trauma of World War II, particularly the threat of a Japanese invasion and Japan's maltreatment of its 22,000 Australian prisoners of war, loomed larger than the war losses in Europe. The country's collective war memory, together with longstanding racist attitudes, gelled the mindset of many Australians into rampant terror about communist victories not so far away.

Some people took a broader view. Mac Ball, who had written the book *Nationalism and Communism in East Asia*,[5] got into a public squabble with Labor's immigration minister, Arthur Calwell, about non-white immigration to Australia. Mac had written an article in the *Argus* arguing for a quota on Asian immigrants. Calwell responded in a pamphlet entitled 'I Stand by White Australia'.[6]

As thousands of Europeans clattered down the gangways of the migrant ships, and the British were courted by offers of £10 fares to migrate across the world, Asians found the doors closed to them. An Australian woman, who had married a

Japanese man and survived the bombing of Hiroshima with her baby boy, had great difficulty getting a visa for her son. (The woman, Elizabeth Kata, later became the bestselling author of the inter-racial love story, *A Patch of Blue*.)[7]

In the end, Indonesia did not become communist. Yet, in the popular mind, Asian countries to the north of ours became a jangling bracelet of unrest, one communist country linking to the next, spreading civil wars south. This became the famous 'domino' theory. It was a convenient visual analogy and played into the century-old terror of invasion by the 'yellow hordes'. As China went, so did North Korea, and Vietnam. Eventually, Australia would fall too.

In this tense atmosphere, the rhetorical genius of Robert Menzies cut through more pacifist voices. In the run-up to the 1949 federal election for which he was put forward as the leader of the new Liberal Party, Menzies pointed out that trade unions promoted communism. Whether this was true or not, a shiver ran through the land.

Although one might think that a manager of one of Australia's companies would not be suspected of having ties to communism, this was not the case. Anyone in a managerial or governmental post could be accused of being a communist sympathiser, sometimes called a 'fellow traveller'. Such accusations could ruin a career. As an industrial chemist, my father had many acquaintances who worked at CSIR (later renamed CSIRO, the Commonwealth Scientific and Industrial Research Organisation). These people, scientists who worked to find industrial applications of scientific research, were among those who socialised with our parents. My father must have been alarmed when a British physicist, Alan Nunn May, was convicted of spying for the Soviets in 1949, and Australian politicians seized on this fact to imply that all scientists were suspect.

When Australian nuclear physicist Thomas Kaiser, an

employee of CSIR, took part in a demonstration in London in 1949 protesting the Australian government's crackdown on striking coal miners, an action that led to his surveillance by ASIO, the CSIR management warned its scientists never to publicly discuss politics.[8] My father had not the slightest sympathy for left-wing agitators. Still, he developed a habit of refusing to say, outright, in public, what he thought about political matters. He deflected such questions with humour. I can see him now, at the dining room table, glass of red wine in hand, adroitly managing not to spill it as he gestured with gleeful emphasis at 'idiotic' politicians.

Suspicion lurked everywhere, so much so that I learned to read by deciphering political graffiti.

'What does "Ming Out!" mean?' I asked Dad one Saturday morning as we drove past a railway siding where the paint dripped its message in white menacing letters. My father took the opportunity to lecture me on the economy-disrupting power of trade unions that hated 'Ming', the nickname for Prime Minister Menzies.

Adoring my father, I accepted this political lecture as gospel. My mother did not respond to this revelation. She was taking in the washing when I told her all about the wicked unions. The wind billowed the big white sheet she was unpinning, hiding her face.

'Here, grab the end of this and help me fold it,' she said.

My mother had never worked in the private sector. Her mother had been a state schoolteacher and her father a clerk in the government-owned Victorian Railways. The loss of her grandfather's substantial family farm 'because of the drought' had made her wary of reliance on individual effort. Dad took quite a different view.

'These blokes in the public service,' he roared, 'those paper pushers, have no idea of the personal responsibility a manager feels for other people's lives! To keep them employed so there's bread on the table, to run the factory so that it maintains safety standards. A company has to make a profit to keep its workers employed!'

With these different positions, our little world at 5 Grange Road reflected the larger world, split by two visions of the future. One saw socialism as inevitable. Far from defining this as rule by government, its most radical proponents saw the working class, through union action, forcing government to do its will. The other side, the business people Menzies exhorted in his speeches, saw private enterprise as the backbone of society. His appeal to the middle class, who did not want their hard-won road to prosperity thwarted by socialists, resonated in a battle for ideas that reached into every household. At least that is how I sensed it, a child who heard heated discussions at the adults' dinner table. I didn't understand the details, but I felt the stress.

Chapter 17

Left and Right in Kew

Given the school's uneven academic results, I am not clear why Mum insisted we all stay on at Preshil after the free and easy preschool years. Yet, such was the school's psychological pull—some would say, cult-like pull—that she never seemed to consider another primary school. One advantage was its location, within easy walking distance of 5 Grange Road. By now, I no longer squirmed restlessly in the back seat of Miss Wren's car beside Ivan Ralph silently clutching his lunch box. Now I set off in the morning with Dymia Bowen, who was my age and lived two doors down, leading a group of children across several busy roads. I do wonder now about the wisdom of sending us off without adult supervision, but with two babies, Kristy and Andrew, at home, and Granny not offering to babysit, our mother had little choice. As we grew older, this practice of independence made us fearless about using public transportation and probably helped us get along in the world.

Our little gang walked to school past the rectangular lawns of the tidy bungalows, where weeds were forbidden and English trees forced out the native gums and wattles. At a time when most schools were built of forbidding brick, our school buildings rambled, long and low, opening to untidy playgrounds. Rules were few, and no one got the strap. Our school preached cooperation, not competition. There were no exams or tests, just reports on the child's development and behavior.

The Preshil method let children learn at their own speed. This worked as long as the child was self-motivated. But those who struggled with learning difficulties proved as difficult to teach, their egos as damaged, as those who remain in traditional school systems today. The school encouraged creativity, and we wrote and acted our own plays, and painted the scenery. We were allowed to hack through the shrubbery in games of explorers and cowboys and Indians, and climb the peppercorn trees, using fallen limbs and pieces of old wood to make huts: forts for the boys, houses for the girls. Not for us were the paper-littered macadam playgrounds of the state schools or the gracious lawns of the privileged private schools.

Preshil had its limitations. The principal did not believe in competitive sport so there were no playing fields. This, of course, seriously handicapped us when we graduated to secondary schools in sports-mad Australia. The headmistress, Margaret Lyttle, known to everyone as 'Mug', had us brainwashed. We were told that state schools were awful places where children were whipped, and that learning at our own pace was the only approach.

If the parents had known what really went on, they might have been concerned. The teachers did not supervise the playground, so there were accidents. My friend Helen fell off the jungle gym and broke her arm and, after another mishap, a girl named Kay sat for an hour outside the classroom with her head wrapped in a bloody tea towel before her mother came to pick her up. There was also sexual abuse of a primary school sort, common, I suppose, in many schools. The boys chased the girls around the yard and pulled their pants down.

In Miss S's second-grade class, we were not provided with

erasers. She told us to wet our fingers with saliva and to rub out the inevitable spelling errors in our writing practice. The memory of this still disgusts me. Nor were the sometimes-addled teachers any good at teaching mathematics. Miss Lyttle confessed she hated teaching it. Even my mother, staunch supporter of Preshil as she remained, became annoyed when our teachers refused to teach the times table by rote. Chanting the tables is a time-honored and pleasurable way for children to learn, but Preshil's philosophy forbade passive learning.

The pupils fell into two groups: those who could take charge of their own educations and those who for academic or emotional reasons couldn't. Because the school ran without academic streaming, friendships were determined democratically. As one of the older girls in my class, I tended to be ahead of most of the others in my work. Yet, my friends were spread among all students in the class, several of whom I remember as emotionally disturbed or struggling academically. The only child I remember we all teased, to my lasting shame, was Alice, who had spina bifida and used a walker. I regret not being kinder to her.

The usual suspects—artists, atheists and foreigners—sent their kids to Preshil. Matthew Perceval, son of painter John Perceval, was in my class; and, for a year, Sweeney Reed, adopted son of Sunday and John Reed, the art patrons. I remember a field trip to Heide, the Reed's home, then farmland in Heidelberg, and to the Murrumbeena pottery of Merric Boyd, grandfather of Matthew Perceval and his three younger sisters.[1] There was also Michael Meszaros, whose father was a sculptor (Michael later became a well-known sculptor in his own right), and Lowan Dalgarno, son of artist Roy Dalgarno. And a number of Jewish children whose parents had been able to escape the Nazis before 1939, including Peter Singer, now the famed philosopher.[2]

Our grandmother was appalled. She opened her purse to pay for the upper-crust private schools our cousins attended, but refused to do so for us. Our school was not 'suitable', she said, refusing to mention its name. Our father took a curiously hands-off approach to our education, perhaps his one indulgence of his wife's desires. The school did not bestow grades and my father never asked how we were faring. He let Mum have her way in the matter of schooling, hoping it would turn out all right in the end. I am still somewhat astonished that my mother, so outwardly conventional and sensitive about reputation, insisted on this educational choice, even when it became apparent that the education itself was lackadaisical.

Mum was a dark horse, in many ways. She kept her opinions to herself, except when she could stand it no longer. She hated injustice and felt personally the petty humiliations of the class system, muted as it was in Australia. She must have believed that Preshil would give her children the confidence to openly question authority. Or perhaps it made no difference at all. I've come to believe confidence is something one is either born with or not. Whatever Mum thought about the school, Preshil outraged the neighbourhood. 'You must be Reds!' people jeered at us. 'You go to a commie school! Commie bastards!'

* * *

One blustery day, Helena Ralph, gentle Ivan's older sister, assaulted me as I sat on the swings in the Preshil playground.

'You're an idiot!' she shouted, as the swing sagged under my weight. I was, at five, a bit too big for it.

'Am not!'

'You are! You're really, really stupid!' ranted the girl.

The attack left me completely mystified. Helena and I had never exchanged two words before. My mother informed me the Ralph family was under a lot of pressure 'just at the moment'. Perhaps the school mothers had started to gossip, noting the contrast between the bourgeois life his house implied and Mr Ralph's political beliefs.

'Can you believe it?' they may have said. 'He lives in a great big house and sends his kids to private school, but he's putting leaflets in letterboxes for the communists!'

Near the corner of Barker's Road, a couple of crosswalks from our school, stood a beige, brick, faux-Georgian house. This comfortable home belonged to someone who had a role in both changing and preserving the country's self-image of the 'fair go'. A country where, while there was still poverty and want, the harshness of the land had abraded much of the distinction between the wealthy and those who worked with their hands, a country where you could think and say pretty much anything you liked.

The house belonged to Cedric, Ivan Ralph's father and our local communist. Cedric Ralph was a well-heeled lawyer. Ironically, his actions preserved what was most precious in our democracy, political free speech and association, while he adamantly insisted on the superiority of a system that banned those liberties. Mr Ralph's law firm helped defend individuals who were being 'outed', that is, identified as members of the Communist Party. A long-time member of the party, Cedric Ralph fought the government's ban on its very existence in Australia.

How odd, it seemed, that he promoted state control of goods and services when he and his family lived in luxury not possible under the communist system. His wife was wealthy, his house substantial. Nevertheless, the couple were true believers. The Ralph's home, where meetings of the Kew Branch of the Communist Party of Australia (the CPA) were held, was the centre of a clandestine world. According to Penelope Pollitt, the Ralph's eldest daughter, the party's network 'determined which doctor you consulted, which lawyer you went to, which trade union you joined, even in some cases which business you dealt with'.[3]

A cabal of six Preshil parents tried to oust Cedric Ralph from the parents' council. In a vote, he won hands down. One hundred parents voted to keep him on the council, with only the six original opponents voting against him. Ralph reported that a neighbour who'd served in the war with him cut him in the street. The incident ended with the two men having a few beers in the pub, but the ostracism obviously hurt.[4]

My mother had not tried to have him ousted. Always compassionate to the victimised, Mum genuinely empathised with the Ralphs, perhaps more deeply than others, because she, too, felt misunderstood. Our mother was not only sympathetic to left-wing causes; she'd been active in them as a student.

In 1934, Egon Kisch, a Czech journalist and communist, was invited by the Melbourne-based Movement Against War and Fascism on a speaking tour of Australia. His mission was to expose Nazi brutality. He had been imprisoned in Spandau concentration camp before being deported from Germany and now wanted to awaken the world to Hitler's evil. For this, he was denied entry to the United Kingdom because the British considered him a revolutionary; Australia followed Britain's lead. Our mother, my brother John wrote, 'was part of the crowd on the wharf when the left-wing writer Egon Kisch, who had been denied entry to Australia, jumped from the ship *Strathaird* to the pier, breaking his leg'[5]

It is ironic that this happened just five years before Australia went to war with Germany. Eventually, Kisch was allowed to proceed on his lecture tour by a ruling of the High Court after a farcical attempt to deny him entry under the *Immigration Restriction Act*. (He had no intention of immigrating.) For our gentle mother, this injustice was a defining moment. John wrote:

> Mum told me that she had been arrested and fined £5, for demonstrating on Princes Pier, a considerable amount in those days. Because of her university activities and her membership of the anti-fascist league it seems likely that Mum would have known many of the people being attacked as 'communists'.

If leftist views did predominate at Preshil, it was an island in conservative Kew. Prime Minister Robert Menzies came from our electoral district, Kooyong. He had been the country's leader in the first two years of the war, and now his Liberal Party squeaked past the Labor Party to win the December 1949 federal election. In his election campaign, Robert Menzies made a straightforward pitch. He warned the people that the communist threat was not just on Australia's doorstep, but in its midst. Communists, he said, threatened from within the unions, and their goal was nothing less than world domination. In September 1949, the Americans announced that the Russians had exploded their first atom bomb. In October, communist leader Mao Tse Tung declared the creation of the People's Republic of China.

On 27 April 1950, the Prime Minister read to the House of Representatives a bill that would outlaw the Communist Party in Australia. His speech announced to the House the names of fifty-three allegedly communist trade union leaders. The list had been supplied to him by ASIO, the Australian Security Intelligence Organisation.[6] While the population and the press, in general, did not view communism favourably, the bill was opposed, in parliament and without, because it made those accused of being Party members guilty until they could prove themselves innocent. Furthermore, the dissolution bill threatened the principles of free speech and free association. The bill was blocked by the Labor-controlled Senate.

Two months later, in June 1950, the Soviet-backed North Koreans invaded South Korea. The Prime Minister promised two Australian warships and an RAAF squadron to the United Nations to assist the South, and left for a previously planned visit to Britain and the United States. Events overtook him, and his government declared common cause with the UK in joining the United States to push back the communists to their side of the 38th parallel.[7]

According to his biographer Allan Martin, Robert Menzies came back from his visit overseas convinced that 'Australia must urgently prepare for the possibility of a third world war';[8] political opposition to the law to ban the CPA immediately weakened. On 20 October 1950, federal parliament passed the *Communist Party Dissolution Act*.

Fine-tuned to my mother's sensitivities, I listened in on the grown-ups' conversations. Sometimes on weekends my parents had a moment to discuss the newspaper over breakfast. Or rather, my mother glanced at the headlines, and my father read the paper at leisure on the verandah.

'Menzies has banned the Communist Party! Not only that, but if anyone says you're a member, you have to prove you're innocent,' Mum warned my father. 'And you'd lose your job.' When she was angry my mother hissed like the kettle.

'Won't happen.' My father pushed his glasses up on his forehead so he could read. He pointed to an article reporting that within hours of the law being passed, six trade unions and the Australian Communist Party filed a challenge in the High Court.[9] Thrusting the folded paper under his arm, he left the kitchen with his plate of eggs and toast. A few minutes later he returned. A cold wind had blown in through the flyscreen on the verandah, disturbing his peace.

A cold wind bringing the Cold War to the bottom of

the world. Houses of suspects and state headquarters of the Communist Party were raided by the police.[10] These suspects were sometimes innocent. After their infamous identification in parliament, many of the named individuals proved to have no connection at all with communism.

As a lawyer and an outspoken member of the party, Cedric Ralph fought this anti-Communist law all the way.[11] He acted as instructing solicitor to Dr Herbert Evatt, who argued the case to the High Court, which overturned the law as unconstitutional. Not willing to concede defeat, the government then took the question to the people in a referendum.

Oh, these were not quiet times in this sunny, sports-mad country. Because of its threat to free speech, the Menzies government's 1951 referendum to alter the constitution to outlaw the Communist Party was vehemently opposed by pundits of all political stripes, from the communists— naturally—to the Australian Labor Party and even the young Liberals. Nevertheless, the referendum question lost by a vote of 49.44 per cent to 50.56 per cent, a very close call.[12] Of course, I understood nothing of all this at the time. My own battles for free speech began and ended with squabbles with my brother John and the occasional tantrum. I am sure I had plenty of them, given the tensions in the household.

But because of our neighbour, a parent at our school, it remained safe to be a communist.

At the same time, our little nexus of adjacent streets engendered a threat from the other side of the political spectrum. Our staid suburb, Kew, represented the political divide in a unique way. A bastion of the middle-class, with its mix of stately homes on leafy streets and cheek-by-jowl cottages near its shopping centres, Kew was a predominantly Protestant town, but had a sizable Roman Catholic population. (Catholic families lived on each side of our house at 5 Grange Road.)

Cedric Ralph represented the extreme left, while to the right, on nearby Burke Road, lived a figure who rose to national prominence. On his way home from work, young attorney B.A. Santamaria dropped in at the palace of the Catholic Archbishop of Melbourne. Santamaria wanted to talk to Archbishop Daniel Mannix about his plans for a new arch-conservative political party.

Bartholomew Augustine 'Bob' Santamaria had started the trade union-based Catholic Social Studies Movement in the mid-1940s to counter increasing communist domination of the unions. Reactionary in the extreme, Santamaria envisioned an Australia where peasants farmed the outback and contraception was banned.[13] At a retreat house at 12 Sackville Street, Kew, just around the corner from our house, Jesuits began secretly training priests in the conservative political activism espoused by the 'Movement'. The Movement's influence brewed a schism in the Labor Party. In 1955 it split into the Australian Labor Party (ALP) and the Democratic Labor Party (DLP), an overwhelmingly Catholic, virulently anti-communist offshoot that was to disrupt national politics for years to come.

Arthur Calwell, a devout Catholic and a leading member of the Labor Party, together with his family, experienced ostracism from fellow Catholics during the dramatic year of 1955 for not joining the DLP.[14] Calwell stated that as a staunch supporter of the ALP, he was both pro-Labor and anti-communist, but such was the authority of the Church that virtually all other Catholics veered toward the DLP. This schism caused the divided Labor movement to lose power in Parliament for the next seventeen years.

My parents were united in their dislike of the DLP, but for different reasons. My mother saw that the cleaving of Labor weakened any possibility of its winning elections; my father held the view that church and state simply should not mix.

He was happy that the Liberals went on to win every federal election until 1972.

The investigative reporter Mark Aarons described the remarkably similar techniques and beliefs of the Communist Party of Australia and the Movement.[15] Throughout the early 1950s, and despite knowing about Stalin's atrocities, Australian communists remained fiercely loyal to Soviet principles. The Party gained power through the trade unions. Meanwhile, the Movement's hatred of communism and its vision for a country based on Catholic principles thundered from pulpits every Sunday, urging parishioners to political action. The Movement infiltrated the Labor Party and unions, and later built networks of influence within cultural organisations and universities.[16] We children understood none of the subtleties, but we did imbibe our parents' and their friends' intense political engagement. Political talk buzzed in the air like a cloud of mosquitoes and was just as discomforting. It was not a good time for nonconformists.

Chapter 18

Gaslighting

After Andrew was born and our mother's spirits took a nosedive, I seemed to develop a sixth sense about how events outside our home echoed both the physical and emotional discomforts within. It must have incensed our mother that her sister, still living with our family but working full time at the *Argus*, wrote on 28 July 1950 that she should 'Be a Happy Housewife'.

'You', Nan wrote, 'are responsible for the health of your family ... The danger spots about your home are the lavatory, the sink, the gully-trap, the rubbish bin. Enemies to rout are noxious insects, rats, and mice'. No mention is made of the breadwinner's responsibility for the upkeep of the home.

Nan was writing for her audience. The idea that a tertiary educated woman should be solely responsible for household plumbing, maintenance, and pest extermination is indicative of social attitudes perhaps unique to Australia at the time. We had no refrigerator until the very late forties, and Mum was still doing the family wash in a large, steamy copper when we moved to Grange Road. The old brick house was freezing in winter and we had no central heating until the sixties. All of us suffered from chilblains. We were not poor. We were middle-class, and judging from Nan's column, my mother's life was better than many.

As Beverly Kingston observed in her groundbreaking book, *My Wife, My Daughter and Poor Mary Ann*, the country's increasing industrialisation did nothing to relieve the burden on housewives. In fact, she noted, Australian egalitarianism had the effect of making women of all classes take on the role of 'full-time domestic service'.[1]

My mother had no household help, except for Mrs Boyle who came on Tuesday afternoons to help with the ironing. Fortunately, a washing machine eventually replaced the old copper boiler, but the ironing piled up like snowdrifts in baskets in the 'sewing room', waiting for Mrs Boyle's assistance. In this room the ironing board stood in permanent position and, in winter, drying racks crammed the small space, making it hard to pass through. This unsightly area provided the only passageway to the back of the house and the verandah, our playroom, and we tore through it, knocking the white cloth nappies off their racks in our rush.

Beyond the sewing room, the back of the house consisted of a damp, cold bedroom and a bathroom—the maid's quarters. But no maid had ever lived there. This, after all, was Australia, the land where the working class ruled. Some transplanted British architect had included an essential room for a maid, but in middle-class Melbourne, no one could afford to hire one.

* * *

Even five years after the end of the war, management and unions remained at loggerheads. Unions, run almost entirely by men, struck for higher wages again and again. These strikes were often aimed at the heart of essential services. The coal strike of 1949 slowed production during an entire bitter winter. The wellbeing of children and their mothers were ignored in this political dust-up.

Inflation surged. I noticed my mother's anxiety as she counted the change at the greengrocer's. The Consumer Price Index showed inflation at a terrifying twenty-three per cent per annum at the end of 1951. Though wages more than kept up (a thirty per cent increase that year), in 1952 a 'horror' budget designed to slow inflation increased taxes at the same time as wool's export price plummeted, causing a slump. According to a study by the Reserve Bank of Australia, the cause of these extreme surges and slumps were complex and were, in some part, due to factors beyond anyone's control, like the Korean War.[2] However, frequent industrial disputes fed the inflationary spiral to the benefit of workers outside the home, but often to the detriment of workers inside it.

The labour unrest and perennial belt-tightening put continual pressure on women trying to manage their households and care for their children. Three months after we had moved into 5 Grange Road, floods devastated the coalfields, causing gas rationing. On the 30 June 1950, Nan, writing in the *Argus*, asked her readers what they thought about the shortages. Apparently, they empathised with the 'women of the flooded coalfields areas (who are) suffering great loss and hardship'.

'Not that hardship is unknown in the gasless kitchens of Melbourne,' Nan wrote.

> We found one little wife battling along in two squalid rooms, striking match after match in an attempt to persuade the reluctant burner to light, soothing her hungry toddler as he wailed for his lunch. She finally resorted to a little spirit stove to heat milk and vegetables, a dangerous contrivance in a small, overcrowded room.

In a week's worth of reporting, Nan, moved by their plight, abandoned journalistic objectivity to assist her interview subjects, even to the extent of helping one overwhelmed mother bathe her children.

> Then there was the little old lady whose one-fire stove kept going out. We helped her stoke it, and watched the green, wet kindling smoulder and sullenly die. We got a few sidelights on the fuel situation generally. The wood supply is a genuine grievance amongst housewives—limited supplies, no deliveries. In one of the inner suburbs, we lent a hand at bath-time. We coped with Johnny, aged two, Ronald, six, and Michael, a football hero of eleven. We heated a bucketful of hot water while the children had tea . . .

With her belief in social justice and her history of financial hardship, Mum might have felt guilty for feeling frustrated when others were going cold and hungry. She knew that every evening at six o'clock the pubs spilled their customers onto the pavement at closing time, filling the streets and the trams with drunken men. Many drank their wages away or lost them on bets at the races. Perhaps she was told, sometimes by my father, that she should be grateful he did not succumb to these national pastimes. He presented himself promptly at six for dinner.

My grandmother and my father must have been perplexed that far from being grateful that she was living in a big house in a fashionable suburb, my mother seemed positively resentful. The big house did offer greater material comfort—or the promise of it—and we certainly had more space than in our previous house in Camberwell with its cold-water kitchen. Despite this, my mother faced the same frustrations as any other housewife in the country.

To be fair, it must have been hard for my grandmother, too. When her children were growing up in the outback, and in Toorak, she'd employed hired help. Now, there were no servants to order around. Except my mother. Unable to complain to her husband about her unending toil, or about her relationship with her mother-in-law, Mum might have felt she was losing her sanity.

The house had certainly looked grand enough, as we'd sat outside that day in January 1950 waiting for my father and his mother to emerge, but with a family of eight actually living there, it seemed to shrink like the house of the old woman who lived in a shoe.

Such nursery rhymes and fairy tales survived the centuries because in the past people lived much more uncomfortable lives than ours. As indeed they still did. Nevertheless, about this time, John and I both took extreme fright at the tale of *Hansel and Gretel*. Our illustrated book showed a terrifying picture of an old woman who devoured the residents of her house.

It was simple for Mum to ban the Grimm Brothers tales from the bookshelf, but we still shared a sense of imminent catastrophe. It came soon enough.

Chapter 19

Our Cousin, Our Sister

Nan seemed as oblivious as my father was to my mother's unhappiness, for Nan was in love. She had met Geoff Hutton, a former war correspondent and later a theatre critic, at the *Argus*. Just as their romance blossomed, the newspaper told Geoff he'd be posted to London as its foreign correspondent. Desperate, she appealed to her editor to be also transferred to London.

Mum sat at the kitchen table shelling peas, the tiny green pellets tumbling from their pods and pinging into the bowl. I stood by the door staring at my beloved aunt, just home from work, her nails glistening with pearl polish as she held her cigarette. She pulled up a stool at the old wooden table and sat down, crossing her legs, her eye shadow as blue as her eyes.

'I'll only be gone six months,' she told my mother. 'Would you be able to keep Kristy with you while I'm away?'

'Well, Nan—' Mum sputtered.

'But you've looked after Kristy since she was a baby. And you're in a much bigger house now, at Grange Road. She doesn't take much room.'

'She is your child, after all, Nan.' My mother paused her shelling, mid-pod. She found it hard to say no to anyone, particularly her charming sister.

'I can't possibly take Kristy with me, Ruth. She would

need a passport, and Dick will never consent to letting me take her all the way to England.' Behind them on the stove the kettle exhaled, then shuddered, working its way up to a slow shriek. I heard a shuffle in the hall. The high-placed brown doorknob turned, and Granny poked her head into the kitchen. Her accusing eyes were level with the knob, peering through the frills of the aprons hung there.

'Is my tea ready, Ruth?' she demanded, glaring at Nan.

Mum scurried to the kettle, poured the boiling water over the leaves in the pot, clattered the cup and saucer on the tray, added two melting moment shortbreads on another small plate, and placed the tray on the edge of the table. Granny took it and retreated.

No one spoke. My eyes darted around the kitchen: the crowded counters; Andrew in his playpen sucking on a rusk; bread still to be cut for tomorrow's school lunches; dinner to shove in the oven; children to be bathed; the never-finished ironing piled in the clothes basket. Nan uncrossed her legs and fingered a run in her stocking. My mother took a deep breath.

'No,' she said.

Nan inhaled cigarette smoke. 'What about my career, Ruth? I can't back out now. The editor is planning on the transfer.'

'You're not yet divorced, Nan. You can't go running off with another man.'

'Ruth,' Nan said, 'you know perfectly well I would be divorced if I could be. But Dick would fight it.'

'You'll be putting your right to Kristy in jeopardy!' My mother's voice rose. Andrew threw his rusk out of his playpen and started to wail.

Nan choked on her tea. She stubbed out the cigarette, swung off the stool, and went to find her daughter. Returning to the kitchen, she lifted Kristy onto her lap and held her close. Mum, at the stove, slammed down the lid on a pot.

* * *

Years later, I asked my mother about this half-remembered scene, the moment when Kristy, who had lived with us for three years and whom John and I loved as a sister, had been wrenched away. She had been pregnant, Mum explained, and she needed to be careful. Her stress level was already extreme.

'I thought,' she said, 'that Nan would see my situation and decide to wait in Melbourne for Geoff to return.' But Nan did not. Nan felt that the moral right, if not the law, was on her side.

'I felt I'd been duped,' Nan later told me. 'It was all so odd, the endless caravan honeymoon, the fact that Dick and I had to be secluded on a farm when I thought I'd married a journalist. I could understand my husband not wanting to tell me, but I can't forgive his mother's betrayal. She never warned me Dick was schizophrenic.'

In 1951, Nan could not divorce her husband on the grounds of mental incompetence unless he had been institutionalised. The grounds of 'lunacy' only applied if the spouse had been 'confined therefore, and . . . unlikely to recover'.[1] Apparently, Dick Nicholl's family influence—or perhaps just good doctoring—kept him out of a psychiatric hospital, at least for the time being.

We children felt the atmosphere in the house thicken, as if the dust motes dancing in the air in the hallway suddenly gathered into a gnat-like cloud. There was a pressure of a looming deadline; a sense of something about to happen.

Then a man came to the house, his legs, a long inverted V, joined to a tall stem-like figure taut with tension. It was Uncle Dick Nicholls, standing alone before the fire. I had run into the dining room and found him there by himself. His wheat-coloured hair flopped about his tight face. I ran out, frightened by his loneliness. Dick Nicholls had come to the house hoping to reconcile with his wife and claim his daughter. I don't remember if either of them actually met with him that day. Perhaps they'd hidden in the woodshed—something I used to do when I'd been naughty. Since she'd taken Kristy from her father without his permission, Nan's right to custody of her daughter was on shaky ground.

Shortly after he showed up, Kristy disappeared. Nan, too, left without a word.

'Nan's gone to England,' Mum said to me. 'She'll only be gone a little while.'

My mother's sense of propriety dominated her thinking. Perhaps the secrecy was the worst of it for her: the lies she had to tell Nan's mother-in-law, Lady Nicholls—that, yes, Kristy was fine, but Nan couldn't come to the phone right now. And how did she tell her straitlaced mother-in-law that the glamorous Nan had left her child to live overseas with a man who was not her husband? Perhaps she feigned a sudden case of deafness if Granny ever asked the question, which she probably did not. Silence about difficult subjects was the unspoken rule in the house.

Nan had called Mum's bluff. She placed three-year-old Kristy in the care of a family who took in children for money. Kristy knows now her mother did it for love. 'I think Mum had to put me in hiding for a while,' she says. But for Kristy, the six months of her mother's absence was a life sentence. 'I felt like a little monkey in a cage who was a hundred years old,' she said as an adult, remembering that terrible time of abandonment.

We children knew none of this. We just wanted our cousin/sister back—as much as she, three years old, wanted to be back with us, the only family she had ever known. We visited her at her tidy foster family's home in the Melbourne hills, an hour's tedious drive away. Dad stayed home with the napping toddler, Andrew.

The polite hosts offered us snacks, pleasant in a distant way as they loomed above us smiling. We were confused by Kristy's delight and distress. Kristy, dressed in her best frock, flung herself at Mother's knees, agitated beyond words to see us all, her face flushed and her blonde curls damp with excitement. There was a patterned carpet and a whiff of furniture polish. In Kristy's room we saw toys stacked neatly away. Just when we were immersed in our play, scattering toys over the room as we did at home, the adults came in, saying the visit was over. As we approached the door to leave, Kristy held her little arms out to us and wailed, a high-pitched ascending scream. We struggled to disentangle her fingers from our clothes as Mum jangled the car keys, stricken.

No one spoke on the way home. John and I sat numbly in the back seat. My chest squeezed from the pressure of my ribs, and it wasn't the seatbelt, because the car didn't have any. It was a long drive down those curving roads in the hills. The rainforest with its huge ferns and towering gums glowered olive-green and dark on the edge of the road, and the rain poured down the car's windshield. Mum gripped the steering wheel so tightly you could see her shoulders twitching through her twinset. The evening came upon us as we entered the suburbs and their sheltering familiarity. The lights were already on at home, and Mum had to hustle to get the tea.

In the kitchen, I picked up my toddling brother Andrew and hugged him so tightly his soaked nappy wet my shirt.

'Cutting onions always makes me cry,' Mum said. But she was peeling potatoes.

Chapter 20

Running Through Her Days

I learned about my youngest brother's impending birth while hunting for something in which to nestle my precious dolls. We had only been at the house for a year and a half when I discovered in the yellow-and-black-tiled bathroom with its lemon-coloured bathtub a satin and tulle-covered basket. It held baby powder and lotion.

'Can I use this for my dolls?'

'It's for the baby,' Mum said.

'But Andrew's not a baby anymore,' I protested.

'We'll need it again soon.' Another baby, another doll for me. I couldn't wait.

Christopher was born a month or so after Nan returned with Geoff from England. My mother's relationship with Nan, strained to breaking point while Kristy lived with her foster family, had been restored by the time of Christopher's birth. Irresistible Christopher, with fat cheeks always in a smile and a full head of dark curls. I carried him around on my hip so much that I developed a lopsided posture for my sisterly devotion, and was prescribed a regimen of exercises and told to stand up straight like Audrey Hepburn.

Soon we had a wedding to celebrate. Kristy was retrieved from the house in the hills, and Nan, radiant in a pretty pastel suit, clinked a glass of champagne with her new husband and our parents in the dining room. The wedding had taken place the week, possibly even the day, after Nan's divorce from Dick Nicholls became final. Rejected by the Church of England because of her divorce, Nan and Geoff chose to tie the knot in front of a Presbyterian minister. Nan had been surprised by the hurt she felt over the Anglican lack of sympathy. Her first husband was schizophrenic and had put her baby's life—and her own—in jeopardy. She chose not to raise her children in any church.

With a new baby to care for, Andrew still a toddler, Kristy two years older, John, me, Granny, and the cats, my mother had her hands full. Nan still needed childcare after she married and Kristy spent most of her daytimes with our family. Mostly I remember my mother running. In flat flapping heels she would hightail it down the hall, fly upstairs to a crying baby, scurry around the kitchen, powerwalk the laden laundry basket outside to the Hills hoist.

Although my parents eventually glassed in the verandah to make an all-season play space, the working areas—the inefficient kitchen, the two rooms at the back of it, and the laundry, which could only be accessed by going outside—were never changed in the forty-five years my parents lived in the house. John noted:

> Because of his peripatetic childhood and then many years at boarding school and university college, I don't think Dad realised it is not frugal to maintain the house—or at least the kitchen, bathroom, and laundry—as it was when built in 1904 or whenever. The only expenditure on herself [Granny] that I can remember is the purchase of the gas fridge, and later the conversion of what had been our living room into her bedsitter by adding a bathroom out the back, taking up some of the verandah. By then people were buying TVs, but Dad held out against the tide for some years.[1]

In his unpublished book on the history of Australian technology, Dad wrote about the extreme inefficiency of the Australian household:

> Australian industry's contribution to the working equipment of the home, such as it was—for cooling, cleaning, heating, refrigeration, ventilating, waste disposal, garden maintenance—was not impressive.
>
> Experimenting boldly in the social sphere, the British–Australians remained almost as conservative in their household arrangements as the servant-saturated British. Leading the world in the liberation of the wages-worker, they left it to the Americans to liberate the housewife through labour-saving inventions. Only slowly and without imagination, waiting to be convinced every step of the way, did Australians allow modern conveniences to force an entry into their homes.

Yet my father, observing all this, did nothing to alter the textbook inefficiency of his family's home. The handsome wood-lined front hall, the dining room, sitting room and Granny's two rooms were all for show. As John pointed out, even when prosperity increased and renovations became all the rage, the Edquists only went as far as central heating.

Recently, I came across an advertisement for a cooktop and oven, and recognised the stove as identical to the cooking equipment at 5 Grange Road. The woman in the photo was wearing a 1920s-style dress, but the oven, grill and stovetop were patented around the time our house was built. By the time my parents sold the house, this appliance would have been eighty years old.

Beverley Kingston, in *My Wife, My Daughter and Poor Mary Ann*, examines the changing role of the middle-class wife in the hundred years leading up to the 1950s. Middle-class women had employed maids to do the heavy work while they took an administrative role, but

> by the middle of the twentieth century, the wife had become a housewife, the servants had disappeared, the family had shrunk to a husband and a small number of children (losing in the process not only the servants but all elderly and unmarried relatives) and the house itself had undergone a transformation in design for the sake of simplicity, economy and labour saving.[2]

At 5 Grange Road, my mother took care of twice the number of children than the average woman, as well as her frail mother-in-law, and had provided a home for an employed sister separated from her husband. She did this in a large house not designed for economy, a house that was the opposite of labour saving. Kingston points out that though this 'levelling of the social classes' was an Australian ideal, it also 'showed the extremely low status of women in the society, their powerlessness and inability to influence or control their own situation'.[3]

Inefficient it may have been, but Granny's purchase of the big house was a godsend. Her widow's income was being eaten into by inflation. My father, with a young, expanding family, could not have afforded a fine, substantial house like 5 Grange Road on his own. The rent he paid to Granny would otherwise have been paid in the form of a mortgage to a bank, and when Granny finally moved into a little flat with a caretaker and subsequently died, the house became ours.

Furthermore, I never remember having babysitters after we moved into the big house. I believe our parents must have left us with Granny if they went out at night. I can see now why my father and his mother thought we'd all benefit from having a grandmother in the house, while he turned a blind eye to her hostility, even neglect.

Granny was supposed to be a built-in sitter when our parents went out, but in fact the situation was reversed. John and I, unbeknownst to each other, lay awake plotting fire escape routes for those times our parents went out. Possibly due to her physical limitations, our grandmother never climbed the stairs to check on us. While I planned to grab Andrew and Chris from their shared bedroom next to mine, and to open my window to sit with them on the roof over the verandah to wait for rescue, John devised a more elaborate scheme.

> My plan, in case of fire, was to break the glass in my window and climb onto the roof, and, having clambered down to the guttering, to either leap into the tree in the front garden that grew closest to the house, or hang from the guttering and drop into the garden bed below. I was concerned that flames leaping up the stairwell might make it difficult to get Andrew and Chris, but accessing their room by clambering around through the ceiling space from the hatch in my room to the access hatch behind the closet in their room seemed impractical in a fire.

Like so many aspects of life at Grange Road, these fears were never discussed aloud.

Chapter 21

On Passchendaele Street

After we moved to Grange Road and our mother sank into a swirl of silent sadness like water down a plughole, John and I spent a lot of time at Auntie Kit's. Whether it was to relieve our mother or to enliven Kitty's days, we were not sure, but it was entertaining for us and, sometimes, a little alarming. We were engaged in a battle with a bird.

Kit's husband Bill's best friend was Pie, his pet magpie. Each morning in the sunroom Bill fed Pie, perched on his outstretched arm. If a crumb fell to the sea-grass matting, Pie dive-bombed to get the morsel before the vacuum cleaner. Jealous, he nipped at our small ankles in a frenzy of cawing. Fearful of Pie, John and I sought refuge in the outside toilet, careful to avoid rousing the black-and-white avian terrorist. The dunny was a pleasant place, with its exterior laced with ivy and passionfruit vines. Uncle Bill Rudd also spent a lot of time out there.

On Passchendaele Street, the radio blared continually. If it wasn't the races or the football, it was the daily talk show with the ever-popular Graham Kennedy and Nicky Nicholls repeating recipes so gravely you knew they were half-mocking the housewife listeners who had sent them in to the radio station, 3UZ. Kit snorted with giggles at their gags, and danced a little twirl with the kitchen broom at the advertising jingles. One day, when the magpie had lost interest in us for a moment, Uncle Bill turned down the radio.

'Listen.' He settled a large conch shell on the side of my face. I gripped the shiny spiraled swell, my small fingers splaying to hold it, the prongs pressing into my skin. The roar of the sea filled my ear, sounding like the crowds on radio when Bill listened to the footy on Saturday afternoons. Roar. Fade. Roar. He'd been a player for one of the big teams long ago, before he'd gone away to war. Conch shells are not native to Port Phillip Bay so I'm not sure where Uncle Bill picked up his. But other shells littered the tideline, and on beaches bordering the Bay the sharp-eyed could discern middens created by the Indigenous clans who had fished there for countless generations, leaving the shells of crustaceans in scattered heaps.[1] To get us out of the house while our Aunt Kit was cleaning, Uncle Bill took us to the beach and pier. We saw the shells, and swarthy Italians and Greeks ripping mussels from the rocks. They threw them into buckets of seawater held by their wives. The women loudly shouted advice, their dimpled, ample flesh jiggling out from skirted bathing suits. We'd heard about the Southern Europeans who'd migrated from their war-ravaged countries and how they would have a better life here. But were they really so poor, we wondered pityingly, that they had to eat shellfish? Even worse, squid! In the 1950s, calamari were not seen on Melbourne menus.

As the men and women gathered mussels, John and I ran along the damp sand, dodging the slapping incoming tide in winter or splashing in the shallows in summer. We kept an eye on the marina, where the hulls of white boats rocked gently in the deeper water. On weekends, crowds of young men pushed the boats down ramps into the sea where, after their owners stood and shouted and ducked the boom and unwrapped ropes, the boats seemed suddenly to find purpose as their sails unfurled. But that was a grown-up activity and we had our own. So much to do! We had castles to build in the wet sand, dunes to slide down. Once, John and I came across a couple wrestling each other in the seaside bushes.

'Come away this instant!' our great uncle rasped.

'Uncle Bill, why don't they have clothes on?' we asked.

'Don't tell your aunt!' Bill said, so rattled by the incident that he locked my brother and me in the car and went to the pub for two beers. It was eleven o'clock in the morning. John and I, cramped and sticky with sand, squabbled and then, tired, cranked down the windows and puffed out the stuffy air, as we listened to the midday sounds of the foreshore: birds cawing after crusts from discarded picnic sandwiches and the rustle of the untidy tea trees with their shredding bark. The sea flapped in the distance.

Perhaps it was the nerves in his stomach, or perhaps it was the strain of child-sitting, but Uncle Bill sought the consolation of a beer earlier and earlier in the morning. He would pull a whole dark bottle from the refrigerator and take it to his chair at the sunroom table. The icy sweat from the bottle leaked downwards like tears. Pouring himself a glass, Bill would drink silently, his face relaxing as the anaesthetic took effect. He lifted his feet obediently as Kitty wielded the carpet sweeper under them.

Kit found little to do. The Axminster carpet required just three or four sweeps with the vacuum cleaner to restore the rooms to spotlessness, so compact was the house. A front porch opened to a hall. In the formal parlour on the left were photographs of Kitty's many nieces and nephews competing for attention with three ceramic geese flying in a diagonal line on the wall, and two stiff sofas lined up at right angles. On the other side of the hall was the master bedroom, with its dark mahogany wardrobe and its double bed under the window. Kitty knifed the cover crisply under the pillows every morning. John and I stayed in the second bedroom, and when we were little, Kitty would slide a chamber pot under our beds every evening to save a nocturnal trip outside to the toilet. The narrow kitchen had a coal range as well as a gas stove, a later addition. Perpendicular to that stood a stainless-steel sink under a window, and across from it a small table with a chrome-bordered linoleum top and two matching chairs. In the middle of the house was a dark den with brown leather chairs and reading lamps, but the family ignored it, preferring the bright sunroom at the back of the house.

Kitty was a whiz at housekeeping, but she found cooking a challenge. She often wrestled with blackened pans on her inadequate stove, pans that had burned while she was hooting with laughter on the phone. Her laugh was like a kookaburra's, cracking and hawing, and could be heard for miles, I feared. Auntie Kit's lively personality rippled from her sunny house throughout the neighbourhood. Trained to suppress our feelings in Granny's presence, Kitty's loquacious manner sometimes embarrassed us.

'They're just stopping with me for a week,' Kitty told the butcher, referring to my brother and me. 'Poor Ruthie has so much to do with the new baby and that enormous house. And so far away! I don't know why they can't live closer,' she said, as he wrapped the fillet. Even then, I sensed that living closer to Kitty's beachside world and the communal play space of its swarming sands would disappoint my grandmother's aspirations for her son and his family.

I tried to toss off the itchy scarf Kit had swathed me in to protect me against the cold sea air. John and I fidgeted as she blithely spilled our family's discomforts: the sense that our mother was drowning, and we were powerless to help.

'We want a hot milkshake,' I insisted, to get her off the subject.

'I don't think they make hot milkshakes,' Aunt Kit demurred, but undefeated by custom, marched us into the milk bar. This venerable Australian institution, on every street corner, sold newspapers, bread and milk, and marvellous concoctions from the blender.

'We don't make milkshakes hot,' said the man.

'But I want a hot chocolate malted, please,' I said softly, regretting asking for something unconventional.

'You can make that, can't you?' said Kit to the milk-bar's owner.

Grumbling, but obedient to Kitty's breezy confidence in his compliance, the man went behind the counter, poured chocolate, milk, and malted milk powder into a beaker, then went into the back room to put it on the stove, returning to whirl it in the blender to give it a satisfactory froth. I was numb with embarrassment, about making so much trouble, and at my aunt for talking so much. She knew everyone at the shops. They seemed to like her, no matter how outrageous her demands. She sweetened those with juicy dollops of gossip and easy laughter. Which neighbour had run off with whose husband seemed to be the staple fare of these exchanges.

I turned to the advertisement of Jane Russell, her face upturned to a bottle of Coca-Cola. Her dark hair tumbling down her shoulders, forties style, she resembled our beautiful mother but, unlike her, Jane Russell looked cool and confident. In America, people were not embarrassed by their loud great-aunts, I decided. Still, the hot chocolate malted tasted delicious, and much fortified by its warmth, I took Kitty's hand as she thanked the milk-bar owner, and we swanned outside into the biting air.

I knew all about America from the *Saturday Evening Post*. Bill was a subscriber. The magazine, delivered by sea mail three months after publication, featured lovely covers that told a story. I knew the charming crew-cut American troops had fought alongside our soldiers to save our country from eating raw fish under the Japanese, even if the Italians had overlooked this benefit by scrambling for mussels.

I could just make out the signature on the paintings by sounding its letters out loud: N-O-R-M-A-N R-O-C-K-W-E-L-L. The name evoked refuge and rocklike stability; the images as static as the magazine cover itself. In my world, stability was the goal of life. Everybody just needed more peace and quiet.

The streets in Hampton were named for World War I battlefields. In the battle of Passchendaele alone, according to the *Sydney Morning Herald*, 'five Australian divisions had suffered 38,000 casualties, including 12,000 dead and missing'.[2] The neighbourhood housed World War I veterans and their families—aging now in California-style bungalows—with the men tending roses and working at humdrum jobs. The kids who had raced down the streets in billycarts were now grown. Another world war had come and gone and some of those boys had lost their lives. Others came back with something missing, as their fathers had done.

None of them talked of the past—the war they fought or the aftermath at home. They suffered subterranean terrors, or the pain of shrapnel wounds flaring, or bronchitis, caused long ago by mustard gas. The men had their consolations: a bet at the races or a beer at the pub. On wintry afternoons, they donned bright scarves and cheered on their football teams.

Uncle Bill and Aunt Kit were typical of their neighbours. In Bill and Kitty's world, bowling was the only social activity shared by men and women. The Lawn Bowling Club mingled men and women in uniforms made snowy by Persil detergent and a good wind-whipped, sunshiny, line dry. The ladies' white skirts hiked up over white stockings in thick, white, rubber-soled shoes as they curtsied to roll an ebony-coloured ball down a green ribbon of grass.

'You beauty,' they laughed as the big black ball swerved slowly towards a white 'jack', sometimes called a 'kitty'. The targets were named after our great-aunt and her twin brother, we thought, taking it all in stride as kids do. The men wore white hats with black bands on them and eased themselves and their beer bottles gratefully into lawn chairs as the ladies prepared the afternoon tea of tiny pikelets, sausage rolls and lamingtons, those luscious little square cakes coated in chocolate icing and rolled in coconut.

For the wives, the steadying demands of family and work filled their need to be needed. They touched gingerly the thin cloth covering their husbands' hollowed hearts. Once couples with a future, now all it took was a shout, a loud noise, a silly laugh, or a cross word to set a husband off. The women's energy turned to repressing their own unseemly desires, and then stemming the exuberance of their daughters.

One day, Kitty asked if we would like to see a bride. At this exciting prospect I skipped down the road to the neighbours', where their daughter Patty was being prepared for her wedding.

'Where is your long white gown?' I asked, in huge disappointment.

Patty, her pale face dough-like at the best of times, burst into tears. With eyes puffy and red, she was being dressed, or rather wrapped, in a bulging ballerina dress of blue tulle. A sickly sweet smell of frangipani wafted from her bouquet and, as she sat down, a woman tilted a crown of flowers over Patty's brow in lieu of a veil. She sniffed and swallowed her tears. While her bridesmaid and mother fussed around her, Patty, the bride, looked at my small self with envy.

'Wish I was your age,' she said.

On the way home, Kitty visibly simmered. 'Disgrace! I had no idea it would be a shotgun.'

What had shotguns got to do with blue tulle, I wondered. My bride doll, after all, wore miles of white, and weddings were supposed to make princesses happy ever after. Only when, a very short time later, a baby came with Patty to visit her parents did I sense a connection between these two facts, a sad bride and a new baby. It was a puzzle. We had a baby at our house, too, and everyone loved him. But people seemed so cross with Patty. And she had cried on the happiest day of her life.

Patty moved away from Hampton, and the memory of her shame gradually dissipated, like the water sprayed by the gossiping hoses over the neighbours' hydrangeas.

Ruth Charlholmes, in a suit of pale blue, marries Dick Edquist,
30 October 1943.

Nan Hutton, journalist, about 1960.

Eva Edquist and her children, 1917.
From left: Bill, three, Eva holding John, three months,
Mary, 17 months (in front), Dick, four.
Eva had this formal portrait taken in Perth before undertaking her
arduous journey with the children to Youanmi.

aint he a Boshter

Victor Edquist admires his firstborn, Dick, at Marvel Loch, 1913.

The house at 5 Grange Road, Kew, as the
family first saw it in 1950.

The mine manager's residence at Sons of Gwalia Mine, WA.
Named after Herbert Hoover, who found the mine and later
became the 31st US President, this house is now a B&B and
function venue.

The family home at 5 Grange Road, 1954. Margaret (far left) bosses the children around in the backyard: Christopher, in the play pool, Andrew, Kristy and John. Neighbor Richard looks over the fence.

Chapter 22

The Stony Rises

'*Coo-ee!*' Auntie Kit sang to Mrs Mason, as if she were way across the paddocks tending the boundary fences. In fact, Mrs Mason lived next door, and Kit's call was a signal to hang her wash on the line so they could gossip over the fence.

'I'm taking the kids on a trip,' she told her neighbour. 'We're going to stay with my cousin, to show them where I grew up.' She turned to John and me, playing nearby, with a smile. 'Near the Stony Rises.'

> Katy, My Dear,
>   Regarding your request about the Lord family history. I'm afraid I don't know very much, wish I knew more, but we don't think of these things until it is too late and there is no one left who knows.[1]

These words began a letter to great-aunt Kit from her first cousin, Doris Draffen. Of all the Lord descendants, only Doris still lived close to her birthplace in an area called the Stony Rises. She was the daughter of Kitty's uncle, Will Lord.

How often Kit had clip-clopped down the narrow concrete path at the side of our house, and let herself in the back door as Mum put on the kettle. Perching her tall frame on a stool at our kitchen table, Kit would spin a tale. For years, the magical past of her childhood in the country had shone like a beacon in Kitty's memory. Her stories were not about loss and war or hardship or worry. They told of a farm, a family, and a house.

My mother and Aunt Nan and Kitty—their mother's sister—talked about Colantet, the lovely house near Camperdown. It lay in a beautiful part of south-western Victoria, and seemed to them a paradise lost. The Lords, they told us, had dreams of wealth when they bought the house. The property was supposed to be passed down in the family, but was lost by the cruelty of nature. The country, so green and fertile at first, turned brown and dry, and the milk and butter on which the farm depended ran thin.

According to notes written by my mother, the Lord land at Pomborneit was 'part of the old Colantet station, which had been taken up in 1844'. It lay at the head of Curdies Creek, between the huge station of the Manifolds—early graziers in Victoria—to the north, the dense and forbidding Otway Forest on the south, and the Stony Rises to the east.

At the beginning of the twentieth century, while Ruth and Sam Lord II were rearing their brood at Colantet, and their two youngest, the twins Jack and Kitty, were very small, all was well with the Lord family and their place in the world, at least in Kitty's memory. This romantic vision of a house in the green countryside never left her, and she passed it to her nieces, my mother Ruth and our Aunt Nan. She wrote in her memoir:[2]

> It was a lovely place. The first settlers, the Duttons, brought from England trees and plants and dozens of rose bushes and fruit trees and redcurrant bushes and blackcurrants . . . The home paddock was four square miles with outlets to roads on each corner and avenues of trees ran down from the house to each gate. The house was colonial style.

The main building had big rooms with French doors opening out on to the verandah, which ran all around the house. The kitchen was a big detached building and, at the back, was a very big chestnut tree spreading its boughs over the roofs. A lovely place to play in. The garden was enclosed with climbing roses all around the fences and big pink cabbage roses looked in my bedroom window. The sitting room and dining rooms were large and had big windows as well as the French doors and were, thus, light and airy. When Jack and I were on our ponies we had to keep in sight of the windows. There was a swift creek running through the home paddock. We used to often take our lunch and play all day under the trees that lined the banks. In the creek were dear little shells out of which we used to make necklaces for the big girls, our sisters, and near the water's edge were lovely coloured irises. We used to call them flags.

'The horses' hooves sang, *Colantet*, *Colantet*, and it was a happy song,' Nan used to say, even though neither Aunt Nan nor my mother had ever been there. Termites had destroyed the weatherboard house long ago but Kitty would not be deterred in her quest for the past. She wanted to show John and me the countryside near where she'd lived as a child and, perhaps, she wanted to return herself, to relive her happy memories. Mum encouraged our journey to the place with the funny name. No doubt she was glad to get her two older children out of her hair for a week to tend to newborn Christopher.

The old steam train that transported goods and passengers all the way from Melbourne to Warrnambool on the south coast was still running in the early 1950s. My brother John has vivid memories of the train—a little boy's dream:

> My first memory of the trip is of Spencer St Station. The platforms were very, very long and the tracks ended with

buffers. So very different from every other station that I had seen. The trip from Spencer St to Camperdown took several hours, powered by a steam engine. The loud shriek of the steam whistle, the whoosh of steam, the chuff, chuff, chuff of the pistons, the rattle of the train on the tracks, the clouds of steam, black smuts of soot floating in through the windows, the stench of sulphur. The noise, the smell, the vibration. It was wonderful!

Kit was as excited as we were, demolishing the sandwiches Mum had packed for us long before we were halfway to Camperdown. She swigged tea from the old green thermos while we children sipped our Kia Ora cordial mixed with water. The filthy dark smoke plumed behind us as we sped past the bush and the paddocks from Melbourne into the south-west. At Camperdown we were welcomed by a big family of second and third cousins, eager to show us life on their sheep station.

Farm life astonished us. The toilet was a stinky outhouse, but inside the house modernity was evident. With two big freezers, the Draffens ate well. The lamb chops came from the sheep outside. Perhaps overly observant of such things and aware of how my mother would feel, I was impressed by the modern conveniences of the country housewife. Tom Draffen's wife, Doris's daughter-in-law, showed off her big white cube. The new washing machine was a marvel. I knew Mum, still twirling nappies through boiling water in the old copper tub, would be envious. In 1952, booming wool prices enabled sheep farmers to live well.

One of the older cousins taught me to milk a cow, to pull the teats in a rocking fashion so the warm milk spurted into the pail. We drank some right from the can as the cow's tail switched, scattering flies. I liked leaning against the warm bulk of the cow, but I was really too squeamish for farm life.

Cousin Tom had taken us in his jeep to check around the property. Uttering a curse, he showed us a dead sheep lying on its side with flies crawling in its eyes.

I failed the farm skills' test during our weeklong stay at the Draffens' when Tom pulled back the head of a ram to cut its throat for a future dinner. The other children stood transfixed as Tom grabbed the sheep's horns, exposing its throat, pink and throbbing under a white mat of wool. Its fearful eyes pleaded with mine, 'Save me!' I ran away and vomited.

Although younger than me, John was not squeamish:

> Tom told us he was going to slaughter a sheep and asked if we wanted to watch. I did. He led the sheep to a tree, then cut its throat. He quickly—everything was done quickly—cut slits between the tendon and bone of each back leg, pushed a stick in, and then, attaching to this, ropes running over a branch of the tree, pulled the carcass into the air, head downward, so the blood drained out. Then he nicked the hide and pulled it off. With another quick cut he laid open the abdomen so the sheep's intestines spilled out onto the ground. The carcass was left hanging there for a while before it was butchered into pieces.

The intentional slaughter of a farm animal was not the only cruelty we saw. Nature had confounded the pastoralists who had settled the countryside. Rabbits, the curse of the Australian farmer, received their start near Camperdown and, nearly a hundred years later, threatened to bring it to ruin once again.

In 1859, Thomas Austin, a squatter of Winchelsea, sent home to England for rabbits. He fancied a spot of hunting. By the time they arrived the one or two pairs had multiplied on board ship to twenty-four rabbits. Released into the wild, they bred without natural predators. Settlers had reduced dingo numbers, so this potential predator was not effective against the rabbits. Rabbits destroyed pastureland, caused erosion, and their population growth seemed unstoppable. They reach adulthood in only three months, and each litter is large. The rabbits caused havoc, ruining the plans of squatter and selector alike as the grass for sheep and cattle disappeared before their eyes.

In 1865, in Colac, not far from Camperdown, 4000 rabbits were hunted and destroyed in a day. By 1868, Colac was considered a rabbit disaster area. By 1875, rabbits had reached the borders of New South Wales to the north and Western Australia to the west. By 1900, they had reached the Northern Territory and Western Australia.

According to *The History of Pomborneit*:[3]

> Prior to 1865, the surrounding country had been leased from the Government by Messrs J. & P. Manifold. In 1865, the part known as Pomborneit was thrown open for selection and allotted by ballot to the various applicants. Of these early settlers only Messrs McGarvie & Boyd remained. All others gradually succumbed to the rabbit pest. Their land was heavily mortgaged and eventually passed into the hands of various Banks. A holding supporting a family in comfort with a herd of over sixty dairy cows, would not provide sufficient grass to feed a horse and two cows—these having to be hand fed. On this rich volcanic country, the rabbits had left nothing but moss.

Pomborneit is the tiny hamlet near the farm Kitty loved so much. The historical note above shows that drought may have helped, but rabbits had been the death knell of Colantet.[4]

John and I were at Draffen's farm the day the neighbourhood joined in a rabbit hunt. Those from miles around collected with the family, adults and children in a line, making noise with shouts, tambourines, and guns fired in the air. The ground undulated, stretching forever into a series of low hills, the grass scrubby and olive-green. Ahead of the advancing army, two fences met at right angles. Suddenly, the land filled with rabbits. They scrambled everywhere, fleeing in all directions, a mess of brown bodies and white tails like powder puffs, running from the humans who were herding the animals into the corner where the fences met. The noise of the hunters rose to a pitch. The terrified rabbits ran for their warrens, and the men and children flung themselves on the ground, catching the feet of the fleeing animals and then clubbing them to death. 'There were rabbit bodies piled several feet high like snow drifts,' John remembered.

This violent and inefficient method of killing rabbits took place around the time of the introduction of the myxoma virus. This natural virus kills the rabbit over a period of ten days. Not a pretty death, but myxomatosis allowed the wool industry to survive, at least until the rabbit evolved to fight myxoma. The virus was killing rabbits elsewhere, but it had little effect on Camperdown's rabbit population, hence the bloodthirsty rabbit cull.

This visit to our cousins opened my eyes to the unglamorous side of farming, so different from Old MacDonald's farm of the nursery rhyme. Nevertheless, this childhood journey left an indelible memory—a joyful one. The story of Colantet had provided a doorway to the past. So insistently did it beckon that as an adult I continued our mother's research into her family's past.

Doris Lord Draffen, on whose son's farm John and I had just stayed, my deceased grandmother Stella, and her sister Kitty Lord Rudd were all granddaughters of the original Sam Lord and his wife, the former Ann Williams. Kitty's mother, Ruth Lord, had left the dairy farm at Colantet and moved to Melbourne with the goal of getting an education for her children. Among her ten children, Ruth Lord had two sets of twins. Besides Jack and Kitty were Annie, known as 'Sis', and Sam. (Yes, another Sam Lord—the third.) Sis died of tuberculosis in 1915, and Sam, who may have caught it from his twin sister, or, the family believed, from sleeping on damp ground while serving in the army in World War I, died of the disease six years later.

Sam was not the only one who'd come back damaged from the war. Two of Kitty's older brothers, Arthur and Frank, served with great distinction, but were away for years.[5] Frank, the teacher who'd helped my mother study for her exam, came back from the war psychologically shattered, leading to the break-up of his marriage.

Kitty's breezy personality would never have led one to guess she'd witnessed such sorrow in her youth. Despite the difficulties of her past, Kitty loved to talk about an earlier time. In particular she liked to tell the tale of her maternal grandmother, an Irishwoman named Jane Leary, and her colourful maternal grandfather, Thomas Constable.

* * *

The Lords spun fables, but they had competition in blarney. Thomas Constable's story about his early life slid over the facts. When Thomas told the tale of his arrival in the colony to guests at his fiftieth wedding anniversary party, he did not mention he was one of the 'Pentonville Convicts'. Nor was this ever revealed—or perhaps even known—by his immediate family. Only research by his great-great-grandchildren has uncovered the truth about our convict ancestor.

Ashamed of his past, Thomas Constable at first hid his real name. The record shows that Jane Leary, aged eighteen, born in Skibbereen, Ireland, married 'Michael Hart', carpenter, twenty-eight years old, born in Cheltenham, England, in St

Andrew's Church in Geelong in April of 1852. Two years later, they registered the birth of their daughter, Mary Jane Hart. According to family history, the family was living on the Ballarat goldfields when Mary Jane, aged two, went to look for her father, out drinking with his friends. She fell down a mineshaft and died.

Soon after this, in November 1856, another baby girl was registered as born to what we assume to be the same couple. Christened Eliza Constable, her parents were Thomas Constable, born Cheltenham, England, and his wife Jane, *nee* Leary, of Skibbereen, Ireland. Given the tiny population of the colony at that time, the coincidence of names suggests that Hart had changed his name back to Constable. According to our family legend and corroborated in an article in the *Cobden Times* in April 1902 celebrating the fiftieth anniversary of his marriage to Jane, Thomas/Michael never again touched a drop of alcohol after the death of his daughter. He became intensely religious. Did he, born again, confess to Jane for the first time that he had been a convict? Did she insist he revert to his real name? Or did he reveal his real name in order to register to vote, a privilege he never would have received in his native England.

I wonder if they—or at least Thomas—took part in the avid discussions held over the Ballarat campfires about taxation without representation and the general discontent that rumbled in the mining township before it erupted at the Eureka Stockade. By 1854, miners wanted the right to own land and to vote. More practically, they wanted the police to stop acting like bullying bureaucrats and to rid the goldfields of crime, especially the bushrangers who harassed the community. At this time, the government insisted that miners obtain a licence to dig for gold. Since finding gold was no sure thing, this onerous fee outraged the miners, who conspired to rebel against the police who hunted for licence scofflaws on horseback, disrupting the digging and humiliating the hardworking men. The grumblings erupted in armed revolt at the Eureka Stockade. The ringleader, Peter Lalor, erected a republican flag—a cross with stars. The hilly ground riddled with miners' holes was a guerilla fighter's dream, but a nightmare for soldiers trying to advance in a disciplined formation. But when the soldiers approached the wooden Eureka fort on a December night in 1854, many of its defenders were either drunk or had gone home for the night. During the mêlée five soldiers and thirty miners were killed. The rest were tried for treason in Melbourne. The jury acquitted them all. Soon afterward, the new Victorian Parliament legislated universal (white) male suffrage.[6]

* * *

How did Thomas come to Australia and why? In 1840 convict transportation to the Australian mainland ceased and, in 1844, a new scheme began. Reformed penal laws, vastly more humane than in previous years, allowed even serious offenders to be given a conditional pardon after two years in prison in England. They would then be sent to Australia to serve out their sentences as virtually free men.[7]

On 9 November 1846, the *Maitland* arrived at Port Phillip from London. It carried 299 convicts from Pentonville and Parkhurst prisons. Prisoner Number 43 was a Thomas Constable, aged seventeen, shoemaker, convicted of stealing lace and sentenced to seven years imprisonment on 17 October 1843 at Gloucester. He had already served his two years in prison, and was about to start a new and reformed life in the colony. It is understandable that he wanted to take on a new identity in the community.

His conditional freedom did not get off to a good start. He fell 'into the company of drunkards', he recalled at his golden anniversary party. Returning to Geelong, he said, he joined the *Matilda*, a schooner sailing to Tasmania. Such a boat did exist and plied Bass Strait till it was wrecked in 1848. In Tasmania, again he was 'guilty of doing wrong, although the crime of smuggling a little grog was only looked upon as a little wrong by the men'.

Then, fate knocked, in the form of Jane. He met 'a certain lady', who agreed to marry him on the condition that he gave up the drink. He promised he would, although at the time he 'had not the slightest intention of doing so'. Only the death of their first child, Mary Jane, led him to see the folly of his ways. He said, 'I asked God to forgive me. God did so and, since then, has honoured me with a life of health and happiness'.

By the time Thomas died in 1911, his reformed ways had made him a popular figure in his adopted town of Cobden. His death certificate records him as a 'Gentleman'.[8] Following the sold-out edition of the issue of the *Cobden Times* containing Thomas's obituary, the paper republished its tribute to Thomas, 'one of the pioneer settlers of the Cobden locality', describing him as 'a fervent Methodist, a strong supporter of the Salvation Army . . . and ever an advocate of Temperance principles'.

Dad wrote about his wife's great-grandparents:

> Thomas and Jane had a lot in common. Both, at the age of eighteen, found themselves infinitely far from home, cut off forever from family and friends, penniless, and at the very bottom of that society's pecking order; he, with a criminal record, and she, Irish and illiterate. What they achieved seems to have come entirely from internal resources.

Jane's story demonstrates courage, resilience and intelligence. New research indicates she may have been only thirteen when she arrived in Geelong, not eighteen. The fact that the marriage record has her age as eighteen, the same age listed for her on the ship she arrived on two years earlier, should have been a clue. Illiterate at the time, she probably did not know her true age. Eventually, Jane learned to read and write and later became an advocate for female suffrage. She must have been happy to see this achieved within her lifetime at the Federation of Australia in 1901. She died in her eighties, of a broken thigh caused by a fall chasing chickens in her fowl-yard.

Jane's journey to a place she'd never heard of was not her decision. Family legend tells that, confused and half-starved in the terrible Irish famine that had killed her parents, teenaged Jane 'lost her brothers on the wharf' and got on the wrong boat. To her horror, she realised when they were at sea that, while the boys were headed for Boston or New York, her ship had its sails set for Australia. She never saw her family again.

What our family legend did not say was that Jane had come from the workhouse. It was not until I went to Skibbereen in County Cork that I learned it was the town hit hardest by the famine of the 1840s. Cork is a place of almost fairytale beauty. Lakes, then the sea, shimmer below rocky hillsides where goats and sheep wander among gorse bushes. But in the town cemetery, a plaque notes that Skibbereen was the 'epicentre of the horror' of starvation, and the graveyard contains a mass grave of 9000 coffin-less and nameless bodies.

When the potato blight destroyed the major form of sustenance, the destitution was overwhelming. If the blight had lasted a year, people would probably have survived, but it continued for five long years, from 1845 to 1850. The English government, which had responsibility for the Irish, treated them as a subject people, and insisted they continue to export corn, even though starving. It offered no help to the people. Instead, it transported them, prisoners of circumstance, innocent of any crime.

One can imagine the terror of the separated siblings. The authorities, without telling the teenagers, herded the boys in one direction to be sent to Canada or the United States, the girls in another. Jane Leary, eighteen, Roman Catholic, of Skibbereen, no parents listed, is on the passenger register of the *Eliza Caroline*, which docked at Port Phillip on 31 March 1850. Research has revealed that girls from the Irish workhouses now have many thousands of Australian descendants. Under the Earl Grey scheme to populate the colonies, between 1848 and 1850, over 4000 girls were sent to Sydney, Port Phillip and Adelaide.[9]

The story of the orphans is not a happy one. Once in Australia, they faced prejudice and anti-Irish hostility. The employers were reportedly disappointed in the domestic skills of their servants who, destitute, usually had no training in the domestic arts. Like Jane, most of the girls were illiterate, and all were penniless and responsible for their own survival. Some, dismissed from their employers' houses, turned to prostitution. It says much for Jane's character that she apparently befriended her employer, Mrs Rice, and insisted that her much older husband stop drinking to marry her. In another family story, Jane wanted to marry in the Catholic Church; her fiancé did not. She then told the priest that if he could find her family, she'd remain a Catholic. The priest failed. Jane lost her faith and married my great-great-grandfather in a Protestant church.

As heartbreaking as Jane's early life was, she ended up a contented woman, long lived, happily married (at least according to her husband) and the mother of nine, none of whom had died of the illnesses that took children so frequently at that time.

The same cannot be said of another of my Irish great-grandmothers, the County Tyrone-born Margaret Connor.

Chapter 23

Hardship,
Best Forgotten

In February 1850, the *Lady Kennaway* arrived at Port Phillip with a shipload of bounty immigrants. Margaret Connor, twenty-seven, a passenger from Cookstown, Ireland, was listed as a nursemaid. Perhaps as one of the twenty-one per cent of Irish working women who could both read and write,[1] she had answered an advertisement for a free passage, the chance of a job at a living wage in a country with plentiful food.

It is possible Margaret met her husband when he drove one of the wool-laden bullock drays to the port of Geelong in late summer to fill the holds of ships returning to England. A bonus for the drivers was a first glimpse at the newly arrived female passengers. My guess is that did not happen. It's more likely she met her husband when both worked at the same sheep station, she as a maid, he as a shepherd or farm hand.

John Wilson Crow and the former Margaret Connor were married in Christ Church of England, Geelong, in October 1852. John is identified as a 'farmer', Margaret as a 'domestic servant'. Both signed their names in a confident and flowing hand. John was about thirty-two, and Margaret, though she appeared to fudge her age, was at least thirty.

Despite the detailed information to be gleaned from the manifests of ships arriving from the British Isles before the time of John Crow's marriage, we have been unable to identify him. Most likely he was a 'bounty' immigrant. These enterprising young people, mostly male, were selected in England or Scotland by agents paid by the ship owners. Their passages were paid by the sale of Crown land in the colony and, on arrival, they were put to work for the squatters.

John Crow seems to have been a man of modest talents and moderate success. Yet he must have been courageous. When he arrived, skirmishes between Aboriginals and white people often disturbed the peace, though the Europeans' overwhelming advantage of firearms resulted in ten times more native than white deaths through open conflict. The gentle but still wild countryside had first been explored by Mr Hawdon and Lieutenant Munday only a few years before John Crow took a job, probably as a shepherd, near Geelong. A shepherd's life would have been hard, monotonous and hungry. Though the Indigenous people (the Kulin alliance of clans in this area) foraged to obtain a nutritious vegetable diet, this fare was unrecognised by the whites. The lonely shepherds often drank their wages away. However, those who saved had a future in front of them, and it seems that John Crow had made the journey from Berwick-on-Tweed, Northumberland, on the Scottish border with dreams of being a farmer.

At least, that is the profession he listed on his marriage certificate, when he chose a Protestant woman from Northern Ireland for his wife. If she thought she'd married a farmer, John Crow, alert to rumours of the possibilities of wealth, had other dreams. They had to do with gold.

Rumours of gold had run around Port Phillip for at least a year before Margaret Connor arrived in the colony. The government at first tried to prevent the news from spreading. But gold proved a lure as strong as the scent of water for the thirsty. A bureaucracy created to maintain law and order over a people who simply did not respect authority soon lost control. Just like the squatters, who had explored and taken for themselves the best grazing land twenty years earlier, a new set of explorers set out to discover the glitter found in rivers and rocks. Control soon became impossible. Within a couple of months, the goldrush became a stampede. Unlike our ancestors Jane and Thomas Constable and Ann and Sam Lord, who went to Ballarat, Margaret and John Crow headed further north to Bendigo. The newly married couple left farm and domestic employment, and joined the throngs in search of a quick buck, leaving chaos behind them, and creating it as they moved.

Only a few months before, Bendigo had been a place of natural beauty. An early settler, Thomas Dungey, reported in a letter to the *Bendigo Advertiser* on 6 April 1906:[2]

> The second week of February 1852, [we] camped at about where the blacksmith's shop was afterwards ... and thought it the loveliest spot on earth, with waterholes with water in them as clear as crystal, kingfisher birds flitting about in the silver wattle, whose lovely foliage almost hid the banks of the creek from view, with occasional splashings as the duck-billed platypus tumbled from the banks into the water. But there was not a human being to be seen anywhere.

By later in the year, according to the *Annals of Bendigo*, the great forests of ironbark that had clothed the hills had begun to disappear. In order to build mineshafts and huts, miners had stripped the countryside of trees. Journalist George MacKay, in a *History of Bendigo*, put it this way: 'After the winter of 1852 almost all of the natural beauty that Bendigo had possessed had disappeared. Dust was everywhere, ankle-deep, blowing in blinding gusts at every puff of wind.'[3]

Margaret and John's first dwelling in Bendigo would have been a calico tent. Perhaps they progressed to a slab hut, with chairs made of tree trunks, tables from chests, and sagging beds fashioned from tree limbs and rags. The miners and their families cooked over outdoor campfires in all weathers. Like the Constables and the Lords in Ballarat, the Crows in Bendigo, a married couple, were in the minority on the goldfields. Most of the miners left their families, if they had them, back in town. That Margaret Connor Crow, Jane Leary Constable and Ann Williams Lord, my great-great-grandmothers, went with their husbands to the diggings suggests they were women of strong character, and much depended upon by their partners.

Margaret Connor Crow gave birth to her first child, William, in 1854. John Crow gave his family's address as View Point, Bendigo. I have a picture of View Point in 1856. It is a beautiful place with fine buildings—churches, banks and shops had sprung up rapidly as a result of the quest for gold. Dr Smith and Mrs Speed, a nurse, attended the birth, so it seems fortune followed the Crows for a time. Despite these attentions, William died as an infant, for he is never mentioned again. In the mud and frost of mid-winter, 1855, Margaret Connor Crow gave birth to a little girl. They named her Margaret.

The Crows had more children: John Patrick, born in 1858, Eliza Jane, born about 1859, and Isabella, born 1861 and alive only five days. By then, dreams of wealth in Bendigo had ended for the Crows. No doctor attended Isabella's birth. The last baby, Matilda, born sometime before 1866, did not survive.

Not far from Bendigo runs the river Loddon, with the towns of Bridgewater-on-Loddon and Inglewood nearby. Struggling with their packs and small children over terrible roads, the Crows decamped to Inglewood. The local paper reported: 'In the winter of '62, long and many were the complaints from those who were obliged to travel between Inglewood and Bendigo. No one made the journey for pleasure.'[4]

At the time of Isabella's birth and death, John Crow is reported to have been a shepherd at McIntyre's station in nearby Kingower. It is here, in the sleepy hamlet of Bridgewater-on-Loddon, that the story of my great-grandmother Margaret Crow intersects with that of her husband, a Swedish immigrant named Adolph Louis Charlholmes.

* * *

A few years ago, my brother John and our cousin Barby travelled to explore the place where our mothers' paternal grandparents lived and died. It is very quiet country now, this part of central Victoria, but in the 1850s and 1860s this somnolent land had exploded with activity as newcomers from every corner of the world bashed the rocks to get at the glinting gold below. Among them were two Swedish men who had escaped the penury of their homeland with the promise of gold in a little town called Talbot.

The settlement at Talbot came to life when Scandinavian prospectors hit it big. The news of the 'Scandinavian Rush' of 1859 may have reached the ears of Andrew Edquist and Adolph Louis Carlholm (as he was then known) in Sweden, or through rumours at ports the sailors visited. Attracted by its goldrush, Adolph Louis came to Victoria in about 1868. My mother believed he had been a sailor because he had passed down to his son Bert some small Chinese artifacts. Adolph Louis Charlholmes, the supposed sailor, and Andrew Edquist, a tailor, might have been employed on ships that blew them all the way from Sweden. Given the unimaginable distance from home, each must have realised this would be a one-way trip. On reaching Port Phillip, the newcomers made their way inland from Melbourne or Geelong on foot or by ox-cart to Talbot, where a 'Scandinavian Crescent' proves that this was a destination for their countrymen.

Five years after the first goldrush, Talbot was hot, dry, and riddled with mine shafts. It had settled its priorities in true Australian style, with courthouse and churches, seven schools, two soap and candle factories, two breweries and sixteen hotels. By the time our two Swedes arrived in Victoria in the 1860s, their future wives, born in 1855 and 1843 respectively, were already on the goldfields. My mother's paternal grandmother, Margaret Crow, born in a tent, spent her girlhood in a succession of temporary abodes as her father searched for gold.

My father's paternal grandmother, Eliza Turner, whose family had emigrated from England, was living in Talbot when her first husband died in a mining accident. She then married the much older Andrew Edquist, by all accounts a 'gentle man, not good at business', according to Granny. Their three sons, including the youngest, Victor, were all born in Talbot, before the family moved to Adelaide and Andrew Edquist supported the family as a tailor.

In the following century the grandchildren of Adolph Louis Charlholmes and Andrew Edquist married and became our parents.

Adolph Louis Carlholm, the Swedish sailor/farmer, changed his last name on arrival in Australia, apparently thinking that the tongue-twisting moniker of 'Charlholmes' sounded more English. You would think an unusual surname like this would make the ancestor-hunting easy. But unlike the Lords, the Charlholmes did not trumpet their history. All we knew of my maternal grandfather's early life was this wistful sentence from my mother's memoir:

'His father was a hotel keeper at Bridgewater-on-Loddon, once a goldmining town I think, but by the time Bertrand was born whatever gold had once been there was gone.'

Swedes are uncommon in early Australian settlement. Except for Germans who founded vineyards in South Australia, most pre-twentieth century immigrants were from the British Isles, like our other ancestors. The Scandinavians were so few—between 1200 and 2000 in the years before World War II—that they had little opportunity to pass along their cultural heritage. It seems that Adolph Louis, like most of the Swedes who came to the goldfields, quietly melded with the predominately British–Irish populations, intermarrying rather than forming group associations with their co-nationalists.[5]

On a May day, only mildly warm, we three amateur genealogists—me, my brother John, and our cousin Barby— poked about Talbot, hoping to find a trace of our ancestors. Hunger had overtaken us. In Talbot, we'd found not a shop open, let alone a café. But, as the website for Bridgewater-on-Loddon states helpfully,

> A problem with most rural towns is the necessity to travel long distances to get most items, whether these items are basic groceries, white goods, clothing or even a haircut. Bridgewater-on-Loddon, however, has a greater number of businesses than the average rural town and, because of this, a far wider range of products and services are available without having to resort to the usual drive to the closest city.

Perhaps, we thought, we could find the pub at Bridgewater once run by our great-grandparents. It was two o'clock by the time we strolled up to the bar of a hotel by the river and asked if they served lunch. The barmaid paused, slapping a rag over the counter.

'What'll ye have?' she asked.

We pointed to the blackboard above her, on which were written the daily specials. Most were now off, it seemed. But we settled on lamb shanks and a bottle of red. Both were surprisingly tasty, considering the smell of mould that lingered over the place. Moving our table away from the bar and its odour of spilled beer brought us closer to the men's toilets. We were the only customers in the pub. Had it been warmer, we would have moved to the neglected patio. From inside, we could hear the River Loddon, a constant flush. Even in this droughty year, the river floated huge fallen logs. Platypuses may still have burrowed into hidden holes on the banks, slinking into the river to fish, but we saw none. Trucks clattered over the bridge.

'Do you know anything about the history of this place?' we asked the barmaid.

'Well, there used to be a lolly shop over the road, but it's gone now.'

'Her history doesn't go back further than her own childhood,' muttered John as we sat down to our table. Perhaps we were the odd ones, asking a teenager about the origins of this place. It was only our generation, the last who heard stories of the very early days, who wanted so much to know and to tell.

Gold prospecting is chancy at best, and for most people resulted in backbreaking work and endless poverty. It is no wonder Adolph Louis discovered that watering the diggers in the form of owning a pub would be more profitable than digging for gold. Then again, with hotels on every street corner in gold towns, the profit in hotel keeping in nearby Bridgewater was also risky.

My great-grandmother Margaret Crow knew about hardship. She'd been a maid at Powlett Plains, a tiny locality about 180 miles from Melbourne, when at the age of twenty-two, she married the much older Adolph Louis. Barby, John and I had just seen the Presbyterian Church, tiny as a handkerchief on the large flat acreage of Powlett Plains Station, where they married. The station was owned at the time by apparently benevolent Scottish settlers who had become so wealthy on their 70,000 acres of grazing land that they built their own church.

Before she died in 1912, aged fifty-six, of a malignant tumour and 'exhaustion', Margaret Crow Charlholmes had given birth to nine children, three of whom lived to adulthood: Alwyn Bertrand, his brother Ernst, and his sister Maud. My mother's eyes always filled with tears as she recalled her 'dear father', who was known by his second name of Bertrand, or Bert.

Bert Charlhomes had died a few months before I was born, as had my father's father Victor Edquist. These men shared some values. Each, despite lack of formal secondary education, had made his way in the world and were honest, intelligent and apparently kind men, devoted to their families. However, though Victor's achievements were legendary to the family, of Bert we knew very little.

I suspect now that, like my mother, he was shy and gentle, not given to storytelling. Indeed, as Nan reported in one of her columns, when she came home from school bursting with an extravagant tale, he would say, quietly, 'Now tell us what really happened.'

But it does seem extraordinary that my mother, who talked constantly about her mother's family, the Lords, never talked about her father's family. She did say that her father had a sister, Maud, and that this aunt and cousins lived in Queensland. She may have mentioned someone called Ernie, but I was not sure who he was.

As I read Mum's memoir last year, a sentence struck me as strange:

> My father, born 25/9/82, was a very well-liked person,
> popular amongst the sons-in-law and accepted as a member
> of the Lord family by all of them. Arthur and Frank were,
> in particular, his great friends and for years they played
> solo or bridge in a group on Friday nights.

This could be a veiled reference to the fact that she was
never accepted by her in-laws, the Edquist family, and felt
disliked by them. But for me, as a girl who adored her father,
it seemed an odd thing to say. My daddy would never feel he
had to be accepted by anyone, least of all his in-laws. He
was who he was. I wondered, as I pondered these lines of
my mother's, why we heard so little of Bert's family if he was
so well liked. Was there a secret somewhere? Perhaps it was
because they were less colourful than the garrulous, fable-
spinning Lords. Or perhaps my mother, the very model of
propriety, did not want to probe. I regret now that I didn't
encourage her to talk about her father.

While researching my family history, I had written to
ask Kevin Poysner, of the Inglewood Historical Society, if
he knew of my great-grandparents' pub in Bridgewater-on-
Loddon. He did not but asked if we had photographs he
could add to the historical society's collection. We did not.

A year or so later, I contacted Kevin Poysner to buy his
book on cemetery records for Inglewood, where Margaret
Connor Crow was buried after she died of tuberculosis
in 1866. Kevin sent me the book. I scanned it eagerly and
found the documentation I was looking for, and, as if in a
fairytale, a note fluttered out of the book and fell to the floor.

'The funniest thing happened', Kevin had written in
longhand. 'A lady has just been here and has been looking
for the same family, the Crows and Charlholmes. I wonder
if she is a relative. Her name is Betty Kellett, and here is her
contact information'.

I wrote to Betty—'great-granddaughter of John Wilson

Crow and the granddaughter of his son, John Patrick Crow'—and got a long reply. Betty's letter provided valuable corroborative evidence about her great-grandfather, John Crow. She confirmed he was born in Berwick-on-Tweed, Northumberland, in 1820, and married Margaret Connor, who died in Inglewood.

And then she told me more. When Margaret Connor Crow died at the age of forty-four in 1866, she left her husband and their children—Margaret, aged eleven, John Patrick, nine, and little Eliza Jane, a year younger. Just like his grandson, my mother's father Bert, many years in the future, John Crow was married fourteen years, then lost his wife and had to care for three children. He couldn't do it. He left his children with a neighbour and disappeared.

Betty's letter explained that forty-six years later, John Patrick and his wife Jane had taken in their nephew Ernst, the second son of John Patrick's sister Margaret and her husband Adolph Louis Charlholmes, after Margaret died in 1912. Ern, a teenager at the time, was ten years younger than his brother Bert. Their sister Maud, then in her early twenties, seemed unable to take care of anyone. Adolph died in 1915 of 'senile dementia', so presumably could not have acted as a parent to Ernie.

Ern fell in love with his cousin Ellen—'Nell'—known as a 'magnificent dressmaker'. Against the family's wishes, they married in 1920, and had two daughters. These children, Shirley and Dorothy, were my mother's first cousins. I had never heard of them.

Perhaps men are less inclined to talk about their relatives. From my immediate family, I know this common belief is not true. So, the question remained.

I discovered, from the Registry of Births, Marriages and Deaths, Victoria, that Ernie had died in 1966 at Box

Hill. I was living at home for most of 1966. Mother never mentioned his death and, to my knowledge, did not go to the funeral, though Box Hill is no more than fifteen minutes from our home in Kew. Yet, my mother knew her mother's relations—uncles, aunts and cousins—and kept in touch with them all.

My mother never wrote anything negative about anyone. She simply didn't speak about matters that made her unhappy.

In a 1916 letter to her sister-in-law Doris Lord, Stella complained of Bert supporting his sister Maud and her feckless husband while they themselves went without. And my mother mentions in her memoir how resentful her parents were when Maud and her three children had come to stay with the family, 'staying on and on' at the time of their youngest child Marjorie's birth.

The favour was not returned. A few years later, Stella was on the cusp of death. Maud did not step in to assist when Bert was faced with emotional and financial disaster. His wife Stella's death coincided with the start of the Depression, and Bert's finances never recovered from the cost of her cancer treatments.

At first, after their mother Stella died, her older daughters Ruth and Nan moved in with their Uncle Ernie and his wife. Ernie was an accountant, and my mother's memoir notes his respectable suburban address, close to her home. Aunt Nell was not just an in-law, but also Bert and Ernie's first cousin. Despite this double connection, it seems that Nell and Ern turned their backs. After helping for a short time, they threw their nieces out. My mother's memoir describes a chaotic period when the girls then lived with 'an English couple across the road' while their father had to board elsewhere.

Eventually their grandmother, Ruth Lord, became the

caregiver for the two adolescent girls, and little Marjorie was adopted by Jinny Lord and her husband Stan Frawley. The girls and their father were enveloped by Stella's family, not his.

No wonder the Charlholmes were written out of the family history.

Chapter 24

Up Above Comes Down Under

When I celebrated my sixth birthday at Grange Road, Dad actually presided at my party. I remember this because it was rare that he involved himself in our events. He organised the Pin the Tail on the Donkey contest. To everyone's dismay but mine, I won.

My father laughed in his good-natured way and suggested that we try the contest again to give someone else a chance. I burst into tears. Granny stormed in and said I couldn't win since I was the hostess. She may even have accused me of cheating. When I cried, she said I was so mean and horrible that all the children would have to go home. More wails. My friends were distressed and, moreover, had no way of going home early because their mothers weren't picking them up for a couple of hours. Mum appeared, looking anxious in her floured apron, to make the peace, and my father loped through the sunroom door to escape.

It was Granny who set the tone for manners in our house. I cannot argue with the premise that children should be taught to be unselfish, and the embarrassment of a tantrum is a small price to pay for this lesson. I noticed, through my rage, my mother as peacemaker, and my father choosing to leave the room rather than confront his mother over her hostility to his children.

I see now that my grandmother had a lofty goal, to

bring up her grandchildren in the English manner of half a century before. With supreme self-control, she believed, an individual could overcome physical and emotional hardship in a manner worthy of a child of the Empire. To Granny, members of the British Royal Family exemplified the values of duty and obedience she sought to instill in us.

In early February 1952, King George VI died. I was still learning to read at the time, and the newspaper printed a photo of the King, bordered in black. In huge lettering, which our teacher held up for us all to see, we read aloud the headline, 'King George Dies'. Outside the classroom windows, the sun beckoned and the tops of the trees waved, a reminder that we had just returned to school from the summer vacation and were trapped inside a hot classroom until three in the afternoon. The smell of bananas in someone's lunch wafted up and drifted over the desks, mixed with the ever-present reek of crayons, chalk and dirty socks. A faraway king meant nothing to us.

A year and a half later, on a wintry evening, our family sat around the wireless in Granny's room to hear the Archbishop of Canterbury crown the pretty young Queen Elizabeth II. As Britons squashed together patiently on their streets, under umbrellas, waiting for the threatened rain on that cool, grey, English summer day in June 1953, we had a greater treat. My little brothers, Andrew and Christopher, had been tucked into bed, but John and I were allowed to stay up late with our parents to listen to the live broadcast of this momentous occasion, Granny in her chintz-covered wing chair, our parents on the sofa, and John and I on the window seat, warmed by the porcelain stove on that chilly winter night. From a stack on the scalloped-edge side table Granny gave us commemorative silver coins adorned with the young Queen's profile.

Forty-five years after she abandoned English shores, Granny remained devoted to the Royal Family. She was particularly interested in Woburn Abbey, near the village of Aspley Guise in Bedfordshire, where her 'people', as she called them, came from. She told us that her not-so-distant ancestors had been in service to Woburn Abbey's owner, the Duke of Bedford. Preserving a link to the nobility, even one of service, was important to her.

In Granny's papers is a letter dated 27 September 1951. It is a copy, addressed to 'Dear All' from a Sister Beswetherick, at Buckingham Palace.

> I do apologise for deserting you in this way and for not being able to tell you about it, but one has to obey a Royal command. It was sweet of you to write and I was so pleased. His Majesty is an excellent patient and is improving daily, and would be out of bed in a trice if we allowed it. He is such a dear and so considerate. He is meticulously tidy person and likes everything in its usual place or he is very put out. His temper is very quick and, until you know him, can be quite frightening, but blows over in a moment and he says, 'Don't take any notice of me. I'm not like this normally. I'm really quite a serene sort of chap.' That's hardly true, but he's so lovable; I find it hard to believe he is my sovereign and I am really here. The Queen and Princess Margaret always come along to say 'goodnight' and stop to have a chat with us on the way. They are both so charming and so easy to talk to.

Was our English grandmother a friend of the letter writer? The faded brown letter, pecked out on a manual typewriter, finishes with a note at the bottom in Granny's handwriting: 'Sister was there 10 weeks. On their leaving, each Sister was presented by his Majesty with a lovely brooch.' Granny kept this letter as a prized possession.

Her devotion to the Royals was not shared by our parents, who had been born in the Antipodes. In those days, Australians had a complex relationship with England. The older generation called it 'home'. My parents and future generations did not. After we children had caught a glimpse of the Queen on her 1954 visit, from a high, portable stadium seat along Toorak Road provided by the local council, we lost interest in the Royal Family, much to Granny's disappointment. She listened faithfully to the Queen's high-pitched tones in her annual Christmas speech, while we ran around in the summer sunshine, screaming in accents that made her cringe.

Granny lived in Australia for almost half a century, yet the local accent had always grated on her. As a teenager, one of my numerous faults was my diction, according to Granny, who advocated elocution lessons. Fortunately, my mother ignored this suggestion. In my world, having a false English accent only made one seem stuck-up.

This muddled attitude reflected the cultural atmosphere of Australia at the time. As the newspapers and our books told us, we were happy-go-lucky larrikins, while the grown-up world in the northern hemisphere was more hard-working, more responsible, and so much closer to the scene of all the action that mattered. The fact that the twentieth century had seen two devastating world wars, both of which started in Europe, while we lived in sunshine and health in a relatively prosperous, casteless society was one of those impossible, irreconcilable contradictions, like religious belief. Our eyes told us one thing, our 'betters' another. And our grandmother believed herself to be one of our betters.

In fact, in the 1950s, our betters from above were moving down under as quickly as possible. In the newspaper we saw pictures of ships bearing immigrants. Not just Britons, but Italians and Greeks by the thousands gathered what they could from the wreckage of Europe and booked passage for Australia. The newcomers settled in, at first in migrant hostels or crowded in with friends. The British among them complained about being housed in Nissen huts left over from the war.[1] These quasi-refugee-camp quarters enraged those who had paid only £10 for a passage across the world, courtesy of the Australian government. If the Italians and the Greeks complained, we could not understand them. The men, who had come first to find jobs on farms and orchards and in construction, now scrambled up the gangways to greet their wives and children. Reunited, these families soon created thriving vegetable and flower gardens in the tiny inner-city lots they crowded onto, with many generations under one roof. Fortunately, with the country needing to establish a manufacturing sector and the government throwing money into infrastructure, jobs were easy to find. The harder part was integration into the larger society.

Kitty's generation was only the second to be Australian-born, but her brothers and sisters had married native-born Australians with Anglo names. So homogeneous had the white population grown by World War I that I wonder how Ernst Otto Charlholmes, Mum's uncle, got by at that time with his German-sounding name.

Kitty warmly welcomed the 'New Australians' who swarmed to her counter at the post office. Kitty had taken a job when Bill's increasing disability, because of the shrapnel lodged in his belly, made him retire early. In Balaclava, where Kitty worked, Italian, Yiddish and Dutch were only some of the languages heard in the bustling shops. Kitty, just as garrulous, joined the cosmopolitan chatter with delight. She developed a new network of friends, not only in her colleagues, but also the customers. It was a perfect career; she could talk all day long. But, with John and I staying with her, as we frequently did, Aunt Kitty faced the problem of childcare for the first time. After Uncle Bill had given John a couple of glasses of beer to make him sleep and I excitedly reported this to my parents, Kit made a quick decision. 'I'll take the kids to work with me,' she told my mother. And so, John and I were introduced to life at the post office.

We felt important behind the counter. Though sometimes a little bored with our colouring books and a lunch eaten by eleven o'clock, my brother and I were nonetheless fascinated by this world of work.

'You send for me a letter?' The New Australians formed a snaky queue in front of Kitty's till. Sometimes they counted out leaves of bills as if they were dealing a pack of cards, exchanging the pound notes for money orders to send home to relatives in the Old Country. The customers took the precious money order to a counter at the side, wrote a note and enclosed it in an envelope. Kitty would then gently affix an overseas stamp on the letter, and give it a satisfactory *thwump* with her hand-held stamper announcing, 'Airmail'.

'I send home to Italy! My family there, they save to come here,' the newcomers said. Their excited voices, in broken English, mingled with Kit's loud laugh.

The pounds, shillings and pence were in different slots behind the counter, like the silverware drawer in our kitchen, but the counting of the money usually sent Kitty into a flap. She liked a bit of excitement. Perhaps, too, she was watching us with half her mind as we made nuisances of ourselves around the back of the spacious sorting room. The letters flowed into big canvas bags, and the postmen hauled them off on trolleys. The stamps changed over the years that John and I joined Kit at her workplace; a side view of King George was replaced by one of the pretty young Queen. The meaning of it all, that a real value was placed on communication, the reams and reams of paper on which people wrote and others read, made an indelible impression on me. People wrote about where they were and how they fared so their relatives on the other side of the world would know, not just that they were still alive, but what they felt. United by the written word, their loved ones far away were not forgotten.

* * *

Radio Australia, where she had once communicated with the outside world, had opened my mother's eyes to a wider vision than the Anglo-centered outlook shared by our Melbourne neighbours. In our childhood, and even more so in theirs, names of non-English or Irish origin were unusual. Our Swedish surname was mangled by strangers. Even though our family had been in Australia for generations, as an adult I was told 'Edquist is not a very Australian name'. Perhaps this helped our parents understand immigrants and their challenges. In her quiet way, my mother had the gift of friendship. Never interested in fashion, tennis, ladies' lunches, or any of the other ways middle-class women spent their leisure hours, Mum's compassion and craving for intellectual stimulation led her to seek out newcomers.

I realise now that the constant flow of ideas from Mac Ball influenced my parents, particularly my mother. Their passionate patriotism, which stemmed more from a sense of the possibilities of postwar Australia than from a sense of power or empire, must have come in large part from conversations with this freethinking man. He saw potential, not problems, in being open to new ideas. Like Mac, my parents made friends with the foreigners who streamed into Melbourne. The people who came to our house at Grange Road—eating peanuts and drinking cheap wine on the stiff blue velvet Victorian sofas—included Czechs, Hungarians, Russians, Americans and Japanese immigrants.

Japanese. How my strait-laced parents befriended the

Tokimasas is something of a wonder. According to the historian Takemae Eiji, 'In 1948, the Immigration Minister, Arthur Calwell saw fit to warn parliament that "it would be the grossest act of public indecency to permit a Japanese of either sex to pollute Australian shores".'[2]

How did Mr Tokimasa get to Melbourne? In fact, Mr Tokimasa was a Nisei, an Hawaiian of Japanese ancestry. He had married his Scottish wife Elizabeth (known as Lebe) in New York and worked there as a journalist for the *Japan Times*. He also worked in Tokyo for the Japanese Foreign Office, and was sent to Canberra to work for the first Japanese Embassy in Australia, which opened in 1941.

Within the year the Embassy closed down because of Japan's entry into World War II.[3] With his usual broadmindedness, Mac Ball saw David Tokimasa's American background and Japanese language skills as a crucial asset, and hired him at the ABC to monitor Japanese broadcasts. That is how Mr Tokimasa became friendly with our mother.

How difficult life must have become for the Tokimasas after hostilities ended! With his name and appearance, David Tokimasa was an untouchable in war-traumatised Australia. The memory of the thousands of Australian servicemen who had died in horrible circumstances in Japanese prisoner-of-war camps was too fresh. So, the Tokimasas became entrepreneurs. They started a chicken farm. They celebrated its opening with a party. All our friends were there. We kids were sent to explore the chicken sheds, of which the Tokimasas were very proud. Parallel lines of coops ran down a huge field as far as we could see. Inside, the squawking birds were organised by colour, placed so they could scratch at the ground and walk around within the cage, yet separated so they could not hurt one another. These were not free-range chickens, yet not battery hens either. As a child whose household chore it was to feed our chooks, this seemed a modern and scientific arrangement, but not the natural order of things. Our hens got into arguments with one another, and all were under the domination of our bossy rooster.

The party was memorable to me because my brother John became sick.

'John drank seven bottles of Coca-Cola!' I tattled as he reeled, puking, around the barbeque.

'Too much of a good thing, eh, boy?' my father said, picking up the little boy gently. My mother stood by, relaxed and decked out, for once, in slacks and a sweater instead of her usual shirt-waist dress. She was holding Andrew and softly laughing. I try to hold on to this memory of my mother being lighthearted.

The chicken venture did not succeed, and the Tokimasas moved on, leaving Australia in 1957 for London.[4]

How did our parents come to have such interesting friends? We were not 'society' people, which no doubt disappointed Granny greatly. Our parents mixed with a different crowd: intellectual, charming and, often, Jewish. Chris has speculated that because Dad did not grow up in Melbourne he was regarded as an outsider, and because Mum came from a family of modest means, they were sensitive to the feelings of exclusion shared by those from less fortunate or more colourful backgrounds.

In a speech, Paul Morawetz,[5] an Austrian/Czech immigrant, spoke about the difficulties Jewish newcomers—with their strange accents and unpronounceable names, their ignorance of football and cricket and their propensity to work hard—faced in the postwar world. One of the 'enemy aliens' who had worked briefly with my mother at Radio Australia, Paul had been born in Austria and raised in Czechoslovakia in wealth and privilege in an assimilated Jewish family. He and his wife Dita managed to avoid the Nazi catastrophe because

Paul was working in Thailand at the time and took a ship to Australia in 1940. Determined to make a name for himself in the new country, he started businesses in Melbourne. In 1941, he took a nighttime job at Radio Australia monitoring German broadcasts. According to his biography, the Australian Security Intelligence Organisation (ASIO) became suspicious. Because Germany had absorbed Austria in 1939, Paul held a German passport. Despite the fact that the German consul in Thailand (then Siam), which had issued the Morawetzs' passports, had them stamped 'Israel' and 'Sarah', thus identifying them as Jews and, therefore, hardly likely to support the Axis powers, ASIO surveilled Paul for years.

ASIO had a vast file on dissenters, especially those with left-wing views.[6] However, not only did Morawetz appear not to have had firm political convictions, he was even asked to run for office for the Liberal Party, the antithesis of actual liberalism. Nevertheless, ASIO hounded him for three decades, and eventually Dita and Paul took up residence in Israel. While not close friends, our family knew the Morawetzs through the Wilkins family and their circle of Czech émigrés. It appears that ASIO didn't like Morawetz's chutzpah, preferring refugees to be humble and grateful.

Dad was diffident, so Mum made the social arrangements. Besides the Japanese–American Tokimasas, our friends included the Czechoslovakian Wilkins family, the Austrian Stevens's, Czech Lotse Santer and his Australian artist wife Edith, and the wonderful Sklovsky family.

Following the tradition of adventurous Australian girls going overseas and meeting an interesting foreigner, Celia Weigall met Grisha Sklovsky in 1937 in the foyer of a movie theatre in Lyon. Grisha was a gregarious Russian whose Jewish family had fled, first, from the Bolsheviks to Berlin, then after the Nazis took power, to Paris. Separated from each other for years, Grisha served in the Free Czech army, while Celia joined the Red Cross, in part to search for him. By some miracle, they reunited in Greece, married, and had three children. Anna, Michael and Jane were roughly the same ages as we four Edquist children. We remain close friends to this day.

Celia Sklovsky painted portraits and landscapes and created beautiful gardens. She spoke slowly and thoughtfully, her head to one side. Sometimes, she took so long to reply to a question or comment you wondered if she'd heard it. Then she'd offer an answer worth waiting for. She took the opinions of young people seriously, which made the Sklovsky house a magnet. In addition to her own three children and various nephews who wandered in and out freely, Celia also acted as informal foster mother to several children whose parents were among the missing. She had come from a large, close family, and had this in common with Mum. Sometimes on Sunday evenings, the Sklovskys came over for a casual dinner. Our mother made kedgeree, that infinitely expandable and inexpensive curry.

Grisha had a great gift for friendship. Although married to an Australian of distinguished pedigree, his Russian name excluded him from top managerial positions in Anglo-dominated Melbourne, though he could have filled them ably. Instead he used his considerable charm to expand his social network, founding several lunch clubs for men, where, unusually in Melbourne at the time, interesting conversation was the point. Twenty-five years after he arrived in Melbourne, he counted among his friends some of Australia's most interesting and influential scientists, intellectuals and entrepreneurs.[7]

The congenial Russian became a passionate Australian. He helped found SBS, the Special Broadcasting Service. Recognising that the massive influx of migrants to Australia since the 1940s had made Melbourne one of the most cosmopolitan cities in the world, Grisha helped bring the polyglot of community radio programs under one agency in the late 1970s and early 80s. Today, SBS is one of the two federally funded public radio and television networks. It broadcasts in sixty-eight languages and features films from around the world.

Australian women brought these ambitious and intelligent men to live in Australia, and the men contributed much to our growing postwar prosperity. All these men, like my father, had professions in the sciences and manufacturing industries. They were, by and large, technical men: engineers, chemists and managers. They worked for what are now called 'multi-national corporations' such as Mobil, Monsanto and ICI. Some worked for the Commonwealth Scientific and Industrial Research Organisation (CSIRO), Australia's national scientific research agency.

The Americans, everyone knew, had saved Australia from the Japanese. But beyond that general gratitude, my parents had genuine friends in two American men who had married friends of my mother's. David Ferber (married to Helen) and Arthur Kinsman (married to Irene) were two of the gentlest and kindest men one could ever meet, displaying the natural courtesy that distinguishes American men, even today, from their rougher ocker counterparts.

The future was beckoning to me, not through the blackened headlines of the newspaper in 1951, mourning the passing of a king, but through my parents' friendships with people from all over the world, including the United States.

Chapter 25

Lifelong Friends

My parents' very best friends were Shirley and Peter Paterson. Shirley and Mum had attended MacRobertson Girls' High School, and Peter had gone to Guildford Grammar, in Perth, with Dad. They introduced my parents when Dad came east at the start of World War II. After a three-year courtship, my parents married. The family friendship has now continued into the fourth generation. Our two families often went on picnics, and one such outing is an early memory.

* * *

The gum trees stretched above the cleared earth of the campsite, their taupe-coloured leaves littering the ground. As I made circles in the dirt with a stick, Mark came running towards me on his short legs, arms outstretched. The campfire behind him blazed, and he looked like a flaming cartwheel. He was older than me, at five, but shorter. His seven-year-old brother John pedaled away on a special tricycle, adapted so his feet could reach the pedals. We all shrieked with laughter. On the way home, I fell asleep in the car. Peter, the boys' father, carried me to the door as I pretended to stay asleep. I liked being carried, but Peter tricked me. He asked me to push open the door and, still with my eyes closed, I did so.

Peter said, 'Somebody's awake.'

My bluff called, I was embarrassed. 'I'm not!' I said.

I liked nestling in Peter's kind and heavy arms, that smell of someone else's father. He felt steady as a rock.

* * *

Our parents' best friends had much in common, including the fact that the wives, Shirley and Ruth, had come from modest means while the husbands came from well-to-do families. Shirley's father had been a tram driver; Peter Paterson was from a family of graziers in the Pilbara, Western Australia. He and my father had been friends since they'd started boarding school at the age of thirteen. John Edquist remembers:

> In those days students were allowed to take their guns to school, and so Peter had his double-barrel shotgun with him. After sitting an exam, the majority of the class, who had not done well, set out to find those who had done well to beat them up. Dad and Peter (who had also done well) hid in the attic of their school boarding house. The mob located them there, and were egging themselves up to climbing the ladder to drag Dad and Peter down, when Peter doused their enthusiasm by waving his shotgun and shouting, 'First one through gets the choke barrel.' The mob lost its enthusiasm after this. Some might feel that the school was perhaps a little too *laissez faire*.

Shirley and Peter Paterson showed their mettle when faced with a potentially challenging family situation, for they had not one, but two, extraordinary sons. Shirley and Peter each carried recessive genes that led to two boys born with diastrophic dwarfism.

Mum looked after John Paterson when his mother went to hospital to give birth to her second child. Showing his

154

flair for the dramatic, his strong personality, and a sense of humour even as a two-year-old, John looked with disdain at the perfect, golden brown slice of toast my mother served him and told her, 'No! Mummy always makes it black!'

My mother's eyes filled with tears when she related how, when she visited Shirley in the hospital, Shirley told her, weeping, that the doctors told her the new baby was 'just like John'.

As Mum described the disorder, it meant the boys' bones ossified when they were young. As adults, each stood only four feet high. With the disability went difficulties in walking, as well as poor fine motor coordination. Both brothers overcame their handicap by sheer hard work and willpower. They refused to let it disable them. Each had a wonderful sense of humour, which stood them in good stead through all the childhood teasing. My brother Chris, then about seven, once asked John, 'Why do you walk like Donald Duck?'

'Because I am Donald Duck,' quacked John, and chased Chris out of the room.

Both highly intelligent, each boy undertook an amazing variety of activities. They attended Sunday school and music camp. Unbelievably, given their blunt, inflexible fingers, they played the trumpet and trombone. Mark was a particular star at this, and later in life played in jazz bands wherever he lived. As members of a model aeroplane club, they made balsa aeroplanes. Both were active in student politics at university—John became president of the Student Representative Council at Melbourne University, the most powerful post in student politics. Both earned PhDs, enjoyed successful careers, and went on to marry and father families.

John Paterson had an eldest child's drive, running for a Labor seat in federal parliament when just out of university. He did not win. His opponent was the Prime Minister, Robert Menzies.

In Australia, only the public service offered a large enough scope for John's reformist ideas. He managed the detail, but always kept the big view in mind. He was fundamentally interested in human systems, and his charisma led him to be one of the most influential people in Australian public management. His reforms made enemies. At the apex of his career, John headed the Victorian Department of Health and Community Services, where he smashed through union cronyism and corruption, and reformed the health system from top to bottom.

John was enormously fun to be with. A brilliant raconteur, he not only wielded a pair of chopsticks like a Chinese-born, he could also cook with ease, was a serious wine buff, an expert jazz trumpet player, and an entertaining dinner companion.

Mark Paterson was a gentle soul with a great sense of humour. I named my second son, Daniel Mark, after him. Like his brother, Mark Paterson always turned thoughtless remarks about his disability into a joke. Once, at a political rally when we were at university, Mark, standing next to me, heckled from the back of the room.

'Would the person who said that have the courage to stand up?' shouted the pompous invited speaker over the restless crowd.

'I am standing up, you dickhead!' yelled Mark, to the chagrin of the men at the podium and the hysterical laughter of his friends.

When I had Peter, my own disabled son, Peter and Shirley Paterson's example of how to live a full life when a family is struck a severe blow gave me great comfort. Their sons had turned out so well, it gave me confidence that I could work with my Peter.

After John's death Mark sent me notes he had made for

John's funeral, revealing how truly remarkable their parents were. Their parenting style, Mark recalled, sparked the 'can do' attitude of the boys.

> Know your strengths, develop them and play to that side of you. Be aware of your limitations and develop ways to get over them. Do not dwell on what you cannot do. Know what others have said, believed, and done. Take on board only so much as you can honestly embrace. Never fool yourself. Don't foul your own nest.

These simple rules for living resulted in two extraordinarily fine men.

Chapter 26

Science at the Dinner Table

Although we grew up in a home seething with opposing points of view about how a household should be managed and children raised, Mum kept her fury with Granny unspoken—to her cost—while Dad turned a blind eye. Neither spoke easily of intimate feelings, in contrast to their political beliefs. Beyond that, they spent weekends together, were united in the common goal of bringing up educated, articulate and reasonably polite children, and made a point of eating dinner as a family every night.

Chris must have been old enough to sit at the table without a high chair when Dad announced we would all eat in the formal dining room. My job was to set the table, and I made a game of pushing the drawers of the pass-through from the kitchen to the dining-room side. I'd take out six sets of flatware and lay them in correct order on the place mats. Table manners were well taught by our parents. In my adult life I've often been grateful for knowing which fork to use or how to eat soup. Table manners have helped in work life as well as in leisure. Setting a pretty table is one of life's small pleasures, and one reason I love giving dinner parties.

Dad took his place at the head of the table during dinner and sat a boy on each side. 'That's so I can whack some table manners into them,' he'd say playfully.

The dinner table conversation, always animated and wide-ranging, covered many adult topics. 'Science will save the world from hunger! Science will send men to the moon!' my father announced, delighted in such prognostications. He banged the dark mahogany table with his fist in emphasis. The knives and forks rattled and his eyes twinkled.

'The Russians have the bomb now,' said my mother. 'We'll all be in smithereens.'

'Nonsense! The bombing of Hiroshima was not mankind's finest hour, but look at how well the Japanese are recovering.' Dad waved a fork over the beef stew. 'The atom bombs on Japan saved thousands of Allied soldiers' lives,' he went on, unrepentant. 'Anyway, they won't bomb Australia. We'll be all right.'

I wonder if my father knew that in September 1952 the British conducted a nuclear test in the Monte Bello islands in north-western Australia, without full disclosure to the participants or the Australian government, or that from 1955 to 1963, the British again detonated blasts in the supposedly empty outback of South Australia, causing contamination lasting decades. These tests were conducted by the British government with little oversight by Australians. Anglophile Prime Minister Robert Menzies, obsessed with the Cold War, gave permission to the British to conduct these tests in the utmost secrecy. He did not even consult his Cabinet. The British Prime Minister, Clement Attlee, had warned Menzies about radioactive contamination.[1]

> The effect of exploding an atomic weapon in the Monte Bello islands will be to contaminate with radioactivity the north-east group and this contamination may spread to others of the islands. The area is not likely to be entirely free from contamination for about three years and we would hope for continuing Australian help in investigating

the decay of contamination. During this time the area will be unsafe for human occupation or even for visits by e.g. pearl fishermen who, we understand, at present go there from time to time and suitable measures will need to be taken to keep them away. We should not like the Australian Government to take a decision on the matter without having this aspect of it in their minds.

The Monte Bello islands, home to mangroves and unique bird species, lie off the north-west coast of Western Australia. In 1983–84, a Royal Commission into the history of these tests found that no one in charge had thought about the vulnerability of Aboriginal populations near Monte Bello and farther into the interior of Australia. Over 4500 people roamed these vast areas, partially clothed and exposed to the open air. The Royal Commission concluded: 'No consideration was taken of their distinctive lifestyles which would lead to their being placed at increased risk from given levels of radiation'[2]

Ironically, given my father's support for the mutual deterrence theory, fallout from the bomb at Monte Bello drifted over areas where he spent part of his childhood and where his father worked—the Murchison, Gascoyne Junction and Yalgoo settlements of Western Australia. The Royal Commission noted, in Section 5.4.5:[3]

> Although there is an element of estimation in Thackrah's population counts resulting from the fact that records were kept of Aborigines residing only at missions, on stations or in towns, his evidence showed that 4538 Aboriginal people lived in such places in the Gascoyne, Pilbara and Murchison regions.

Fallout may even have spread as far as Mt Isa in central Queensland, where, only a few years later, Dad's brother-in-law Peter Wreford would manage the Mary Kathleen uranium mine. That mine, which operated from 1958–1963, created tailings which continue to seep radioactive waters into local drainage systems, leading (at the least) to the death of native vegetation.[4] It can be confounding to realise that uranium sales have contributed greatly to Australia's present-day prosperity.

An optimist, Dad thought the fact that both the Russians and Americans had the atom bomb would prevent another world war. But Mum feared scientific progress as much as my father embraced it.

'Absolutely not!' she told the salesperson who suggested we put our feet under the X-ray machine in the shoe store. We saw other children do this, their foot bones outlined in eerie green, so the shoe could be fitted correctly.

Worried about radiation, which had not cured her mother of cancer, Mum also later campaigned against a misguided Victorian government program to X-ray everybody's chest every three years to diagnose tuberculosis. This overzealous use of technology and social control is hard to understand, given that Mantoux tuberculin skin tests were widely available and given free to schoolchildren since 1948. The compulsory X-ray program lasted from 1963 to 1974.[5]

My mother even protested the government's decision to put fluoride in the drinking water. She saw cancer looming in such tinkering with nature, and she believed the government had not done sufficient research.

'Don't be ridiculous, Ruth!' my father said. 'Many countries put fluoride in the water, and it stops dental decay.' Undeterred, my mother wrote letters to the paper protesting this action by the government. Her protests went unheeded.

My mother believed in egalitarianism and the rights of Australian citizens to demand a response from the government, but this ideal did not manifest in our home. Granny did not believe my mother had a right to her opinions, nor did she believe in equality. She instructed the puzzled butcher boy not to ring the front doorbell, but to go to what she called the 'tradesman's entrance'. This side door to the house, alongside the gully trap and next to the laundry, was the door through which we all habitually entered the house, including Kitty tottering in for her cuppa and a chat. Naturally, Granny's instructions irritated my mother. 'We don't believe in that class structure,' Mum said. 'We don't keep servants.'

She was not, of course, talking about herself. Then again, perhaps she was.

Defiantly, Mum treated the two elderly gardeners who came on Tuesday afternoons as honoured guests. As they crept crab-like around the garden, one desultorily mowing the lawn, the other slowly clipping the oleanders, she prepared them an elaborate afternoon tea. Homemade cake. A pot of tea. Served on the best china. My mother carried the tray to the porch and placed it gently on the slatted table.

'There we are,' she said, and the old men hoisted themselves up the steps to their repast.

Compared with my mother's heroic unsupported efforts inside the house, the two sweet-natured gardeners seemed slow and ineffectual. Yet no one questioned their role in maintaining the garden—my father's domain. My guess is that this was work my father understood. The company he worked for made products that made our arid earth more arable. An industrial chemist, he was engaged in the unglamorous but useful business of making detergents and phosphate-based fertilisers.[6] Fortunately for the business, fertilisers had a ready market in the suburbs as well as on commercial farms. Despite his concerns about Australia's industrial dependency on England and America, as the 1950s progressed, my father grew excited about the future of manufacturing. After all, he argued, 'the age of steam arrived in Australia with the commissioning of a steam-powered flour mill in Sydney in 1815' and inventions such as the stripper-harvester in South Australia in 1843, or the fact that '20 or 30 models of automobiles were made in Australia, by Australians before 1905' meant that our country had proved it could be an industrial powerhouse on a level with other first-world nations. He remained frustrated that Australians, on the cusp of a burgeoning local aircraft industry just before World War II, acceded to Britain's demands that they hold back and that the car industry was now totally under foreign control. These attitudes were part of a legacy of colonialism, my father believed. But also, he wrote, in his unpublished manuscript:[7]

> In the wage earner's view, the function of industry is to provide jobs while paying not less than a specified minimum wage. The property owners, other than some manufacturers, consider that an Australian industry has to justify its existence by standing unaided against import competition from anywhere in the world. The result is a compromise with most industry dependent, directly or indirectly, on tariff protection. However, the prevailing economic philosophy is in favour of free trade while the wages system is inviolate. Consequently, Australian industry is contracting.

Dad wanted Australian technical know-how to take the world stage. Progress, in his view, meant scientific advance rather than gains in humanitarian values. He just wished others could see it his way.

These thoughts were apt to disturb my father at the dinner table. He would discuss these grown-up questions as if we children were old enough to understand. Perhaps he admired our foreign friends because they were not afraid of hard work, and willing to work long hours. Easy-going

Australians were shocked when 'New Australians' broke trading laws and sold bread on Sundays, not because Sunday was sacred, but because it violated the eight-hour day and the five-day workweek. When baffled migrants persisted in opening their bakeries on the weekend, they were threatened with violence.

'Everybody needs the weekend off!' Mum said, in support of the protests. She had never lived in a country where people could shop all weekend and every night of the week, and could not believe that such a system would have merit. Of course, she may have been making a point about her own absence of free time. No bread maker, on Sunday nights she'd have to make scones for our school sandwiches because, like locusts, we'd eaten everything over the weekend. My mother, who identified with the less fortunate, did not see the irony. Industrial action had made life harder for her own sex. And immigrants who work harder than the native-born are typical of any society; they self-select for initiative and drive. Life was changing and Mum read this as an assault on her socialist values.

It was ironic, my father often pointed out, that in a nation devoted to sport there was no leisure class. Everyone had to work to survive. With an inflation rate in the double digits, frugality—at times, necessity—meant that middle-class families had to use their leisure time to grow food. In the 1950s, the degradation of soil and plant life caused by monoculture and genetically modified foods had not yet occurred. The food farms we knew, like the Balls' farm at Eltham, and those of market gardeners who supplied the greengrocers and the Camberwell and Victoria markets, grew multiple crops. Our father did the same. He took great delight in his vegetable and fruit gardens, proud of the old-fashioned way he provided for his family. He took a scientific approach to it, forking compost in huge piles, while experimenting, too, with superphosphates and pesticides made by the firm for which he worked. The results were impressive. The big compost pile beyond the backyard's rosemary bush contained our weekly scraps from the kitchen as well as chicken droppings. Each weekend Dad turned the pile with his huge pitchfork to side-dress the rows of beans, Jerusalem artichokes, potatoes and other vegetables he grew between the Hills hoist and the chicken coop. In addition to the vegetable garden, he tended trees, including two varieties of plum, a pear, lemon, orange and an inedible crabapple. My mother made ample use of the oranges, squeezing them for our morning vitamins. Her lemon delicious pudding, an Australian classic made from our own fruit and eggs, the lemony sauce swimming under its cake-like top, remains one of my favourite desserts. The plum trees grew at the bottom of the garden, and each year we had a surfeit. They fruited in late summer, which gave my father the opportunity to buy the perfect Christmas present for my mother—a canning set.

The canning equipment sat there, unused, until March. As the summer wore on and the harvest season approached, Mum seemed to bend under the weight of the plum-burdened tree. Perspiration discoloured the pastel armpits of her shirtwaists as she marshalled her children to gather fruit. Dad's invention of an old stroller topped with a laundry basket did double duty as we bore the baskets of plums inside, never minding the many that splattered to the ground. Mum stewed plums, baked plum tart and plum cake, and we grew to hate plums in any form. And still, they came. Eventually, reluctantly, Mother pulled the bottling equipment from its cardboard box.

We never saw the results, because she hid the hated jam jars at the back of the cool cupboard. It was winter before my father remarked, 'It's about time we had some of those delicious plums. Didn't you bottle some?'

Our mother looked at her plate.

'Plums. Fantastically good for you,' Dad enthused.

'You can't eat them,' Mum said, finally.

'Why not?'

'I'm afraid you'll get botulism,' she said. Dad shook his head with bemusement at our mother's lack of confidence.

Mum's fears were not unfounded. Bottling is a tricky business. It takes a long time, directions must be followed to the letter, and cleanliness at every step is of vital importance. I doubt Mum ever had an uninterrupted hour, let alone several, to safely put up our abundance of fruit.

Our father believed in fresh food, but our family's livelihood depended on Albright & Wilson's agricultural chemicals. In addition to artificial fertilisers, the company made pesticides. Dad, a fan of DDT, kept the chooks' nesting boxes free of pests by a liberal use of spray. Years later, our dinner table talk was enlivened by a debate on Rachel Carson's book *Silent Spring*, published in 1962. The differing world views of my parents were on show. While my father did not like to hear his industry disparaged, he did see the dangers of an indiscriminate blanketing of the environment with chemicals, and was acutely aware of the balance of nature in Australia's often inhospitable landscape.

Artificial insecticides and even artificial fertilisers are now known to be a cause of many environmental ills. Dad realised this. But, as a trade-off, he considered feeding the planet to be the greater good, and believed this achievement would not be possible but for the 'green revolution' of the twentieth century.

Having grown up in the driest part of the driest continent, Dad noticed how much of the landscape—which, to the first settlers, had seemed almost park like—had, within fifty years, given up much of its fertility through mismanagement. He saw artificial fertilisers as the quickest way to restore the land to productivity. Furthermore, under Australia's unique climatic conditions, he saw industrial-scale agriculture as the only way that farmers could overcome 'salination, erosion, proliferation of unwanted species, notably rabbits, and unforeseen climatic variation'. He also believed that the only way to overcome these issues was 'through more science, more precisely tailored pesticides and fertilisers, more ingenious machines'.[8]

My mother could see no good in change, even if the convenience it offered would benefit her, while my father's twentieth century belief in technological progress has led to climate catastrophe and, arguably, to as many health problems as were averted in the previous age. He always said that in looking at history, we have to remember that people cannot foresee the future. We solve one problem only to create another.

Chapter 27

Food of the Past, Food of the Future

My father had no doubt learned early gardening skills from his father, who fed his family from a prolific garden he made, extraordinarily, at Youanmi, Western Australia. My cousin Harriet Edquist wrote of this garden:[1]

> Other photographs taken at the same time show this boy and his siblings holding other large vegetables or standing beneath a vine of truly gigantic beans. Their father Victor Edquist took the pictures and behind the lens we can sense the satisfaction of a gardener who has produced such wealth in such a place.

It is not clear how much meat the family ate, given Youanmi's distance from markets. But we made up for that a generation later at 5 Grange Road. In Australia in those days, meat cost little. We ate lamb chops and beef stews and had roast lamb or beef every Sunday.

My brother John wrote:

> In my childhood, lamb was very cheap, basically because Australia had a lot of sheep—about 113 million in 1950. These were mainly raised for their fleeces, and there were more than enough to feed the then population of eight million Australians. According to my parents, there were times when a lamb loin chop was cheaper than an egg, so

at times we had chops for breakfast. Of course, this was partly because eggs were very expensive and rationed. Those who could, kept their own chooks for eggs, but this had the undesirable consequence that rats became common throughout the suburbs.

Dad built the large chicken coop behind the woodshed at Grange Road and we always enjoyed the fresh eggs I collected. In December, he would eye an ageing hen, contemplating the rare treat of a roast chicken for our Christmas meal. He caught the squawking victim, tied its legs together, laid it on his tree-trunk chopping block, and decapitated it. The deed done, soon the chook was draining into the laundry sink, waiting for Granny to pluck and gut it. She was practical and matter of fact about this procedure; we kids found it disgusting.

She muttered under her breath at my squeamishness as she attempted to demonstrate the essential housewifely skill of plucking and gutting. I stood by her, gripping the side of the sink as I balanced on a wooden crate and leaned over, getting in the way as her reddening hands plucked feathers in the steaming water, and grasping one or two as they fluttered past. Water sloshed on Granny's shoes as I pranced, but her apron kept her striped cotton dress almost clean as she prepared the so recently alive bird.

Once it was plucked clean, Granny drained the scalding water and closed the laundry door against the flies. Here came the yucky part. She laid the chicken on a bench covered in newspaper, pulled from her pocket a very sharp knife and, with an expert hand, sliced the chicken at both ends, pulling out guts and crop to throw in a bucket under the counter. As the smell of blood and guts rose, the hot, closed room became claustrophobic. Sweat beaded on my grandmother's brow.

It was hard not to flee at this point, but a sharp reprimand that the flies would get in if I opened the door left me stuck by Granny's side till the job was done. My task then was to turn on the water in the sink so she could rinse the bird over and over before leaving it to soak in cold water. Then, she carried it by the legs into the kitchen to nestle it in the refrigerator. Later, it would be stuffed with milk-softened stale bread, apples, onions and herbs from the garden for our festive dinner.

Trained as a teacher of domestic science, Granny's views on nutrition were modern by the standards of her day. She was a proponent of homegrown foods. Our meals were almost always cooked from scratch, and my father's garden provided many of its fruits and vegetables, as well as its eggs and chickens. Composting would have come naturally to my grandparents, aware, too, of the benefits of that potent fertiliser, chicken manure. Did she chop off the bird's feet, boil and declaw them, and make a nutritious broth from the collagen-filled feet? Probably, for nothing was wasted in Granny's world. Even the chicken guts were buried near the fruit trees, fertilising as they decomposed.

Christmas Day at 5 Grange Road was a time of stress for my mother. After all the food shopping the week before, during which the back of the Morris Minor would be filled with vegetables and beverages and the dreaded (to me) Christmas ham, Mum would rise extra early on 25 December to put the festive bird in the oven. She'd then haul to church on this one day of the year those of us who did not resist. I could sense her tension rise as the minister droned on, could feel, perspiring through her dress in the stifling hot pew, her panic that the food cooking at home needed her attention, and that the guests would come too soon.

We ate Christmas lunch with Nan and her family, never with the Edquist cousins and their parents, Uncle Bill and

Aunt Judy. They came over in the afternoon, to pay their annual visit to Granny and eat Christmas cake. This much-anticipated event sometimes ended in disaster. We enjoyed our three Edquist cousins, close to us in age, all unconventional and funny. Running around outside, we roared with laughter, splashed each other with a hose, messed up the tools in the garage. The screams set Granny's teeth on edge and she was soon seized by heart pain. An ambulance screeched onto the gravelled drive to take her away as a sombre quiet settled over the house and my father, his brother, or both, backed out the curving driveway to follow the wailing ambulance. The rest of us slipped into the cool of the long, wood-panelled hallway, padding over the oriental rugs to the safety of the dining room and a drink of calming lemonade, or, in the case of the grown-ups, a fortifying glass of sherry. This guilt-inducing episode happened at least twice at Christmas, and each Boxing Day Granny reappeared, to make our mother's life a misery.

As our family became older, with bigger appetites, we began to eat turkey on Christmas Day. Chicken had lost its special occasion status as the plucked birds started to appear in the windows of fast-food establishments, browning slowly on the rotisserie. Some people—but not us—would pick one up on the way home from work. Possibly meat started to become more expensive at this time or, possibly, as her family grew older and ate more, Mum's meat-buying habits became more frugal. Her meat mincer, an iron contraption clamped on to the side of the kitchen table, got a good workout when she bought the cheaper cuts of meat at the butcher's. Sometimes I helped her grind it. By the time I was seven or eight, I had learned a lesson in where food came from, and the practical skills of preparing it.

It was not just me. In my family boys were also allowed in the kitchen, despite the risk of becoming the focus of

Granny's wrath. She didn't much like children. Or so it appeared to us. My brother John wrote:

> Granny used to make the Sunday apple pie from scratch, making the dough herself and then rolling it out with a rolling pin. This involved an extraordinary amount of violence and noise as the rolling pin hit the kitchen table. I used to try to snatch little bits. (I loved eating raw dough.) On the breadboard and right next to my thieving fingers, Granny would bring the rolling pin down with a crash, hard enough to have broken bones had she actually hit me. Only as an adult did I realise that as she never actually did hit a finger, she probably didn't intend to. I suppose she was working out all the frustrations of the preceding week. I don't think she liked living with us, and she certainly wasn't happy that our father had married our mother, rather than the daughter of one of Melbourne's better families.

On Sundays, Mum or Granny made apple pie in an old rectangular dish. They kept the upper crust from collapsing on the apples by shoving an eggcup or upturned tea cup under it, apparently on the theory that the crust cooks better if not sitting on the damp apple. Despite these moments of agreement, the kitchen was the battleground for territorial control. They might have both made a pie with an egg cup in the middle—I find this extraordinary and have never seen anyone else do it—but Granny otherwise found our mother's housekeeping methods slapdash and inclined to the shortcut. Mum would make a bed without ironing the sheets. This horrified our grandmother, who could give an entire lecture on the right way to hold a broom. Sometimes, when her bridge group was about to visit, Granny wielded the Sunbeam Mixmaster to make her Victoria sponge, with its layers of strawberry jam and whipped cream. She could slice a loaf of bread as thin as cardboard, and was annoyed when we sawed great hunks of it for our toast-and-jam snack after school.

'When I was your age, children ate bread and water,' Granny admonished.

* * *

The black-garbed Italian and Greek wives who lived secluded, mysterious lives behind closed doors in the inner suburbs were largely responsible for the liberation of the Australian housewife. As I had seen at Aunt Kit's house, when Bill took us to the beach, the immigrants from Mediterranean countries missed the dishes they had grown up with. So, they recreated them. They started cafes and bistros, introducing a new and more casual way of dining out. A food revolution began.

The newcomers changed the concept of home life. Friendship could be more public, exist outside the confines of the house. God forbid, some brave publicans even allowed women into the bar! Though admittedly, that didn't happen until the era of women's liberation. Before that, pubs required women to drink in the 'Ladies' Lounge'. This dismal situation made the new cafes even more attractive. Liquor licences allowed patrons to bring their own wine into the new cafes, and life relaxed. An expensive restaurant meal, for special occasions only, gave way to cheap and cheerful bistro eating. In the later 1950s and into the 1960s, increasing affluence meant such luxuries were more affordable, and helped to alter the roles of men and women in Australia and their attitudes to one another. Before, men drank in the pub, away from women. Women kept charge of the kitchen, men ate what they were given. Now everyone was talking about food.

Coffee led the way. Cappuccino had made its way into the essential national diet by the late 1950s. So popular is the Australian take on this Italian drink that Aussie visitors to Italy often find themselves disappointed by the native version. American companies trying to break into the Australian coffee market had their hopes dashed. Takeaway coffee is just not the norm in more laid-back Australia. If you're going to pay for café-brewed coffee, the thinking goes, you may as well drink it in the company of friends.

Cappuccino wasn't the only extraordinary discovery; New Australians ate *al fresco*. The tiniest of establishments under Greek ownership managed to offer souvlaki and pita bread and delicious fresh salads to patrons who sat outside enjoying the sunshine. Inner-city cafés pulled chairs onto the sidewalk, while vine-bedecked patios appeared behind buildings in areas once used to house rubbish bins and outside toilets. Suburbanites soon followed suit. Grilling became the thing. Backyards, no matter how tiny, now sported barbeques made from bricks and metal grilles, umbrellas shielding tables and chairs from the sun, and the occasional bar built close to the pool.

With 5 Grange Road under Granny's strict control and my father's lack of interest in home improvement, the Edquist household did not adopt this new trend. My father barbequed only on picnics, and we never ate out. The bread was wholegrain, the oranges freshly squeezed. I longed for white bread and soda, but these were only allowed at parties. At home our Sunday treat was cream on our dessert—that is, the fat of the milk that rose to the top of the bottle and was carefully skimmed off and saved.

What we couldn't have, we desperately wanted. It was at the beach with Kit and Bill that I associate the pleasure of shrieking in the waves, and the splatty joy of a sweet, soft, vanilla ice-cream cone eaten with table manners forgotten.

And once in a while, Kitty let us have fish and chips. The Italians ate shellfish pulled from the rocks, other Australians made a packet out of eating shark. The killer fish was a popular snack, renamed 'flake' by some marketing genius and sold, steaming and delicious, in paper packages. You'd never find fish recipes in our mother's repertoire; Dad refused to have it in the house. Probably, the memory of reeking fish transported by camel train to the mining towns of the outback put him off.

We children had never been to a restaurant. Our father hated to pay for food that would be better cooked at home. So, my first taste of eating out was with Kitty and Bill. In those days, when only men were allowed in public bars, women and children headed to the citrus-shaded beer garden. Kitty's birthday was in September, the first month of spring, and Uncle Bill took us to the beer garden at the back of the pub to celebrate. I still remember the enticing smell of the beer garden; the yeasty waft of Foster's mixed with the salad, barbequed steak and fries of the counter tea, the frangipani perfume of a passing waitress, the scent of the courtyard citrus trees, and the sound of relaxed laughter and joking around us. We sat under the sun-splashed umbrellas. The grown-ups' beer frothed and glistened on their baton-shaped glasses. Bill gave out a whole-body sigh as the beer sank in. John and I sipped lemon squash, the drink with the funny name, not squashed at all but tingly, tangy and sweet at the same time.

I started as a bee buzzed nearby and burrowed into an orange blossom. Kit caught Bill's eye and smiled, and I heard the hum of happiness.

Chapter 28

A Rightward Turn

As a fourth-grader, I read avidly, even the newspaper with its photos designed to shock. So my nine-year-old self reacted with dismay at a picture of a woman being dragged to a plane. Her shoe had fallen off and the two men pulling her didn't let her bend down to put it back on. This was Evdokia Petrov, a Soviet spy. The men who manhandled her were Russian officials, intent on bringing her home to face justice for being outed publicly in Australia as an agent of espionage. Mrs Petrov and her husband Vladimir had been 'diplomats' in the Soviet Embassy in Canberra since 1951. With the death of Stalin and the execution of his successor Beria, the Petrovs were in danger at home. They were, apparently, Beria protégés and, moreover, had been unsuccessful in establishing a Soviet spy network in Australia. The Australian Security Intelligence Organisation (ASIO) knew about the Petrovs' activities, and tried to 'turn' Vladimir Petrov. He decided to defect and did so without telling his wife.

No wonder she cried hysterically at being dragged to the plane. Crowds of Eastern Europeans who remembered Soviet tyranny surrounded the three trying to board. The strongmen shook them off and pushed Evdokia onto the plane. But ASIO had a trick up its sleeve. At Darwin, where the plane made a stop, they managed to separate her from her guards, and asked if she wanted to stay in Australia. She said she wanted to talk to her husband.

One can imagine the phone conversation between Evdokia in Darwin and Vladimir in Sydney: 'Why didn't you tell me? Do you really want to send me to my death?' Notwithstanding his answer, which must have been unsatisfactory at best, Evdokia decided to defect as well. Protected by a new identity, the Petrovs lived out quiet lives in a seaside suburb of Melbourne, their whereabouts hidden from the public.[1] For years I focused on Mrs Petrov's shoe. Someone even wrote a play about it.

As it turned out, the Petrov Affair turned Australian politics to the right—a swing of the pendulum that remained until 1972. The Labor Party leader, H.V. Evatt, accused the Menzies government of doctoring the Petrov documents, which revealed three members of Evatt's staff were Soviet informants. Evatt gave a speech in October 1954 blaming B.A. Santamaria and his anti-communist 'Movement' for Labor's loss of the federal election in May that year. In consequence, the Democratic Labor Party (DLP) split from the more leftist Labor Party. This split prevented Labor from electoral victory for almost a generation.

In 1956, the Russians brutally suppressed an uprising in Hungary. In what must have been sheer panic, Hungarian intellectuals used whatever pull they had to get visas to leave the country. Some came to Australia. My mother must have been involved in some organisation helping these refugees, because I was sent along Sackville Street to befriend some recently arrived Hungarian children.

It was not a success. The bewildered boy with his strange haircut and his blonde sister stared at me through the doorway as I tried to converse. They spoke no English. But even if we had shared a language, I doubt we could have communicated. I, with my comfortable suburban childhood, could not have comprehended their dangerous journey to cross the border to the free West, their arrival in the new country, and their adjustment.

Mary, John Paterson's widow, described just such a journey to me. Her family had fled Hungary in November 1956, her mother carrying three-year-old Mary through snow to the Austrian border. A group of students passed them, and one kindly offered to carry Mary. Not wanting the family to be separated, her parents declined. The students were shot by the Russian border guards. Somehow, in the horror, Mary's family slipped through to safety.

Since the death of Stalin in 1953, stories like this had seeped into the consciousness of even the most ardent Soviet followers, and an aversion to communist ideology gained momentum. Over time, as our parents' friends from Soviet countries became ever more vocal about the evils of communism—Grisha was a prime example—even my mother lost any idealism she may have had. She once believed in the idea of 'to each, according to need', but developed a wariness about conformity and bureaucracy and overzealous government control. In fact, as I remember, she became agitated over several national budgets—yes, she actually read them—which gave more power to Canberra. She bristled at the thought of states' rights being diminished.

The times were against her. Central planning became the mantra of the day. In 1957, Europeans launched the Common Market. In fact, the Australian experience was no different from trends worldwide, up till the present day.[2] Politicians' ability to overlook local needs in the service of streamlined societal functioning became the story of the second half of the twentieth century and the beginning of the next. And the world became wealthier. These two facts are not unrelated. By the mid-1950s, increasing material prosperity made any notion of a communist electoral victory in Australia a pipe dream. Enhanced by more or less instantaneous communication across time zones and distance, globalisation occurred ever more rapidly. 'Small and local', the backdrop against which our mother had spent her youth, seemed, as time progressed, quaint. This must have caused great frustration for someone who, despite her timid nature, actually wrote letters to the authorities and stood up to developers and government agencies to express her individualistic, somewhat Luddite, views. Her conservatism extended to technology. She hated television because she believed it shut down conversation.

Even the country's increasing prosperity offended her values. Our mother dressed and behaved so as not to be noticed, yet her dislike for people who wanted to 'keep up with the Joneses' made her stand out. Her views on personal conduct became so increasingly out of touch with the times that it became impossible to live within her framework of proper behaviour. In that, she'd barely moved out of the Victorian age. If she and Granny had actually been able to have a conversation, they would have agreed that the country's lax morality was not moving the country in the direction it should go. Her conservatism was of the Puritan kind; she had a Quaker-like honesty and compassion for the underdog, and she hated prejudice.

My father was tolerant, though a better phrase might be *laissez-faire*. While conservative in politics, his sense of the ridiculous grounded him. Dad expostulated frequently on the stupidity of politicians. So, I wonder what my father thought when, in 1956, he received a letter from England. It was from Margaret Greene, a connection of his mother's. Granny maintained an active correspondence with her English relatives. One of her unmarried sisters, Annie Marguerite (known to us as Daisy, or Great Aunt Margaret) had adopted one of her pupils, and the girl, Lesley, had married a man named Ben Greene, a cousin of the novelist Graham Greene and a man with political aspirations. Margaret Greene was their eldest daughter.[3]

Her letter[4] was written on the stationery of the League of Empire Loyalists. The letter thanked my father for 'being so kind to Paul while he was with you—he wrote with such warmth and happiness of his time in Australia that it has made you seem completely part of the family'. Completely part of the family? Who were these people? Who was Paul? I have no memory of him sitting for dinner at the round mahogany table with its curved-backed chairs. For a guest, my mother would have gone to extra trouble to make a special roast. If it had been winter, there might have been a steamed pudding in honor of the English visitor, perhaps her lemon delicious. If Paul came, let's hope he talked in polite generalities, charming her, and did not touch on the purpose of his visit.

The letter offered to introduce my father to Eric Butler, of the Victorian League of Rights in Melbourne.[5] Butler was a notorious anti-Semite and right-wing nationalist; the League of Empire Loyalists[6] was a group of radically right-wing Britons that included ex-fascists like its founder, A.K. Chesterton, and Ben Greene. Furthermore, Margaret Greene, the sister of the young naval officer Paul Greene who had come to dinner, suggested my father join the League of Empire Loyalists.

My father did not. His sense of humour would have steered him away from the lunatic Britain-for-the-British fanaticism of the Empire Loyalists or the Victorian League of Rights. Furthermore, my parents had befriended European immigrants, many of whom were Jewish. I hope my father never showed this letter to my mother. I found it in our grandmother's papers after the house was sold. I imagine that our father wanted nothing to do with the League's recruitment effort and immediately gave it to his mother in order to shield Mum from its contents. Most likely, his mother kept it as some kind of historical or family record.

My father's sister, Aunt Mary, recalled in a letter to Dad that the Greenes were unrepentant Nazi sympathisers. She wrote,

> Mother was most annoyed about 1939 or '40 when some sort of Fascist literature began to arrive from the UK. I think she suspected it was connected in some way with Ben Greene. She returned it and said very firmly, 'No more.' Ben was interned for a time during the war—he could possibly have been an admirer of Mosley's—Lesley and [great-aunt] Margaret were very indignant when he was interned.[7]

Nevertheless, like the Empire Loyalists, my grandmother Eva, along with her daughter Mary and Mary's husband Peter, approved of South Africa's apartheid system and other ideas antithetical to my mother's family. While visiting Johannesburg just after the Sharpeville riots in South Africa in 1961, Mary wrote to her mother: 'The white people all wonder what is going to happen. They all regret the withdrawal from the Commonwealth.'

Mary went on to express her views on the matter. 'I cannot work up any feeling of horror at the segregation of the blacks to their part of the post office and their own homes, for instance. It's a peasant population and it keeps to itself. We have not met an educated native.'[8]

My father always said that people are the result of their childhood experiences. Mary, he would have said, was reflecting her own upbringing in relation to the treatment of the Indigenous people of Western Australia, where segregation was the norm. When Mary and Peter voiced such opinions, which they did quite forcefully on their annual visits to stay in our house, my mother cringed and told me she even felt 'violently sick'.

Although politics impinged on our lives in unexpected ways, some of these intrusions were delightful. When Melbourne hosted the Olympic Games in late 1956, my father managed to obtain three tickets. He took John and me to see the cyclists at the Velodrome and we saw the Russian Vladimir Kuts win the 5000 metres race. Never had we heard a crowd roaring in such a cacophony of languages.

The Cold War had stalled, somewhat, by 1956—unless, of course, you were Hungarian. The talk of communists hiding everywhere in plain sight, just waiting for the chance to pounce, had pretty much dissipated. Revolutionary fervour, if there was any left, had a hard time competing with the prosperity coming our way. Some people even had television. The government had made this available just in time for the Olympics.

The Olympic Games were exciting, but they were also unsettling. Watching the athletic prowess of the citizens of the USSR was stirring, and also a little intimidating. A month earlier, we had learnt what the Soviets could do when they put their minds to it.

Sputnik energised us all. Shock reverberated throughout the United States when the Russians launched the first spacecraft in October 1956, and the space shot's fear effect electrified Australia. My father, the scientist, was in his element. Here was his chance to expound on the importance of a scientific education. Chemistry and physics, that was the thing! The humanities were for sissies. Mum squirmed at that statement. Geoff, her beloved sister Nan's husband, was a theatre critic.

Night after night at the dinner table Dad would elaborate on his theme. We sat there, rapt, a willing audience.

'Do you think we'll explore other planets, Daddy?'

'Even your grandmother thinks the Americans will get to the moon in your lifetime!' Dad exclaimed. 'But other planets?

Maybe. And there is probably life out there. They're listening for it.'

'Who are?'

'The Americans. They're listening for radio waves made by other civilisations.'

'Why would they send radio waves?'

'If you study physics, you'll learn why,' Dad said.

He directed this to my brothers. I, as a girl, was not expected to excel in science, as indeed I did not. But I took my father at his word. America and progress shone in my imagination, linked together.

'This is the American century,' my father said. 'The one after that will be the Chinese.'

He was good at foreseeing big changes happening in the world. He predicted email too, in the 1980s. 'Instant global communication systems' he called them. If he had foreseen the dominance of computers in the next century, he might have insisted his daughter persist at mathematics. Fortunately for my sanity, he did not.

Chapter 29

Private School, Public Transportation

With some trepidation at first, I set off each morning on the tram to my new secondary school. I entered seventh grade at the age of eleven, not because I was particularly bright, but because of a clerical error.

At the time we attended, Preshil only catered to sixth grade, so we were all enrolled in private secondary schools. Under the system then in place, a child had to be enrolled at birth or soon after, in order to be admitted up to ten years later. Then, unless one was the son or daughter of an alumnus, entry was conditional on the child passing an IQ and general knowledge test. The final goal of education, entrance to university, was extremely competitive. Schools jostled to have the best 'results', i.e. university places, at the end of the year. Therefore, they took no chances in their intake; all new pupils had to be reasonably intelligent.

My parents had booked me in to two secondary girls' schools for 1957. However, the secretary at the smaller school had made a typo. Accordingly, a notice appeared at our house asking me to show up for the school's entrance test a year early. Mum called the school and was told to 'take it or leave it'—because there were now no more places left for the following year. This school had a reputation for offering a nurturing environment, and it was also much closer to our house than the other, more prestigious academy. Thus, my parents arranged for me to take the entrance test to Fintona Girls' School. I took the test, and my parents were told that I was more than ready for the seventh grade, though I was only in fifth. Flattered, my parents sent me off the following February, apparently confident I could sail through, despite having missed an entire school year. It was an academic disaster at first. Having missed instruction on fractions and decimals, for my first arithmetic test I got correct answers for four questions out of fifty. I was painfully shy, totally unused to a structured academic schedule, and way out of my depth. It was not a good start. I had been at the top of my class at Preshil and ever after I had to play catch-up. It affected my academic confidence. In the end I imagined I had been put in this position to take the wind out of my sails. My last report card at Preshil said: 'Margaret is bossy and a show-off.'

No one seemed to notice my academic struggle. At home, we did not discuss our school achievements, academic or otherwise. At the time I felt relieved, knowing that my best friend at school had to endure her father's grilling and goading her to come top of the class. Whether it was my mother's compassion or my father's lack of interest in our results, this apparent apathy still strikes me as odd. My parents had invested financially in my education but, possibly, they sent me to this school for benefits that had nothing to do with learning.

Australians believe they enjoy one of the most egalitarian societies on earth. However, in Melbourne, the snobbery that surrounds where one went to school was an enormous factor in the disdain Granny held for my mother. After she died, I found in Mum's papers a letter from a sociologist at Melbourne University. The researcher said she had reached out to investigate the career and life path of girls from 'the lower middle class'—my mother's cohort at the state-run

MacRobertson Girls' High School. Even in the late 1990s, when I read this missive, the words stung. To be put into a class category, thereafter to remain for life, on the basis of one's school, is unjust—and so very Melbourne. I am glad my mother was too beset with Alzheimer's to understand this letter, let alone to reply to it.

In the United States, one of the first questions a person asks another on being introduced, is, 'What do you do?'

In Melbourne, the question is more likely to be, 'Where did you go to school?' School meaning high school, not university. As the social historian Janet McCalman noted, 'the private school did more than educate—it *made* you middle class, it gave you lifelong, indestructible membership of the caste, not for anything learned at the school, but just by the fact of "being there" '.[1]

Present-day Australia is committed to free public education, but that commitment was not universal until the beginning of the twentieth century. By 1893, the Anglicans and the Catholics had created competing school systems. However, these were mostly fee-paying schools. State secondary education existed in the cities, but not in the farming communities or country towns. Until 1905, schooling ended after the eighth grade for most country children. Those families who valued education therefore sacrificed to pay for it.

Even elementary education was not guaranteed in country districts when my grandparents were children. In rural areas, the parents had to guarantee that at least thirty children would attend the primary school, and parents had to provide a third of the teacher's salary. One can imagine the financial hardship for struggling farm families who had to pay for their children's most basic literacy and numeracy. Teachers were also hard to find outside the cities. Then, as now, the field of education was not one in which to make a fortune. Wages averaged £40 a year—approximately the same wage as a shepherd.

Indeed, one educational strategy was to employ, at minimal wages, a recent alumna to teach the younger children. My maternal grandmother, Stella, started teaching at the local one-room schoolhouse where her younger siblings were enrolled. This greatly confused her youngest sister Kitty—my great-aunt Kit—then about five years old. She wrote in her memoir,

> Jack and I started school at Pomborneit, Stella, Frank, Sis, Sam, Tom, Jack and I—quite a number. Stella was in her last year when we started. She went down to Warrnambool to take an exam which qualified her to be a Junior Teacher. I was so confused. I didn't understand why I had to call my sister Miss Lord and instead of explaining to me, Mr Mumby hit me with a cane over my shoulders each time I called Estell.

Kitty reported that she and Jack and their older siblings ambled to school on their ponies. A family would have to be reasonably well off to provide a pony for every child, and so it is little wonder that lack of transportation cut short the education of many country children. According to one historian, the average child in the Victorian countryside attended school for four years. According to another, only half the children of school age in 1861 could read and write. According to a third, the real reason Australia proved so tardy in providing free secondary education was the population feared the intellectual arrogance it would bring.[2]

Be that as it may, an alternative to the state-run school has always been the denominational school—if a student could get there. Private boarding schools dotted the countryside and, in the larger towns, Catholic elementary schools were often attached to rectories and convents. Parochial schools, in general, presented an affordable opportunity for parents seeking a faith-based education for their children.

While Australians in the majority claimed to be members

of the Church of England, they were not a religious lot. However, religious schools helped shape a distinctive Roman Catholic identity. Catholicism was a force in Australian civil life and politics from the country's earliest days, when Irish people were accused of crimes out of proportion to their numbers and were sent to the colony as convicts. Later, like my own ancestors, others fled the famine of the 1840s. More than a residue of class resentment continued into a sectarian divide between the Roman Catholic population and the dominant Protestant elite, and the historical division of church-based schools appears to have contributed to the notable social layering that marked my childhood.

The area around Grange Road was crowded with private schools. Most were denominational. Two of the best boys' schools were Scotch College (Presbyterian), where my brothers and my future husband, John, toiled at their books, and Xavier College (Catholic). Nearby were Carey and Trinity grammars, which then accepted only boys. For girls, the mega school, Methodist Ladies College (MLC), and the smaller schools, like Ruyton, Genazzano Convent, the tiny St Mark's and, further to the east, my school of Fintona, which paired itself with the Camberwell Grammar School for boys, offered a multitude of educational choice.

When, in the 1970s, some diehard purists in government, in favour of separation of church and state, took on the issue of private school funding, which had always tacitly occurred, the private schools rebelled. The Catholic school administration threatened to close their schools and send their pupils to the state schools. Seeing that the state system would be flooded and unable to cope with the influx, the government backed down. Since then, this partially state-funded private school system has remained the education of preference for parents who can afford the fees. Some would argue that the state system is too linked to the values of the political party in power to offer a consistent educational philosophy. For instance, under a radical Labor government in the 1980s, Victorian state schools were told that they had to produce equality of outcome, not equality of opportunity for their students. Out the window, then, went any consideration for gifted students. Diversity of educational philosophy may be one reason private schools are so popular in Victoria. But even at the federal level, there has been a steady drift to funding non-government schools more generously than government schools. Today, fully forty per cent of Australian children attend non-government schools.[3] Inequality, the bane of the American educational system (where property taxes in local municipalities fund schools), was and is as prevalent in classless Australia.

To get to Fintona, I went on the tram. As soon as the bell rang to end the school day at 4 pm I raced to catch the tram home before it got too crowded. I did not wait to play after-school sports as my subsequently more popular class-mates did.

I had fallen in love. Not with a boy, but with a baby. While my classmates were changing into their hockey uniforms, I was belting home to wolf down our after-school snack of bread and jam and tea. I then ran over the road to 'help' Mrs Gabriel with her new baby, Alex. He was adorable. I spent every hour I could with him, learning the ins and outs of little babies' bodies. Alex's four-year-old sister, Melissa, and my brother Christopher were contemporaries and played together. At the time I remember begging my mother to have another baby of our own. But she smiled and said she had plenty already. I think this year with Alex (I grew bored when he started to walk) gave me stability in what was a pretty difficult start to my new school.

Fortunately for my shy nature, my school lay to the east of our house, in the opposite direction to the city-bound commute and the pandemonium that occurred every afternoon on the Cotham Road tramline, the No. 42 tram to Mont Albert, at its busy intersection with Glenferrie Road. In mid-afternoon the teenage rush for the tram home began. Adults would do well, even today, to avoid the afternoon crush of smelly adolescents, with their rucksacks and raucous laughter, as they packed the trams like sardines.

Harried tram conductors, many of them recent immigrants struggling with English, made half-hearted efforts to keep control, threatening to throw the most rambunctious off the tram. The No. 42 tram was an oasis of calm, however, compared to the commotion that occurred at 4 pm at the corner of Barkers and Glenferrie roads. Crowding onto the No. 69 (now No. 16) tram at this stop, the scarlet, yellow and blue blazers of the Scotch boys brushed up against the green and grey uniforms of the MLC girls, while one or two of these girls, adventurers in trans-sectarian flirtation, might, with downcast eyes and a smirk, nestle against the red-piped black blazer of a Jesuit-educated Xavier youth.

There was no respite for the poor tram conductors after the last of the after-school sports players stumbled off the tram steps, for the drunks got on at 6 pm. In the Melbourne of our childhood, the six o'clock swill was the result of a law that closed pubs at the dinner hour. Men who drank—and there were many—rushed to the pub from work at 4.30 or 5 pm, guzzled as many beers as possible, then staggered to the tram, where they rocked smelling and belching on the outer seats, the inner ones being more or less reserved by custom for women and children, assuming anyone could get a seat at all.

I became an old hand at travelling into town on the tram because of my teeth. The office of severe Dr Spring, the orthodontist, became my second home for years in secondary school. My overbite, inherited from some unknown ancestor and exacerbated by thumb-sucking, was a challenge to orthodontia. However, by the end of a harrowing four-year epic of retainers or plates, braces and various hooks and eyes, my teeth emerged triumphantly white and straight. Dr Spring was so pleased he took photographs so he could show off my corrected overbite at a conference in America. So my fame, in the form of X-rays and teeth pictures, preceded me to my future home.

Chapter 30

Holidays and Happy Times

On weekend excursions we packed so much equipment we may as well have gone camping. We'd head up into the rain-forested hills to places like the romantically named Ferntree Gully. There, in the designated picnic areas, our parents would unpack a plaid rug and a straw picnic hamper filled with a homemade lunch. In winter, people were allowed to cook sausages and steaks on the grills provided by the local council. Our favourites were snags—sausages, dripping with fat and lathered with tomato sauce, wrapped in a slice of bread.

On summer weekends, Dad put up a canvas play pool in the backyard and, yelling happily as water hit our shoulders, we hosed each other down. As time went on, summers became hotter. No one had air conditioning. On very hot evenings, we'd come downstairs with our pillows and try to sleep on the faded Persian rug on the cool dining room floor. From my room, a child could climb the white, stepped bookcase up to the windows and climb out onto the roof. When we grew older, on hot nights my brothers and I would sit on the terra cotta roof tiles and look at the stars. Sometimes the sky lit up with the red, smoky aura of distant bushfires.

In the May or September school holidays, Mum would gather her friends and we would go off to the hills or the beach. Several families of mothers alone with their children, staying in flimsy fibreboard houses with their thin mattresses and tiny living spaces. In these rented houses my mother had only exchanged one kitchen for another. But it was a kitchen without Granny in it, which I suppose was the point.

As we grew, we swapped these tame little holidays for more adventurous and far less comfortable camping. Dad appeared to feel right at home in this environment; it must have reminded him of his childhood. Mum tolerated the situation and its many inconveniences. The vacation of January 1956 became memorable because of two linked incidents. Walking over rocks in the shallows near our campsite at Anglesea, three-year-old Chris, usually a sunny child, complained his tummy hurt. Eventually our mother became so worried she drove him to Geelong Hospital, where he was immediately operated upon for appendicitis. We visited him in the hospital. With his black curls and ready smile, he became a favourite of the ward. One day Andrew, who'd climbed a tree to wave goodbye to Dad, whose turn it was to take John and me to visit Chris, fell down and broke his arm. Dad quickly reversed the car and we all piled in, Mum cradling a sobbing Andrew, to take him, too, to the hospital.

The next year, we began to have our summer holidays—again shared with family friends—at a magical place called Apollo Bay. To all of us who went there, Apollo Bay was as beautiful as its name. We camped in its rolling hills, not far from the cliffs and surf, on a dairy farm run by an enterprising fellow named Ken Watkins. Each January we'd descend in a horde on the quiet hamlet in a cloud of dust from the utes, the pick-up trucks holding our tents and boxes of provisions.

I can still smell the green fresh grass of the camp. The cows grazed the scrub between the gum trees on the almost vertical ranges and, when they came down to the creek, sometimes poked their curious heads into our tents.

Comfortable our campsite was not, but it was tremendous fun. The toilets were flyblown outhouses. We showered in the changing sheds at the beach.

A sheltered inlet on the spectacular Great Ocean Road between Lorne and Warrnambool, the little town of Apollo Bay quadrupled in size in the summer months. At its most prosperous, it had a pier from which fishermen sold their catch directly to customers, and a foreshore with picnic tables and trash bins. On the other side of the road, overlooking the sea, sat the classic Australian retail strip: a newsagent's shop, petrol station, chemist, bakery, fish and chip shop, small supermarket and competing pubs. Just out of town, a Mechanics Hall drew locals and visitors to dismal dances once a month. On occasion, the hall doubled as the town's only movie theatre. Breaks to splice a new piece of film into the projector were met with catcalls by an often-drunken audience.

We loved trips to town to buy milk and bread, daily papers and fish. We loved flicking each other with towels, and we loved the silly old films. We loved crabbing and fishing and walking for miles along the beach, and we loved surfing. We loved the sea.

We loved sleeping on air mattresses and waking up to the sweet smell of grass. It is hard to say whether we loved best our morning swims, walking along the side of the cliff till we slid down to the beach, or the nightly singalongs by the campfire after a meal of eels, crayfish, steaks, or sausages with toasted rolls. We loved all of it.

'We live from siesta to fiesta!' laughed Grisha Sklovsky, whose élan and gift for friendship made him the joyous leader of our group.

We shared our meals with the other families around a campfire. Late afternoons, we placed squat round bottles of cheap Chablis in the creek to chill, piled into the truck, and rattled down the dusty road to the town to buy the crayfish from the dock for our feast. This now-expensive treat could not be more easily prepared—the crayfish were simply boiled in a big pot.

At other times, we'd eat eel, which swam in the creek. No one seems to remember how this was cooked. My brother John thinks the eels would have been gutted and pan-fried with lots of garlic to make them palatable.

Much less exotic, but particularly wonderful, were our treats of Chiko rolls. I'd always believed these had been around forever. But, according to that font of all knowledge, Wikipedia, Chiko rolls were invented in 1951 by a man from Bendigo, who sold them at football matches. They peaked in popularity in the sixties and seventies. The extremely unhealthy snack consisted of a thick pastry exterior over an interior of cabbage, barley, lard, celery, carrot, corn, onion and beef—with plenty of salt—then deep-fried. How we loved them!

Because getting our bread and milk daily at the shops gave teenage girls the opportunity to meander along the high street looking in shop windows and making eyes at teenage boys, our trio of best friends—Anna, Angie and I—eagerly offered to 'do the shopping'. Therefore, we did not have to resort to making that classic Australian campfire bread, damper. This yeastless bread, a staple of legend, probably tasted like a rock. However, I have come up with a couple of recipes of my own which make a tasty loaf.

The memory of Apollo Bay was so vivid and happy that I used it as my own personal anaesthetic at the dentist. Our dentist did not appear to believe in anaesthetics for routine fillings. Which just goes to show the calming effect of the memory of these seaside holidays. To my surprise, as an adult, I found that others who shared that farm at Apollo Bay with us felt the same. A respite from the real world. But where, exactly was the 'real' world? And what was our relationship to it?

Chapter 31

Cultsha

In January 1959, *On the Beach* was filmed in Melbourne. In the movie, as in Neville Shute's novel of the same name, the Northern Hemisphere is reduced to rubble by an accidental nuclear war. Australia is cut off from the disaster until, slowly, radioactivity wafts through the air and drifts in on the tide, killing everything in its path.

The film's bleak story, and their sudden world fame, thrilled Melburnians. In a nuclear disaster, they would be the last people to remain on Earth. They took pride in this, delighted that Gregory Peck, Ava Gardner, Tony Perkins and Fred Astaire brought their sprawling seaside city notoriety. It seemed a strange kind of patriotism. Possibly jealous that the southern metropolis had been chosen as the scene of a movie, a Sydney journalist made up a quote from Ava Gardner, in which the actress claimed Melbourne was an appropriate place to make a film about the end of the world.

In Shute's imagining, the world ends, as in T.S. Eliot's poem, not with a bang but a whimper. The citizens of Victoria line up quietly to get their government-issued suicide pills. There's no anguish, no debauched partying, no histrionic weeping, no unseemly fuss. At least, that's how I remember the story. After all, as my mother reminded me, Melbourne is not Sydney. Everyone knows that's a raucous, uncouth city; its humid weather corrupts.

Mum visited Sydney only a handful of times. For her, Melbourne was a place of safety, a place of moral rectitude, a place where bad things didn't happen or, if they did, only after they'd happened everywhere else. Naturally, I was desperate to go to Sydney.

A few years later, I went for the first time to the city of sin and stayed with a schoolfriend at the YWCA. We viewed the sparkling crenellated harbour from a ferry, stared up at the protractor-shaped bridge and, as instructed, avoided King's Cross. We were at the YWCA that August of 1962 when we saw the newspaper headline announcing Marilyn Monroe's death. I devoured the somewhat lurid details of her life, imagining the United States as a place of glamour and danger and, therefore, an attraction. That moment began a lifetime of travel or at least, of dreaming of it.

For my mother, as for many of her generation, lifestyles of other cultures both repelled and attracted. She befriended foreign newcomers, but could not imagine living anywhere but Melbourne. She heard her friends' stories and tried to imagine the wonders and horrors of Europe. For her, as for many Australians even today, the country's distance from the rest of the world protected it. Yet, it tantalised.

Granny was not the only one to make condescending remarks about Australian culture. Our teachers and intellectuals generally believed that the 'real world' took place overseas. We learnt from English or American textbooks, the only ones available. Living, as our schoolbooks said we did, at the end of the civilised—that is, the English—world, our first history lessons were of the explorers. We drew pictures of brave Captain Cook, landing at Botany Bay with his cocked hat askew. We knew that irascible Matthew Flinders skirted the coast of the enormous continent, mapping it. We were taught it was incredible luck that Flinders beat the Frenchman Baudin, by only a few miles, to be the first to set foot on Kangaroo Island, off South Australia, and claim it for the crown.[1]

'Can you imagine,' my father expostulated, 'what Australia would be like if the French had settled it?'

He was thinking of the degradation of the Congo, the indolence of Vanuatu, the decadence of Tahiti. We took his word for it. Not till I actually set foot in France did I have a pang of regret that Napoleon had not claimed the far country as his own. This was not the general view. Having so recently escaped invasion by the Japanese, I suppose it was natural for the nation to revel in its British roots. Those roots now struggled to break through the soil to grow in their own direction. That the colonisation of our country had destroyed thousands of years of successful habitation by Indigenous people did not occur to us.

My parents and their friends talked politics loudly and with relish at dinner parties. What excited them was a new sense of national identity. It is said that all politics is local, but for Australians in the fifties, the idea that local could be as important as Great Britain, the distant realm in the Northern Hemisphere, elated them. Their boosterism was egged on by their émigré friends who saw the new country as a salvation from war-ravaged Europe, still torn between East and West.

Our family was not the kind to call England 'home'. Not even Granny did that. She looked back to England, but never expressed regret in leaving it. In her bookshelves, she displayed novels by the Brontës and Dickens. They described a forbidding world. British children's stories were replete with nannies, sickly children in pinafores, and animals we'd never seen. This alien world was dark, cold and comfortless. In short, unimaginable.

Much more fun were our own Australian books, and there were many. We started with May Gibbs' *Gumnut Babies.*

Their adorable dimpled bottoms had made Gibbs one of the country's most famous illustrators. *Dot and the Kangaroo*, a cautionary Edwardian tale, frightened us with its warning about getting lost in the bush. Our favourite was *The Magic Pudding*, Norman Lindsay's inventive story of a bad-tempered pudding that kept remaking itself no matter how many times it was tucked into. We moved on to Ethel Turner's *Seven Little Australians*, a family saga set in 1890s Sydney. In the fifties it was serialised on ABC radio's *The Children's Hour*, and I still remember weeping and being unable to eat my dinner after listening to the chapter when my favourite character Judy was trapped under a fallen tree.

'How would you like to die when you're only thirteen?' Judy asks breathlessly from under the eucalyptus trunk pinning her to the ground. The tears that poured down my cheeks then were only matched by the scene in *Little Women* when Beth died.

We were great readers in our family. When we went to friends' houses, we kids would disappear to read their books. In retrospect, it seems anti-social. I can only say that Granny's training had made its mark; children were silent.

Later, I became enraptured with tales about the *Heroes of the Outback* by Ion Idriess, and recollections of pioneering families such as *Kings in Grass Castles* by Mary Durack. These books reinforced my mother's stories of the Kelly Gang, bushrangers who had terrified her grandmother's people in the 1860s, even though the gang never operated in the Western District of Victoria. At the museum we were fascinated to see Ned Kelly's famous armour. The Robin-Hood-like Kelly tales were familiar to Victorians long before they were immortalised in the famous series of paintings by Sidney Nolan, who iconised Kelly. Nolan attracted the world's attention to a new Australian art, based not on the sentimental landscapes of

England, but on the harsh reality of social injustice and the implacable forces of nature versus man.[2]

The literature and art of our country told two stories, both gritty and unsentimental. One pitted people heroically battling an unforgiving landscape. The other told of cities where, because the land itself was so hard to conquer, most people lived and struggled for better lives.

No one realised that we, the descendants of the colonial invaders, did not know how to work with the land; nor did we let the land tell us how to live harmoniously with it. No one asked the Indigenous people for advice. Only one artist, Russell Drysdale, even made them a theme in his paintings. His painting, *Shopping Day*, shows an Aboriginal family, dressed in European clothes, standing desolately in an empty township. Their haunted dark faces show the shame of dispossession, not dignity and pride from having lived in balance with this arid country since before the Neanderthals died out in Europe. Only in the 1980s did art by Aboriginal people become recognised by art dealers who saw beauty and meaning in its patterns. Also unknown to the general public in the 1950s and 1960s were an extraordinarily beautiful series of rock paintings in the Kimberley region of Western Australia. Brilliantly depicting dynamic movement, possibly a ceremonial dance, the figures wear tassels, belts and headdresses. Today, our familiarity with abstract art allows us to access the haunting beauty, if not the meaning, of these images of humans and animals. Research is ongoing, but it is now thought the paintings date from around 17,000 years ago.[3] Blinded by a European-based lens, we did not recognise what was in front of our eyes. Our schoolbooks taught that 'culture' meant the Anglo-based art forms imported from Europe. The curriculum appeared to be designed by people who didn't trust originality. But outside the schoolroom, things were stirring.

Nan and Geoff Hutton were heavily involved in the development of Victorian theatre and ballet companies.[4] Both were excited by the 1955 performance of the first Australian play to show working-class life, *The Summer of the Seventeenth Doll* by Ray Lawler. In his review in the *Age*, Geoff called it 'an event worth seeing and celebrating'. This perhaps did not do the play justice, since it became a nationwide success and was exported to similar acclaim in London.

My mother had season tickets, with Charlie Wilkins, to classical music concerts. We went to the National Gallery of Victoria to see the paintings and, in my late teenage years, Mum enjoyed taking me to art gallery openings and auctions. Occasionally, she bought an inexpensive painting. We had an artistic tradition, albeit only a century or so old. It developed in parallel with European art trends of that time. Australia's isolated painters came to their own understanding of impressionism and, later, modernism, at the same time these trends were shocking viewers in Europe or America. Our authors and poets wrote as well as any abroad. Ruth Park's tales of impoverished people in Sydney,[5] for example, are as memorable as those of her contemporaries in the Northern Hemisphere. It was just that there were so few artists, musicians and authors, and so few to appreciate them. It was hard to make a living in the arts in Australia, so many went overseas. This left those who stayed behind with a sense of betrayal, and defensive about their own achievements. Critics, teachers and students were confused. With the universal egocentrism of a small society, we exaggerated the importance of our own artists, while simultaneously deriding them, constantly denigrating them in relation to the work of artists living far away and, especially, long ago. Our schoolbooks told us real culture happened elsewhere.

Not that overseas culture was all that edifying, in the minds of the censors. A group of nameless bureaucrats at the Literature Censorship Board, all men, avidly inspected every book coming through customs and declared it fit or unfit for local consumption. This applied to books for adults as well as for children. Thus, Australians were not permitted to read about Holden Caulfield's teenage angst in *Catcher in the Rye*, nor about the shenanigans of the poverty-stricken residents of a New Hampshire town in *Peyton Place*, nor of James Joyce's Ireland in *Ulysses*. (A perplexed judge, when asked to rule on its banning, asked if it was a translation of the original.) Australians were not allowed to read William S. Burroughs' *A Naked Lunch*, or *Brave New World* by Aldous Huxley, or Vladimir Nabakov's *Lolita*. All were deemed obscene. Prime Minister Robert Menzies thought those who wanted to read James Baldwin's *Another Country* were communist sympathisers. In 1966, Penguin Books Australia (where I was working at the time) challenged the ban on D.H. Laurence's *Lady Chatterley's Lover*. Using a clever stratagem, John Stephens, Penguin Australia's manager, had the books printed in more liberal South Australia, then quickly dispatched them to Victorian bookstores. They sold out before the police could pounce. Defeated, the government retreated. By the middle of the year *Lady Chatterley* was released throughout the country.[6] But that was all in the future. Censorship did not release its hold until the Whitlam years.

In the 1950s and '60s, returning residents reported customs agents ferreting through their suitcases, ripping open brown-paper packages and confiscating the books therein. Not surprisingly, those who had never left Australian shores wanted to know what they were missing. It was an extraordinary contradiction. Adults were treated as if they had no right to read what they wanted, and children were told their country's culture was worthless. Native infantilism and overseas superiority infected our thinking.

My mother, who had focused her studies on Shakespeare and Milton like every other Australian university arts student, wanted to go to England to experience the wellspring of culture for herself. Like most Australians, however, she had ambivalent feelings about the English. She lived under Granny's thumb like an underling, and three of her great-grandmothers were Irish.

Dad had returned to company headquarters in England several times since his first long trip to the UK in 1946–47. The trip took three months: a six-week voyage by ship, a couple of weeks at the home office, then another six weeks to return home. As his career progressed, he did this with increasing frequency. On his visit in 1959, Mum decided to go with him.

Miss Skog, a Swedish martinet, lived with us children while our parents were away. Despite her delicious, brownie-like 'hedgehog slices', we were not happy, and Miss S. complained about us constantly. I realise now that poor Miss Skog, with her grey hair and apron, was too old for the job. In addition to looking after four noisy kids, she also had to care for Granny, who by this time could barely see due to cataracts.

I was at a difficult age, at least according to Miss Skog. My great excitement at the time was going to Saturday night dancing lessons at Meyer's Dancing School. Each weekend I put on a custom-made frock made by Auntie Kit's dressmaker, Mrs Thom, and Kitty—who by this time lived in the War Widows' flats only a mile or two from our house—drove me to dancing class. She drove nervously, under the speed limit of thirty miles an hour, swearing at all those who passed her because they were breaking the law. But Kitty loved dancing and a good time, and thus braved the night and its drunken roadsters to give her great-niece her launch into the social world. A boy from dancing school rang me, and although I can't actually remember this, he must have asked me out. Miss Skog had a fit. She'd listened in on the other end of the line and reported the conversation to Kitty. She thought it her duty to tell her, and, of course, I couldn't possibly go with my parents being away.

So did my foray into the teenage social world begin— or not begin, as it happened. Kit was amused, Miss Skog vowed never again to keep house for a family with a teenage daughter, and my parents toured Europe, blissfully unaware. As for my mother, that first trip away from Australia changed her life.

Chapter 32

My Mother's Secret Studies

While in England my mother got to know English people quite different to Granny. The British she encountered were friendly and had shared interests. She visited galleries and museums, seeing for the first time works of art she had only read about in books. When she came home, she could not stop talking about all she had seen, and then she took action. My mother enrolled in the Fine Arts Department at Melbourne University. She loved it. Somehow, she managed to get her classes done by the time we came home from school, so our home life, with dinner on the table, laundry and housework done, was not disrupted. Perhaps this was the agreement she'd made with our father or, more likely, it was a tacit assumption on both their parts. In my parents' eyes, her foray into scholarship did not merit more help at home.

As she progressed in her studies and the time came to write her master's thesis (quite a few years later), our mother decided to learn something no one else knew. In the University Library, she had discovered a book of engravings by a family of obscure sixteenth century Flemish engravers. She was entranced. No one—at least no one in Melbourne—seemed to know anything about the Sadeler brothers. Mum could find nothing about them in English.

Having obtained her professor's permission to study and

identify the prints for her thesis, Mum then found she had to learn German to follow the trail. She went further and further into her subject, corresponding with experts all over the world. Her enthusiasm later encouraged me to study art history and travel to see the originals.

By the time I was married and living in Boston, she was still pursuing this work. She collaborated with researchers at the Rijksmuseum in Amsterdam and the Fogg Museum at Harvard University. I asked why she didn't convert this highly original thesis to a PhD. She said she could not. She slaved away at her thesis for years, at a table in the sunroom. She lived in a house with thirteen rooms. By the time the children were grown, Dad had taken over a bedroom as his study, and Mum could have taken another as 'a room of her own'. But she could not bring herself to demand this. She worked under great inconvenience, self-imposed, gathering up papers and putting them away when people came to visit. When she finally presented her thesis to her supervisor, he gave her a less than stellar grade. As usual, she hid her crushed spirit.

Later, as her friends' children and a relative or two pursued doctorates, she grew agitated. She had achieved much through her diligence, but the time and place in which we lived did not allow her the glittering prize of academic acknowledgment. It did not help that when our mother began studying to get her master's degree, my father would not let her talk about it. He said it would hurt his career. 'I won't have a blue-stocking for a wife!' he declared.

After I protested at his unfairness, he explained his rationale. 'Most of the blokes at work have wives who never went to university. It would be pretentious for your mother to get another degree.'

My father's family had no time for the arts; they actively despised any but conventional painting, and they never listened to music. My father thought education was necessary for scientists and engineers, but seemed to think an arts degree a frivolity. I doubt he realised that study was my mother's life blood. And she never dared tell him.

Opposing intellectual interests led to silent battles of values between my parents. At least my mother felt it was a battle. My father had such a strong personality he may not have been aware of her views. It is no wonder Mum lapsed into long periods of silence. Sometimes, when surprised out of a reverie, she would say something to reveal she had been holding an argument with Dad in her mind. But it was in her mind, not in reality; she never took up the verbal cudgel.

When I was a young woman, Mum would advise, 'Don't say what you really want, the Devil may hear you.' She meant the Devil would thwart you, just for the heck of it. So Mum went through life with her wants and needs veiled. She did her best to conform to her husband's expectations of a corporate wife, and quietly got on with the ironing and her surreptitious studies.

Chapter 33

The Corporate Wife

I'm not sure if my father's colleagues found out about his wife's dangerous academic bent, but as I became a teenager my father's career took off.

In her 1960 Christmas letter to a cousin, Dad's proud mother bragged about her son. Eva wrote:

> Dick has been promoted to be managing director of the Australian branch of his firm, Albright & Wilson, makers of phosphorus products, an old, well established English firm. A successful well-conducted firm, affiliated with I.C.I., but not conducted in the body and soul-destroying way in which American firms are.

The additional responsibilities must have been stressful. After work my father headed to the gin decanter on the sideboard in the dining room. I followed him like a puppy. It was our special time together, and I spun it out as long as I could.

'You don't want a drink, dear, do you?' he called to Mum.

I pulled out the placemats from the drawer, sprinkled knives and forks around them, and waited, feeling slightly disloyal, for Mum's inevitable reply.

'You know I don't drink,' she retorted, her voice muffled, her head bent to the oven.

My mother was allergic to alcohol. The histamines in red

wine made her break out in hives, as did the sun. This inability to join my father for a quiet drink before dinner emphasised the disparity in their roles.

My father's elevation at work seemed to have an inverse relationship to Mum's intellectual aspirations. She said she could never find a job as interesting as her years as Mac's assistant, but I suspect my father would have forbidden her to take any job at all. Even though her beloved Aunt Kitty worked at the post office, and Nan had never stopped writing for a living, the social status my father's job now conferred made a low-level position—the only job my mother would have been offered, given her absence from the workforce for so many years—an embarrassment to contemplate. She could no more take a job, say, at the post office, as Kitty had, then fly to the moon. And she regarded with ambivalence Kitty purchasing splendid clothes with her earnings. Mum regarded self-display and self-promotion as grave sins. Self-promotion would have been required for her to get a job.

Flamboyance, on the other hand, was in Kit's nature. She hired a dressmaker. Auntie Kit found a genius of creativity in the diminutive Mrs Thom, still working at eighty-two. In a flash Mrs Thom could whip up a Vogue pattern, or a picture in a magazine, into the real thing. Of course, speed was not the point. Innumerable fittings, conducted over cups of tea, converted yards of raw silk, velvet and other gorgeous fabrics into garments fit for a queen. And Kitty, six feet tall, smiling and elegant, sallied forth on her many excursions in her new clothes with the confidence of royalty. These expeditions often took place on the bus. Settling her splendid, custom-tailored coat and skirt on the seat, Kitty enjoyed the opportunity afforded by public transportation to be admired, and engaged other passengers in conversation. We children, captive in her company on many a Sunday afternoon, would be introduced to the conductor, and our perfectly ordinary achievements made public, while we prayed to be let off soon. At home we were being trained to abhor public spectacle.

For me, Kitty's joie de vivre, if mortifying, was also captivating, as was my aunt Nan's. The message from my mother and my grandmother, for once on the same page, was that adornment was somehow tacky. Yet this instruction conflicted with the racier American values of *Seventeen* magazine, and with Mum's behavior as Dad's career progressed. Sitting at the hairdressers, her hair being transformed into permanent waves, my mother possibly found herself intrigued by the marital advice offered by women's magazines. She took to freshening her lipstick, changing into a clean dress, and running to the door when Dad came home.

Late afternoons, Mum listened without comment as her aunt and sister gossiped over our kitchen table. If she envied their freedom to work, she did not say. She might have said, if asked, that the nine to five was hardly freedom. Did she not have her own car, free to whisk her children to the dentist, to their lessons? Did she not accompany my father on occasional business trips, upon which the spouses' program offered full opportunity for shopping? Did she not belong to a women's club? How could she possibly complain about the benefits of middle-class life?

She could not and she did not complain. My father's rise up the corporate ladder should have eased my mother's burden, allowing her to live more like 'a lady', but her reticence to ask for help—or my father's obliviousness—meant that little changed in our household.

English executives of my father's firm visited several times a year, and Mum was expected to entertain them. Dad could have taken them to a restaurant, but he hated eating out. He felt the food was better at home. Whenever company was expected, Mum, panic-stricken, leapt into action. On a limited food budget, she pounded beef strips thin with a mallet so she could top them with breadcrumbs and herbs, roll them up, and secure them with a skewer or string to make her 'veal birds'. One of her more successful desserts was the classic Brockhoff chocolate biscuit log. However, on at least one occasion I remember, she stared with disappointment at her coffee flummery, which shimmered—a little too much—under wax paper in its crystal dish on the sideboard.

'Too runny,' she said. But it was too late, and Mum rushed from the dining room to shower and change from her shirtwaist to dressier, but still plain and proper, attire. Still scurrying in her unaccustomed high heels, Mum flew through to the sunroom, where her typewriter lay on a blond wood table and her fine arts books were piled next to the thesis she was writing. Mum picked up her papers, slapped them into a folder, put the books back on the shelf, and whipped out a tablecloth, hiding the offending typewriter, the symbol of her urge to learn.

I was often marshalled to help serve the food at these dinner parties. Sometimes I noticed the men talking animatedly, while Mum sat at the end of the table in what seemed to be stunned silence, ruminating on her dissatisfaction with the meal. Thankfully, her English guests did not seem to notice the food.

The day after one of these events, my father chortled with amusement at dinner, when he reported that the Englishman had remarked on the 'coolie-like' labours of Australian middle-class wives. I watched Mum's face stiffen. But she said nothing. I was shocked. It was true that women in our circle did not have *au pairs* or maids like their English counterparts, but to be compared to a coolie—a near-slave who in the old days worked the Queensland sugar plantations—was too much.

'How can you say that?' I asked Dad in teenaged indignation.

He, in his turn, looked startled. 'I was paying your mother a compliment,' he said.

He simply didn't get it.

And, in my outrage, I didn't get it either. He *was* paying her a compliment, based on his recollection of a mother who saw her role in professional terms. Eva provided the best possible home life in straitened circumstances, contributing to the family's welfare just as importantly as her husband's salary did. My Aunt Mary, remembering life at Leonora, wrote:

> 'Housekeeping was a serious and responsible job in the early settlements'.[1]

My father did not see that the endless repetitive round of housework, with no opportunity to earn money and thus feel validated in the way that males did for their work, would erode our mother's self-esteem. Apparently, he also believed that studying for an advanced degree was reaching too far. In this, he reinforced our mother's secret belief that she did not deserve her education and the opportunities that went with it.

My mother had no experience whatsoever of what was expected of a 'corporate wife'. My grandmother Eva, however, had lived this life to the fullest. Far from being a junior partner in her husband's rise from gold prospector to manager of the Gwalia mine, her participation was equally important, and regarded as such. The difference was that when Victor achieved the pinnacle of his career, Eva lived more or less like a duchess. Even if the time and place we lived in had allowed this for our mother, her sense of social justice would not. So, she escaped to the past in her studies. Nan, with concerns for the present, had a more clear-eyed view of what work could mean for women. And that working in a man's world need not lead to a loss of femininity.

Chapter 34

The Companionate Wife

With her blue, made-up eyes and blonde hair, Nan epitomised glamour. She wore sheath dresses and high heels, and sat with her legs crossed, a cigarette in one hand and a half-filled glass in another. She had pizazz, our Nan. She displayed her femininity exuberantly, without submissiveness. She wore makeup to bed. I absolutely adored her.

Nan and Geoff bought a charming terrace house at 14 Stirling Street, Kew. I learned to traverse those streets, only a mile or so from our house, so frequently my feet tramped without conscious effort down Sackville Street, up Davis Street, and around the corner to Stirling Street. I walked there, countless times, drawn like a moth to my aunt and her two daughters. The family had expanded with the birth of Barby, born at the beginning of 1953. The baby was premature, and Nan and the frail infant spent a month in the hospital. Kristy must have come back to live with us at the time, but such was our family fluidity that I can't remember.

Nan's career had in fact been greatly enhanced by her time filing newspaper articles from London in 1951–1952. Her entertaining and thoughtful stories from England were reflections on women's lives there, rather than on politics. On her return, this body of work allowed Nan to launch a successful freelance career. She wrote about matters of concern to women at *Woman's Day* and the shelter magazine

Australian House and Garden. She continued to advocate for equal pay for equal work, highlighting the difficulties facing women. No doubt her dreadful experience with her first husband made her sensitive to how women were still hamstrung. Until mid-century, they could not sit on a jury in Victoria, they could not initiate a bank loan without a husband's permission and, until 1966, they had to leave employment in the public service when they married. In 1973, she advocated for legislative change to allow the right to abortion.[1] After time on maternity leave in 1953, Nan settled into a routine which seemed a model of domestic bliss. She and Geoff lived a life combining work at home with a career that mandated visits to the theatre and an attendant social life I envied. She called it a 'companionate marriage'.

Each week, 'Nan Hutton on Thursdays' entertained readers of the *Age*, and she advised the lovelorn in her lonely-hearts column for *Woman's Day*. Nan wrote her columns at an old Royal typewriter in the family room. She cut up cheap butcher's paper into strips about four inches high. If she made a typo, as she often did, her fingers flying along to keep up with her thoughts, she could whip the offending piece of paper out of the typewriter and thrust a new piece into the carriage.

This beloved aunt presented a model of working for money while remaining at home for the children. She was a trailblazer in her advocacy for the right of women to work and attain pay equal to men's. In 1955, she wrote an article in *Woman's Day* about how the multiple roles expected of middle-class women made their homemaking enterprise commercially valuable, despite being uncompensated. She suggested her readers come up with a better name than 'housewife', choosing to use the word 'calling' in her writing.[2] Nan also saw that not every woman could afford not to work. She was way ahead of her readers. A year later,

Woman's Day asked them for their opinions on women's right to earn a wage outside the home and found the readers six to one against.[3]

Nan is quoted numerous times in the book *Imagining the Fifties*, by John Murphy, which examines 'Private Sentiment and Political Culture in Menzies' Australia'. He calls her a proto-feminist. She may have been a feminist, but if he'd met her, Murphy would have seen a woman who relished being feminine. Her husband and her children stood at the centre of her world.

Nan coped in combining a career and childcare, but she often struggled to stay on top of the chaos. Many a time I would go over to find her in a dither. Like my mother, she could not say 'no' to anyone. Visitors were forever dropping in, and Nan entertained them while ironing. In the scramble, the cat could be on the kitchen table, lapping up the milk from a jug left over from breakfast, while the phone rang unanswered as Nan typed away on her paragraph-sized bits of paper, agonising over her word count as her newspaper deadline approached. If I appeared, I'd sometimes be dispatched to the butcher to fetch the lamb chops and feed the kids.

This was a busy, happy home and Geoff Hutton doted on his two girls. It seemed an enchanted female world, their family bathroom closet shelved floor-to-ceiling with perfumes, makeup, hair colours and other essentials of female existence. Living as I did in a male-dominated home where the soap was unscented, I found their house a paradise of femininity.

The Huttons were pioneers in home renovation. Over the years, Nan and Geoff made improvements to their nineteenth century house, including creating a family room with seagrass matting on the floor. Large windows opened onto a spacious backyard where children climbed the mulberry trees. The family room, an innovation at the time, doubled as Nan and Geoff's office, the desk and typewriter strategically placed so the writer looked out the window.

Geoff was as gentle in manner as he was handsome. A master of anecdote, he chuckled in retelling stories of his war correspondent's days in New Guinea,[4] or of his meetings with politicians, finding pompous powerbrokers ridiculous.

Nan, too, could tell a funny story, so their social life was as busy as their work life allowed. Often, I went to babysit because their jobs called them away from home on weeknights. Geoff had become the *Age's* theatre critic, and he and Nan would rush off to the city. Afterward, Geoff would stay up to the wee hours writing his critique.

As I grew into my university years, I was sometimes invited to their dinner parties, possibly to help look after the girls or help Nan serve the meal. Nevertheless, I felt welcome and grown up enough to join the lively banter and laughter that burbled around their table. Nan's dinner parties were always interesting, and not just because the wine flowed and laughter echoed on the deep stone walls of the house. I was a budding chef, fascinated by her simple and small first courses, true appetisers. She could make hard-boiled eggs glamorous, the split halves of the egg upside down on the plate, clothed in a homemade mayonnaise—made the French way—and topped with parsley. Or, she'd take three asparagus spears per person and top them with a lemony sauce.

As early as 1950, Nan lamented Australia's monotonous, if nutritious, diet.[5]

> How many of our recipes are derived from the countries where cooking is an art? It's easy enough to blame the sameness of the recipe books on the market, but the reading public, including recipe readers, usually get from publishers what they demand.

Nan went on to suggest to readers of her column that they befriend the 'New Australian' next door to get tips on braising meat with wine, and other relatively inexpensive ways to make food delicious at little cost.

In 1957, Geoff became the *Age's* correspondent in Europe, and the family went too. How Nan managed to file stories with a nine-year-old and a four-year-old constantly in tow, I cannot imagine. While in Europe, Geoff developed a passion for French food, which he brought home. Back in Kew, with a map of Paris on the wall and the smell of French cooking wafting from the kitchen, he would put on his beret and dance the girls or Nan around the family room to the songs of Edith Piaf.

Thereafter, Nan created a repertoire of French dishes. Since the French have a genius for making the most delicious repast from almost any ingredient, Nan learned to imbue the cheapest cuts of meat with savoury flavours. She made friends with the butcher, as she did with everyone, and he often slipped odd things like pig's trotters into the white-wrapped parcels she hauled home.

Nan did not realise that I loved offal. Mum's dishes of brains or tripe in white sauce and parsley disgusted the rest of the family, but I lapped them up. An aroma of carrots, onions and apples wafted from the kitchen one afternoon when I was at their house. I asked Nan what was on the menu for the evening. Hesitating, she hummed a little tune.

Finally, she said, 'Oh, just a little French dish. You know Geoff only likes French food.'

'What?' I persisted.

'Well,' she said quickly, *'tripes à la mode de Caen.'*

'Ah,' I exclaimed loudly, 'tripe! I love tripe!'

'Shh,' she whispered. 'Geoff hates it.'

At this, I happily set the table. I kept looking from under my eyelashes at Geoff and the girls throughout the meal, with sidelong glances at Nan and our conspiracy of silence. Everyone ate the tripe long braised with calves' feet—yes, an essential ingredient!—onions, carrots and Calvados apple brandy. It was delicious.

You will not find recipes for *tripes à la mode de Caen*, or anything like it, in my repertoire. Whatever is done to it, tripe still looks like popped bubble wrap. I don't mourn my lost love for tripe. It has gone the way of other offal in my cooking repertoire. Out. Nevertheless, I think of Nan as a role model for cookery and gracious living as well as a writer. Chris, too, was greatly charmed by her, recalling that she and Geoff ate dinner at 9 pm after the newspaper had gone to the printers. 'Nan would throw a blue-and-white checked tablecloth, in the French style, over a side table under a standard lamp, and serve dinner for two with a carafe of wine. Very civilised.'

In 1961, Nan and Geoff took advantage of the credit squeeze of that year[6] and bought a block of land in the upscale beach suburb of Portsea. There, surrounded by more salubrious houses, they built a fibro-cement-sheeted house. The humble 'fibro shack' has to be one of Australia's great contributions to its famed pleasant lifestyle. The one-bathroom, closet-less, two- or three-bedroom, one-storey house clad in asbestos-cement, launched in this era, enabled families living on workingmen's salaries to sample the good life near a beach. Today, these simple 'fibro' houses are making a comeback in popularity (presumably cleansed of their asbestos content). However, in the 1960s, the socialites of Portsea must have shuddered to see such a modest home in their midst. Situated at the end of a road, the house was soon covered in vines. With a pretty garden created around it, the house was transformed into a warm and wonderful gathering place for Nan and Geoff's many friends and vast family.

Nan put a sign on the gate. Meaningless to others, my mother smiled when she saw it. Her sister had called the beach house Colantet.

Chapter 35

Aptitudes, Attitudes and Ambition

One day, I found Simone de Beauvoir's book, *The Second Sex*, on my mother's bedside table. What Mum thought of de Beauvoir's analysis of patriarchy I am not sure, since she never discussed it with me. She probably considered it too dangerous. But feminism had begun to stir, even in the Antipodes.

As their children reached the teenage years, many of my mother's friends returned to the paid workforce. When asked why she did not join them, Mum said she would hate to go back to work 'to be bossed around by a young man'. She may have been reacting to the poor feedback she was getting at the university for her work on Flemish artists of the seventeenth century. Her supervisor seemed threatened, as my father almost certainly was, fearing her master's degree would lead to an actual career.

When I was a teenager, the question of careers for women was jousted at, but not taken seriously. The all-girls' school I attended did have loftier ambitions for its students than secretarial work, but we, along with most of the parents, were loath to embrace our options. Teachers, parents and girls would circle the career question, make a stab at it, and retreat. Were professional aspirations for women desirable, we wondered. A career might put off the men we were being trained to marry. The spiderweb of convention had enmeshed us in its silken net.

Still, our headmistress made an effort. Mr W., a lone male in our all-girls' school with its all-female staff, was a psychologist employed to administer 'aptitude tests' to the girls. Aptitude, of course, is a very different thing from attitude, let alone ambition. Mr W. had wispy fair hair and a droopy posture. We gave him no credit at all. Some of the parents encouraged this attitude, suspicious of the psychologist who would probe too deeply into their daughters' minds, uncovering unseemly motives or unacceptable desires.

'Mr W., do I trouble you?' we giggled, feeling threatened by his intrusion into our thoughts.

Anxiety frizzed the air on the day we were to discover our true abilities. We were near the end of eighth grade. The test, we knew, would determine our classes for the next year. We were academically 'streamed' at our school. Those in the 'A' classes were headed for university, while those in the 'B' classes took less demanding subjects. I was in the A stream, but my mangling of mathematics landed me in big trouble. Why 'x' and 'y' should hide the identity of a number in algebra mystified me, and so did the Pythagorean theorem.

'Can you explain again about the hypotenuse?' I asked our mathematics teacher. Her short, iron-grey hair swung by her chin as she whipped around from the blackboard, her navy pleated skirt shuddering, her black lace-up shoes stamping the floor in fury.

'A2 + b2=c2,' she said, her voice rising to an angry quiver. I remained unconvinced.

Given my obvious stupidity at simple mathematics, it mattered how well I did in Mr W.'s test. I wanted to stay in the A stream with my friends. (By now, I had settled in, and except for mathematics, loved my school.)

That Friday, each girl sat at her desk and pencilled in answers to questions about comparisons, questions about how we liked to spend our time, and one peculiar question.

'Who,' we were asked, 'would be the one person you would choose to be with if you were stranded on a desert island?' I answered, 'My brother, Christopher', and hoped this would not condemn me in some unseen way. The test was unlike any other, not about what I knew, but how I thought. I felt spied upon.

A few days later, Mr W. called me into his office to discuss the results.

'I think,' he said, cheerfully, 'you'd make a fine lawyer or a librarian.'

I took it meekly, but felt downcast. The drab women who checked out the books at the municipal library did not inspire, and I had never heard of a lady lawyer. I felt the letter 'L' emblazoned on my brow, marking me as an untouchable among the girls and boys I knew.

Instead of taking his remarks as a compliment, I sulked.

'You can do anything you like, then,' the psychologist said, his face defeated and his shirt cuff riding up at the wrist as he held out my paper.

I stomped out of his office feeling dull, dull, dull. How unfair to be steered towards a boring career characterised by brainy single ladies dressed in grey! A future self flashed before me—plain, earnest and bookish.

It appeared that even a career as a teacher could not be reconciled with family life, at least at our school. The teacher we most admired was Miss B., our third-form English teacher. With her wavy red hair, pencil skirts and jewel-coloured twinsets, she looked the way we all wanted to look—a model of feminine perfection. When she turned to write on the blackboard, we avidly inspected the straightness of her stocking seams. But she married and left. Marriage meant a teacher would lose her job.

I wanted a bit of glitter. Nan seemed to have the perfect combination of a glamorous career, enhanced by eye makeup *and* a family. In a rage, I told my parents about Mr W.'s advice. I could not imagine, I told them, a more inaccurate reading of my skills and interests or a more unsuitable career for me. I wanted to be a writer. But it seemed this had not come out on the check the boxes test.

In the A classes for the next two years, I struggled through arithmetic once a week, geometry and algebra twice a week. I remember the torture. Fortunately, electives were allowed in the last two years of school and, to my great delight, I was able to take art, while the brighter students toiled over trigonometry. My pleasure in no longer having to struggle with these hated mathematical subjects more than made up for my being no longer taken seriously academically.

Our art teacher, an artist herself, inspired me. I was a mediocre painter and sculptor, but Dawn—she urged us to call her by her first name—also set us readings and essays in art. Not just conventional art history, either. We were encouraged to go to galleries, to explore the moderns. I wrote my first essay in her class on the abstract painter Piet Mondrian. It was pure pleasure to write each word, and to try to explain, in the English language, what the Dutch artist was trying to convey in shapes and colours. The wonder of learning about fine art led to a life-long passion, one that had nothing to do with logic, librarianship, or the law.

I will gloss over the raging argument that ensued my last year of school. I was young for my class (due to skipping sixth grade) and finished school two weeks after my seventeenth birthday. Granny and my mother, in a rare moment of agreement, decided I should enroll at Invergowrie. Before her marriage Aunt Mary had been the school's bursar. That school's curriculum—I am serious—trained young ladies of a certain class for housewifery. I would have none of it, even though my housekeeping skills could have benefited. I wanted to go immediately to university, to sit in a classroom (as I had at Preshil) with boys. As for a career, I still had not thought of one.

Such were my formative years at 5 Grange Road. My life, in its freedoms and constraints, was typical of girls in mid-century Melbourne. Our family life, however, was not typical at all. Nevertheless, I grew up believing I would always live in Melbourne and would have a life similar to my mother's, even though I saw that she struggled to find her true path.

I saw before me three models of womanhood, models that played ping-pong in my head: that of my saintly mother, who put her needs aside; of my glamorous and witty aunt, who combined family with a successful career, but had been transgressive; and of my paternal grandmother, who had bravely struck out on her own, had overcome adversity bordering on deprivation, and with a remarkable man had experienced a happy marriage. Yet no one liked her.

What had happened to Eva to make her the way she was?

Chapter 36

A Journey Back in Time

Although the quartz rock with its veins of gold sat in Granny's cabinet as we were growing up, we children had no first-hand knowledge of Australia's goldfields or the way mining had touched our father's life. Granny was not like Aunt Kitty, a woman who could paint a picture of yesteryear and draw others into her tale. Our grandmother's personality pushed others away. And we were not the only ones to think her standoffish.

Granny's daughter Mary had married widowed mining engineer Peter Wreford and travelled to the other side of the continent to raise a family. At Peter's funeral, his youngest brother approached my brother John and announced, 'Your grandmother was a bat!'

Apparently, at the time of Peter and Mary's marriage, Peter's mother, Wilhelmina Wreford, had presumed to ask Granny to call her 'Mina'.

Granny had reportedly replied, 'Oh no. If I did, I would have to let you call me Eva, and only my close friends do that.' John Wreford went on to say Granny had 'crushed' our mother, and he didn't understand why Dad had allowed it.

My father was actually a kind man who loved my mother very much. I can only speculate that he had no idea what was happening to his wife's emotional health at 5 Grange Road. In Dad's world, you just got on with it.

'Never apologise, never complain,' he said. His upbringing had been spare, with a father absent for months at a time, sometimes years, and a mother whose English background contributed to her chilly personality. It's been said the English treat their dogs better than they treat their children. As far as I know, Granny didn't like dogs either.

Perhaps it is not surprising that a capable but cool woman appealed to the young prospector Victor Edquist in 1909. Eva Litchfield might have reminded him of his own stern mother, whose life had been far from easy.

'Yesterday, late in the afternoon, a very shocking accident happened to a miner named Daniel Davis [sic], while he was engaged in cleaning out an old shaft', a story in the *Talbot Leader* claimed on 16 April 1869. An inquest found that Davis, a twenty-nine-year-old Welsh miner, had died of a compound fracture of the skull when he fell as the hook holding his bucket loosened from the side of his mineshaft. The paper went on to say that Daniel Davis—his real name was Davies—'has always been the best of characters for industry and sobriety ... has been married about three years, and has two children'.

His widow was my paternal great-grandmother, the former Eliza Turner, whose family had come from England to Australia when she was a teenager. After the death of Daniel Davies, Eliza was left alone in the small mining town of Talbot, Victoria, with a two-year-old boy, Will, and baby Elsie. Eliza struggled, naturally enough, until five years later when a sweet but impecunious Swedish tailor, twenty years her senior, proposed. Eliza and Andrew Edquist had three sons, Alfred, Arthur, and Victor, born in 1879.

Andrew Edquist, for whom our brother was named, moved his family to Adelaide where, according to Granny's notes, he followed his tailoring trade, and his wife fed the family from a garden featuring 'grape vines, a quince, and a prolific almond tree, as well as many vegetables'. These crops became necessary for the family's survival when the tailor, Andrew Edquist, died. Victor, his youngest son, was only eleven.

Victor's excellent school reports raised his mother's hope that he would get a scholarship to continue his education at a private high school, since there was no public high school nearby. But he failed to do so. In her memoir, which dwelt lovingly on her husband and their marriage, Eva wrote of her husband Victor's early life.[1]

> This failure was a terrible disappointment because Victor knew that his mother could not possibly afford to pay for him. Victor felt he had failed and had laid his plans not to hang about or be a burden, or to face his mother until he had a job. He knew the results [of the exams] would be published in the morning newspaper and took care to see it first. He had no pocket money, but his last term's season train ticket to the city still had a few days' validity, so he went looking for a job. On the train he met a boy he knew who was already working, who told him that the bookseller E.S. Wigg & Son needed an office boy. So Victor applied for and got the job, and so made a start.

A year later, gold was discovered in Kalgoorlie, far away in the west. Victor blazed with gold fever, but having lost her first husband to the mines, Eliza discouraged her son from taking up the dangerous underground trade. According to Eva, 'His mother, who took everything the hard way and did not believe in sudden fortunes, was a damper on wild ideas so Victor contented himself with attending the Adelaide School of Mines night classes as a preliminary to a metallurgy course'.

Victor's ambition flared when he sold tickets to miners on ships bound for Klondyke, Alaska, where gold was discovered in 1898. But his first real chance came when his half-brother, Will, then working as an accountant on a mine in Reno, New South Wales, cabled Victor and asked him to apply for a job that had just become vacant at the mine, located about 100 kilometres south of Canberra, the nation's capital.

Their mother protested. Will wired back, 'Don't be a fool!'

The brothers soon went into business together. Will and Victor bought and sold mines, made money and lost money, all in the mines around Reno. According to Eva,

> Victor took an active interest in all the mining activities going on around him, especially in the residues. These were slimes and sands remaining after the ore had been crushed and processed to extract as much gold as possible. Before the cyanide process was introduced, extraction was often very poor so that the residues still contained a good deal of gold. Victor studied 'cyanide' and most carefully experimented, tested and cross-tested the heaps of sands etc. He concluded that if he could get the financial backing he could build the simple plant necessary and treat the stuff for a very handsome profit. His brother Will and one or two others backed him and he carried through the project most successfully. The result was plenty of good experience and about £2000 each for himself and Will.[2]

With this early entrepreneurial success, Victor's confidence soared. Eva continued:

> He never actually said so, but I am quite sure the next five or six years were the happiest of his life. He was young, strong, and interested in his work, which was well within his capacity. It was a bracing climate, and he had a number of pleasant, congenial friends whom Victor very much enjoyed. He used to describe what fun it was to rush down to the river to catch fish and to raid the garden for

melons for breakfast. Then there were dances at Reno and Gundagai. The young people would ride over, often in snow, their evening gear carried by them in some sort of bundle or box. Victor could not decide for a time whether to take up land, but gold-fever had him in its grip, and perhaps his very success had blinded him to the hazards of mining and treatment. Both he and Will moved to Western Australia, to Kalgoorlie, then at the height of its fame. Victor bought some heaps of residues on a 'pay as you earn' basis, but found this a very different proposition from Reno. These new ores were sulphides and most refractory. Successful treatment of the sulphides was a problem many people wanted to see solved, and Victor worked so hard and intelligently that he found backers when things became hard. He did not lose courage, kept on trying, and in the end solved the problem, and won the admiration and respect of all who were interested and understood the matter. Bewick Moreing told him they would give him a job whenever he wanted it.[3] However, the problem had not been solved in time to save his small fortune, and he lost the two thousand pounds.He went on, in partnership, to treat other dumps in the district, [but] with only fair success.

As Victor's and Eva's grandchildren (and as adults interested in learning more about our family's history), my brothers and I had talked for years about visiting the goldfields of Western Australia. During Easter 2007, my brother Chris (from Melbourne) and I met my brother John and his wife Deborah (from Canberra) in Perth. For me, coming from America, it was literally the longest journey in the world. Farther away still are the goldfields that fuelled the wealth of this vast state bordering the Indian Ocean.

Because our grandfather had worked in mines all over the region, we wanted to go to the goldfields at Youanmi and

Day Dawn. However, even in the twenty-first century, the distances from Perth to these historic mining towns were so great that we had to limit our journey. We were heading to Kalgoorlie, Kambalda and the township of Leonora, where the great Sons of Gwalia mine was located, a mine that had played a key role in Victor's career and the place our father had spent years of his youth. The Sons of Gwalia mine was also where our mysterious Granny had been living before her move to Melbourne. We wanted to understand not just Victor's role in the region's mining endeavours, but also mining's impact on our father and grandmother.

Our route, 538 kilometres by air from Perth to Kalgoorlie and then by car to Gwalia and back, covered an eerie landscape of copper-coloured earth under astonishingly blue skies, and skirted the remains of ancient dried lakes. In the distance they glisten as if filled with water—and you see how beautiful this country is, and how its lack of water tantalises and frustrates all attempts at permanent settlement.

As a student, years before, my brother John had worked one summer as a labourer on a nickel mine at Kambalda. It is within sight of Red Hill, where our grandfather Victor and his half-brother Will had started prospecting in Western Australia. They worked an old abandoned goldmine overlooking a dry salt lake, the arid but beautiful Lake Lefroy. The place is desolate, stony and, as the name implies, a small mountain of red earth. On our journey in 2007, John drove us off the road to the spot, the car rocking as it crushed the rusty gravel. We climbed the hill and looked out at the vast, uninhabited landscape below, a scene of incredible beauty. In front of us were the remains of dried silver lakes, miles and miles wide. Millions of years ago they were great inland seas. What is left is salt. What is not left is any trace of Victor's and Will's mine. They worked it until the gold ran out.

A problem on the mines near Kalgoorlie was that the ores contained many metals besides gold, and were difficult to refine. Victor tackled this problem at Red Hill, apparently seeking another entrepreneurial success. Ironically, according to my father, who was himself a mining engineer in his youth, 'The Red Hill concentrates contained 0.5 per cent nickel, but all that signified at the time was another complication for the cyanide process'.[4] Notwithstanding his only 'fair' results, Victor pressed on. Victor's eldest brother Will was the major investor in their Red Hill mine, but he remained in Kalgoorlie, working as an accountant.

It must have been a lonely life for Victor. A crack shot, he sometimes shot rabbits for the local Aborigines, and every couple of weeks he packed up the gold findings, got on his bicycle and, riding carefully with his pistol at the ready, cycled the fifty-eight kilometres to Kalgoorlie to deposit his earnings. One afternoon, dropping in for tea at his sister-in-law's house, he met an English home economics teacher named Eva Litchfield.

'He came in looking very hot and red, but with a nice smile', Eva wrote in her memoirs. 'I soon felt at home, especially when he told me this amusing little story. He had enquired at the stationer-bookshop in the town for Dr. Johnson's *Rasselas*. The girl, never having heard of it, went to enquire and came back saying they had a book on wrestling, was that what he wanted?'

Having established their bookish credentials and their superiority to the local yokels, Eva recalled she felt 'still more at home when at teatime he offered me the last cake on the dish with a smile and a twinkle saying, "A handsome husband and £10,000 a year"'. Victor was handsome, but the £10,000 was no more real than Jane Austen's description of her fictional character, Mr Darcy, to whom Victor referred.

These lines from Granny's memoir about how she and

Victor had joked about a bookstore employee's mistake—she'd thought he was asking for a book on wrestling when, in fact, he'd wanted Samuel Johnson's *The History of Rasselas, Prince of Abyssinia*—give a hint of a woman we never knew. Well read, and with a sense of humor, she was someone with whom Victor, also well read and with a sense of humor, must have felt an immediate rapport. The two understood each other, and Eva had kept the quartz rock from Victor's early diggings with her all these years.

After they married, my grandfather needed a steady job. He became a metallurgist for Bewick Moreing & Co., at that time the biggest mining company in the state, and earned a steady salary. But life was not easy.

A year after they married in 1912, Eva gave birth to my father, Dick. Without any of her family to turn to after the birth, Eva went to Adelaide to stay with her mother-in-law, the formidable Eliza Turner Edquist. Eliza was seventy years old by the time her first grandchild was born in April 1913, and she and Eva did not develop a close relationship. Eliza died in 1919, never seeing her grandchildren again, and Eva endured the isolated life of a miner's wife.

At a mine at Marvel Loch, with the beautiful name of Mountain Queen, Dick, aged one month, began his life on the goldfields. Marvel Loch, named not after a vanished lake but after a racehorse who won the 1905 Melbourne Cup, is today a five-and-a-half-hour drive from Perth along the road to Kalgoorlie. According to my father, 'living conditions at Marvel Loch were not far removed from camping out'. The family lived in a two-room cabin, its hessian walls sagging and torn. It did not rain much at Marvel Loch, but when it did, his parents put an umbrella over his crib. The sanitary facilities consisted of an outhouse over a hole in the ground.

My father wrote in his memoirs that at this time his mother was happy. 'The climate was not too harsh there,' he said, 'and for an English girl life in a mining camp was still an adventure.'

There are signs that in fact Eva was under considerable strain. My infant father failed to thrive—until saved by goat's milk. He was allergic to cow's milk. Since infants are not allergic to their mother's milk, one has to assume that Eva's milk had dried up or was not sufficient, usually a result of stress.

Dad wrote:

> I have before me a photograph, marked 'Marvel Loch, 1914', of my mother tending a pram in front of what appears to be a two-roomed hessian cabin; but the earliest construction I can actually remember was that of the metallurgist's house at Gwalia, about 1924. The walls of this house, inside and outside, were of hessian [cloth] nailed to the usual timber frame and whitewashed. The roof was of corrugated galvanised iron; the ceiling, sheet metal, impressed with a pattern. The kitchen and laundry were separated from the living quarters by a kind of enclosed connecting verandah called the 'vestibule' which acted as a breezeway and housed the perishable food storage: a Coolgardie safe and a hanging meat safe . . .
>
> Imagine cooking over an old-style, wood-fired cast-iron stove, boiling washing in a copper, and ironing using flatirons heated on the stove in that climate! My mother always had hired help, but even so, when she made a return trip to England in 1930 to see her family they were shocked, I was told later, to see how she had aged and lost her English complexion.

The family was soon to move farther into the remote interior. In 1914, Victor took his wife and year-old son Dick to Fingall's Mine at Day Dawn. A map of Western Australia shows the Murchison Goldfields right in the middle of the vast state. The map also shows a lake next to Cue, which is three miles from Day Dawn.That would be Lake Austin—another dried remnant of an inland ocean. By the turn of the century, mining optimism had created a thriving town in Cue/Day Dawn.[5] The town enjoyed sports meetings, including a 'novelty race' involving bottles of beer, and councillors unsuccessfully proposed a law to reduce the number of stray goats—'one man, one goat'. Here, Victor's career started its upward trajectory, with 'very satisfactory results on the modified plant', according to his manager, W. Blyth. He went on, 'Mr. Edquist has these matters in hand and we have great confidence that in a few weeks we will have the simplest flowsheet of any mine in the state'. At Day Dawn, Eva gave birth to another son, Bill, and then a daughter, Mary. Soon they moved again, this time 115 kilometres away to another mine with a lovely name: Queen of the Hills, Meekatharra.

At the beginning of 1916, Victor was sent to 'size up an option', in remote Warriedar, about 112 kilometres south of Yalgoo, the nearest railway point. The family situation became extremely difficult. My father said, 'It appears ELE (Evangeline Louisa Edquist) had to move out of the house and stay at a hotel in Day Dawn from March to June 1916, before joining VTE (Victor Thomas Edquist) with the children at Warriedar.' Though my father was too young to remember, he wrote: 'There (at Warriedar), I think living conditions would have been about as primitive as at Marvel Loch.' The Warriedar venture did not work. The treated ore did not reach the predicted values. For Bewick Moreing, the losses incurred were described as 'an expensive disaster' and the entire operation was written off.[6]

Eva, pregnant with her fourth child in three years, traipsed the 340 kilometres back to Perth with Victor, arriving in September 1916. They were hoping to find a more comfortable place for the family to live. Later that year, Victor moved to a new job at the mine at Youanmi, even farther away, 570 kilometres north-east of Perth. Eva stayed in Perth to give birth to her last child, John, on New Year's Eve 1916. Eva reported she employed an English girl, Kate. 'A big strong girl. She seems willing and good natured. She does the housework and children's washing every day, and I do the cooking.'

Free from Victor's watchful eye, Eva indulged herself in a splurge of new furniture buying, even as she deplored the mess the children made. And my father—whom she called 'Dickie' in this letter to her friend Hay Marmion—she'd already cast in the role of eldest child, of whom much is expected.

> Victor says I have spent so much money he will not take a holiday, but I hope he will come after all, though I don't want him to see the garden, or the dining room walls, or the sideboard with which Dickie has apparently been amusing himself by picking at it with a piece of pointed iron! ... Dickie still calls me occasionally in the night to my intense indignation as there is never anything the matter—he may want a sip of water. Since the new maid came, I have Mary back in my room and needless to say I do not spend several half hours during the night singing her to sleep. She seldom wakes at all now, even when I have the light on to breastfeed baby.

It is not recorded whether Victor came back to Perth to see the new baby, but we do know he soon returned to the interior. For Victor, hired as the mine's metallurgist, the job in Youanmi was to test his abilities and his leadership. Labour was hard to find because almost every able-bodied man had gone to war. The rest were internees. Italians, Serbs, Croats and others from the old Austro–Hungarian Empire had come to Western Australia to work on the 'woodlines'. These railways ran deep into the bush where the workers cut timber to feed the mine's incessant demand for wood. Suddenly, in 1915, the government rounded up all the non-naturalised workers on the mines and woodlines and sent them to camps for enemy aliens. As overseas investment focused on war-related goods, mining slumped. Nevertheless, Victor persisted.

Marital duty—or the expense of keeping a house in Perth— drove Eva to join her husband in the stony desert. She gathered her four children and their suitcases, and followed him, arriving at Youanmi on 11 April 1917, with Dick, just turned four, two-and-a-half-year-old Bill, Mary, eighteen months, and John three months. It is hard to imagine how she managed to get to Youanmi, juggling her suitcases and several little ones in tow. Yet resourceful Eva managed to secure a compartment to herself by 'pottying the children one after the other, thus driving the male passengers out'. The train took passengers from Perth to Mount Magnet but after that travel was by bicycle or cart or, if one was lucky, by car. The dirt track wound its slow way through the scrub another 111 kilometres from the railway station to the mine where Victor worked. Eva reported in a letter to her friend Hay Marmion, that 'Our new furniture has been terribly knocked about. Bottoms of the wardrobe smashed and splintered and the dining room table split across'.

Reunited with Victor, the family settled into the metallurgist's house, such as it was. Like the one described earlier by my father, the hessian-walled, white-washed, corrugated-iron-roofed house was lit by carbide lamps and Eva cooked on a wood stove. This provided warmth in winter, but no relief from the desert summer heat. Winters were so cold that a basin of water would freeze inside the house, and summers so blistering hot that temperatures exceeded 46°C for weeks on end. Nevertheless, the children found the place enchanting.

The Aboriginal name, Youanmi, refers to a spring in the area. Its greenery delighted the children. My father said:

> My earliest memories of the bush quite close to the house at Youanmi are of abundant life of trees and bushes and creepers, bearing flowers and nuts and pods, alive with birds and lizards and insects, including edible grubs and bats in the evening.

Dick, at three and a half, marvelled at the natural environment, but Victor's work life challenged him as never before. Ironically, a process that my grandfather later patented to extract gold was responsible for the deforestation of the area, as the woodlines encroached further into the forest and the workers felled more and more trees. Called the 'Edquist Process', it used charcoal to precipitate gold from a cyanide solution. His innovation then recovered the charcoal by flotation. The Edquist Process was a forerunner of methods of extraction used today.[7] At the time, Victor's ideas were the key to the mine's survival.

Now that the family had been reunited, the immediate problem was how to feed them. Dad described their diet. 'Food was transported by camel or donkey team from the railway head at Mt Magnet—it took four days to get there— otherwise we lived off my father's vegetable garden,' my father recalled, adding 'the kids were all pretty healthy in that solar radiation'.

> In the absence of refrigeration and convenience foods, our diet was somewhat restricted, judged by the standards of today. Fresh fruit and fresh fish were of course unknown. Fruit and vegetables brought up from the coast were available, but not at their best after some days in the railway system in summer. We generally had dried fruits. On the other hand, what we did have fresh was fresh

indeed: eggs from the fowl-yard, milk straight from the cow or goat, meat not long killed, as it did not keep long in that climate ... My father always kept a vegetable garden, which flourished for part of the year ... on plenty of animal manure and relative freedom from pests. Rockmelons grew well in that climate, too ...

Some local genius invented a swamp cooler-type contraption called a 'Coolgardie Safe' to preserve food in the withering summer heat. It served as a primitive refrigerator. My father remembered 'on really hot days you might put the baby in there'.

As always in the outback, water was incredibly precious. Dad said each bucket was used three times, for cooking, washing and throwing on the garden. The water itself had several sources, he reported.

'Scheme' water was reticulated from the mine's supply ... which came from wells some kilometres away. It was very brackish, and we children were forbidden to drink it. Distributed in pipes laid on the ground, it came warm to scalding during daylight hours most of the year. 'Condenser water' was condensate from the mine's steam engines. It could be used for washing ... Rainwater was collected off the roof and stored in corrugated galvanised iron tanks.

With four small children, Eva would have spent her mornings bent over a copper cauldron, twirling a stick around in the steaming water to do the family washing. The water, condensate from the mine's steam engines, smelled of engine oil, and her waist, gripped by a corset, dripped perspiration as her long, heavy skirts clung to her damp stockinged ankles. Her face would have turned brown as an acorn, not helped by the soot from the wood stove.

One day Eva, fed up with the life, threatened to leave Victor. Family legend has it that 'out the door she stormed, with the four wailing children waddling after her like ducklings'. She marched several times around the few wide blocks that made up the town, then came back.

'Fortunately,' she recollected, 'Victor said nothing,' thus allowing her dignity to be restored, as well as her entrapment.

While Eva struggled with the chores of keeping her children clothed and fed, these years in Youanmi seem to have formed the basis of my father's optimistic attitude. In a warm climate, with parents who worked hard but were no longer separated, he was a happy child with few material possessions and no need of them. He started school—shoeless—at the Youanmi State School where, as in similar one-room schoolhouses, the older children taught the younger ones.

At the end of 1920, the family returned to Perth to live in the seaside suburb of Nedlands. Six months later, Victor took another job away from them all, as manager at the Big Bell Mine in Cue. There he worked until 1922, when he was appointed to the Sons of Gwalia mine as its metallurgist, and the family joined him in Gwalia.

Chapter 37

Ruination

In 1922, the local paper in Gwalia reported that the metallurgist on the Sons of Gwalia mine had been sacked. His offence was commenting that the newborn son of the Mine Superintendent, Mr Jock Adam, was as dark skinned as an Aborigine.

'It is rumoured,' noted the paper, on 1 March 1922,

> that a remark was made a couple of days ago concerning Mrs. Adam's baby boy, Donald, who apparently has dark hair and is dark complexioned like his father . . . The word 'Warragul' was used; this is a well-known Aboriginal word for a male child. This somewhat misplaced observation was not well received by Mr. Adam and W. Eyres was dismissed soon after.[1]

Mr Adam felt that he and his wife had received the worst imaginable insult. But Mr Eyres' views did not have him ostracised. He immediately received two job offers elsewhere, and the paper devoted several paragraphs to the farewell parties for 'Bunny' Eyres, noting that 'he has many friends in the district and will be greatly missed'. He was replaced as metallurgist by Victor Edquist, who five years later became the mine's manager.

Three days after Victor's promotion to manager on 23 April, 1927, the local paper noted that there were only fifty-five full-blooded Aboriginals in Victoria. (New research indicates that in fact there were about 60,000 full-blooded Indigenous people living in the area in 1770. This was reduced to 15,000 by 1835, 2000 by 1845, and only 600 by 1901.)[2]

The conjunction of the news of my grandfather's appointment as manager of the Sons of Gwalia mine and the report of the decline of the Aboriginal population can only be a coincidence. It is unlikely that Victor's attitudes to the original inhabitants were any more enlightened than those held by Jock Adam or Bunny Eyres, or of any of the Europeans living in Western Australia at the time. Humans have lived in Western Australia for at least 40,000 years and the Kimberley region of north-west Australia is cited as a place of possible entry from the north even earlier. The First Peoples believe they have lived in Australia since the beginning of time.

People had inhabited the land for so long that by the time the Europeans arrived there were several different language groups in Western Australia. Their culture was rich in complicated kinship relationships and marriage taboos. Ochre paintings have been discovered in the Kimberley that are believed to be up to 40,000 years old. Over 100,000 rock art sites have now been recorded in Australia, many from sparsely populated Western Australia.[3]

The haunting, poetic creation stories of the first inhabitants of Australia were already packaged in bright covers and sold as children's books by the 1950s, but the true story of their degradation was only hinted at. Did my father and his parents know that Indigenous people in Western Australia were hunted down, slaughtered and enslaved? Or did they shove that unspoken knowledge aside?

The books I have read about race relations in Western Australia refer to 'race riots'. What the authors mean by this is the unhappy relations that existed between workers of British stock and Southern Europeans. According to mining historian Patrick Bertola, it was only in 1963 that Aboriginal people were allowed to work in mining on lands they had occupied from time immemorial.[4] Not only had they occupied these lands, they had also mined them, particularly for ochre, which they traded over long distances. According to the NSW Department of Primary Industries, they excavated to a depth of twenty metres using 'pole scaffolding' and 'heavy stone mauls and fire-hardened wedges'.[5] Between them, the white settlers, graziers and then the mining companies depleted the Aboriginals' mining lands and their hunting grounds, forcing them to work for rations only, or to beg.

Not far from where my father spent his early years is 'the rabbit-proof fence'. This wire fence, running north and south for 3000 kilometres, was meant to keep out rabbits from pastoral country. But it also ran right over Aboriginal clan land, ignoring ancient boundaries. In my grandparents' time, policemen roamed the outback looking for 'half-caste' children. With the idea that the half-white children would be better off trained to be domestic servants or stockmen, police tore the children from their parents and settled them in orphanages, boarding schools, or foster homes. One man, in particular, deserves attention.

At the very same time and place that my grandfather was making his career in gold, Auber Octavius Neville was making life hell for half-caste children and their mothers. Neville, wielding the title of 'Chief Protector of Aborigines', gradually accrued more and more power over Aboriginal lives. Believing that the Indigenous people were dying and he was doing those children born of Aboriginal mothers and white fathers a favour, Neville mandated the removal of these children from their mothers. They were placed in institutions and given a basic education in numeracy and literacy so they could get low-level jobs. The aim was for the mixed-race children to marry whites and thus to be gradually assimilated over the generations.

Neville's policies were not universally admired. In fact, a neighbour of my grandparents criticised the policy so determinately that the forced removal of children received international notice. Mary Bennett, my grandmother Eva's exact contemporary, taught at Mt Margaret Mission, located between Leonora and Laverton in the vicinity of Gwalia. The mission, run by the Reverend Shenk, had a reputation as one of the more humane mission schools, but Rev. Shenk was criticised because, while he disapproved of government policies, he vehemently opposed Aboriginal customs.

Mary Bennett brought British press attention to the plight of the Aboriginals in 1934. She testified before a Royal Commission on the treatment of Aboriginal people in Western Australia, on the sexual abuse of women and children, and the policy of removing children from their families. The Commission found problems with Neville's policy, but allowed him to continue. As researcher Elfie Shiosaki reported,

> Mary Bennett, an activist for women rights, had denounced the forcible removal of Aboriginal women and children as 'akin to slavery' and in violation of the League of Nations Covenant and Slavery Convention which had been signed by Australia in 1929. . . . In reacting to these widespread revelations, the commission seemed to become some kind of performance by the State to reassert senses of nationalism and national identity in Australia, which had been deeply unsettled by these revelations.[6]

If my grandmother knew Mary Bennett, she never mentioned her.

The removal of Indigenous children from their mothers took place all over Australia, and continued in some states until the 1970s. My brother Chris, then a partner at a national law firm, appeared on behalf of eleven members of the Stolen Generation at the 1997 *Bringing Them Home National Inquiry into the Separation of Aboriginal and Torres Strait Islanders from Their Families.*

The degrading treatment of fellow human beings in this area was obvious to anyone who cared to look, but there was no mention of it in our schoolbooks. A hundred years before the original occupants of Western Australia were banned from land their ancestors had roamed from time immemorial, they were also removed from their ancestral lands in the east, in Victoria, the process accelerated when gold set off a rush.

Victoria, my home state, was named after the Queen at the time. Imperialist values reached their zenith under Queen Victoria, and it's no surprise that Granny never questioned colonialism; after all, she was a child of the British Empire.

Chapter 38

A Daughter of the Empire

Gwalia and its sister town of Leonora were far indeed from what my English-born grandmother considered the apex of civilisation. Evangeline Louisa Litchfield was born in Bedfordshire, England, on 15 September 1881. Queen Victoria had been on the throne for forty-four years, and Britain's influence stretched across the globe. The atlas Eva would have memorised in her geography class showed countries in every continent mapped in the colour of watered blood: the red of Empire. Britain's vast reach did offer opportunities for the enterprising but, at home, class strictly defined career options. This was the era of *Upstairs, Downstairs*. Eva's family was decidedly not upstairs. But, as her memoir relates, her family had aspirations to rise above their station.

From the faded lines of my grandmother's memories of her childhood come hints of the family's striving to attain middle-class respectability—in other words, ideas and values that made them better suited for the New World than the class-bound Old. Eva had been born into a family that knew difficulty and struggle, but believed hard work would lead to a better life. In this, her family was not typical—their ambition belies most of the literature about Victorian England.

Eva's maternal grandfather George Hobbs was a saddler. Apparently, he struggled to make a living. Eva said, 'He held Liberal views, but whether that was because he was not successful, or he was ignored because Liberals were anathema to the powers—squire and parson—I do not know.' Elizabeth Hobbs, Eva's mother, married a man, who, like Eva's future husband, Victor, determined to educate himself. Eva wrote:

> William Litchfield was not an active athletic type, and was not clever with his hands, but he loved books and words and tried to improve himself at night school. He left Aspley and went to London about 1870, and at once got a job in an environment which suited him—with a bookseller. He took evening classes to learn shorthand and other subjects, and years later amused and impressed us, his daughters, by describing how he kept himself awake to study by wrapping a wet towel round his head and drinking black coffee. In the later '70s, he was recommended as English private secretary to a Spanish gentleman ... he seems to have been a man of wealth and position and an aristocrat ... My father and mother always mentioned Don Calvo in admiring tones. My father seems to have mixed a good deal with Don Calvo's household—and learned to speak Castilian Spanish fairly well. This was the language of the educated classes and was a great advantage to him.

It is to this mysterious Spanish gentleman that Eva's father William owed his career and, ultimately, his death. He set the stage for Eva's own fearless attraction for distant parts of the world. She said that Don Calvo obtained for her father a consular job as Vice-Consul for Uruguay. In her memoirs, Eva shows an eldest daughter's acute understanding of the family's social and financial situation.

> Three daughters were born, and all went well until 1886–87 when a revolution in Uruguay put the government out

of office and all government servants lost their jobs. This was a sad time for us and, to economise while my father found another job, we moved to a cheaper house in a poorer neighbourhood. At last, he applied for a position advertised by Peak, Frean & Co. that wanted a man to travel and represent them in South America. A requisite accomplishment was good Spanish, and some Portuguese was desired.

Peak, Frean & Co makes biscuits. My great-grandfather William's nervousness at having to apply for a job in sales is apparent in the next part of Eva's memoir.

Many years later my mother told me that when my father applied and looked at his competitors waiting for an interview, he felt pretty confident. He was not too old (35), had always been careful to dress well, and knew he spoke good Spanish pretty well and enough Portuguese soon to improve. He did succeed and went on his first voyage in the summer of 1889 after a few months travelling in England with an experienced (commercial) traveller who instructed him in the business. He made a success of his work in South America and remained with the firm for the rest of his life; after a year or two adding one or two more agencies. Later he was offered, at a higher salary, a settled position in Barbados as Peak Frean's agent, but neither he, nor (particularly) my mother, thinking the place suitable for bringing up white girls, it was not accepted.

Meanwhile my poor mother must have had a harrowing time, left with three little girls and a fourth on the way. No certainty the journey would be a success, and at that time the threat of sudden or quick death by yellow fever always hanging over them. It was arranged that we should move to a cottage near Aspley Guise, so that we should be near my aunts and great-aunts. Hilda, my youngest sister, was born in November 1888.

I find this passage remarkable in its empathy. Clearly, a younger Eva than the one we knew understood her parents very well, alert to the challenges they faced.[1]

To Eva, her father's voyages sounded romantic and exciting, a model for her later confidence in tackling her own journey. Eva's memories show that, like the man she later married, her father was not afraid of adventure. Like Victor, he overcame the obstacles of limited formal education and job insecurity to support a growing young family. Like Victor, he took jobs far from home, leaving his wife to look after the children for an extended period.

Eva's tone grows wistful as she recalls her early childhood, when her father was alive. 'They called the cottage near Aspley "Esperanza" and their "hope" was fulfilled. We returned to London and settled in Lewisham, then a pleasant suburb. We had four homes there . . .'

Intensely practical Eva now turns to what would become an abiding interest—how to live well on a modest income.

> Large families had necessitated large homes, and how cheap they were compared with today. Our largest house in Lewisham, in one of the best residential areas, had eleven rooms besides kitchen, scullery, pantry, larder, bathroom, internal toilet, linen cupboard, and store cupboard. This was ground floor, and first and second floor leased for a rental of £75 per annum, but the occupier paid rates and taxes. All the rooms except two small bed- or dressing-rooms had fireplaces.

The detail is amazing. Eva is recalling a house from her childhood, and she knows exactly how much rent the tenants paid, and who paid the rates and taxes!

After four girls, Elizabeth Litchfield presented the family with a boy, Horace Courtney, in 1891. When Eva was fifteen and little Horace only five, their father died of the yellow fever so dreaded by travellers to South America. His widow had to manage five children by herself. Eva recalls how she and her sisters suddenly had all joy, and most prospects of marriage, ripped out from under them. Their mother had to lay off her domestic help, and the girls spent every afternoon after school, and all weekend long, cleaning the large nineteenth century house. No wonder Eva became a teacher of home economics, at that time a new profession encompassing novel ideas of efficiency, diet and hygiene. Elizabeth Litchfield told her daughters they must train for careers. 'The boy,' she said, 'can fend for himself.' Sadly, Horace's life was shortened by war. He was killed in action in France in 1915.

As Eva's only daughter, Mary speculated that the sisters were victims of the shortage of eligible males caused by World War I. Actually, these sisters were already in their late twenties and early thirties when war broke out. But without a father or an older brother to make introductions in their teenage years, opportunities for girls to meet the opposite sex were few. Schools, at least classrooms, were segregated by gender at that time, so Eva recalled that naturally enough, most of the families they knew were families of girls.

'They went to few parties,' was my aunt's explanation.

All the sisters—Eva, Agnes (Nessie), Annie Marguerite (Daisy or Margaret), and Hilda—became schoolteachers and, apart from Eva, none ever married. My father remarked:

> They all rose to the upper levels of the only profession that was really open to women in England before World War I—teaching. Two of the sisters instructed at teacher training colleges. Nessie became a vice-principal at forty-one, and Daisy was a principal before she was forty-five. Hilda, too, became a school principal.

Eva's youngest sister Hilda eventually became an Anglican nun, and taught in India. When I met her in her convent near Windsor,[2] she was seventy-eight years old, tiny and charming, her face so tanned by service in India that she reminded me of an acorn. She was full of admiration for Eva. 'It is so exciting to think of all you exotic relatives on the other side of the world,' she said, making little of her own adventurous years of service in Calcutta as head of a boarding school for a 'very nice class of gels'.

'Will you stay for Evensong?' she asked, as I sipped the last of the tea from my china cup.

Being young and anxious to get back to the more exciting life I imagined I was living in London at the time, I declined, saying I had to catch my train. It is one of the small regrets of my life. I could have given this last survivor of my grandmother's sisters—the only one I ever met—another hour of my company, and have given myself the precious memory of ancient nuns chanting the ancient creed in an ancient abbey. I find it remarkable now that both Eva and her sister carved out new lives for themselves, one in teeming Calcutta and the other in Western Australia's desolate goldfields. They faced hardships they never would have known had they not ventured forth into the unknown.[3]

While men have traditionally been explorers and adventurers, women tend to stay by the hearth. After I met my great-aunt Hilda, and began to think for the first time as an adult about the life of my grandmother, a sneaking admiration for them grew. I am still amazed. Hilda, at least, had the community of her religious order to back her up, but Granny did it all on her own. In this she acted more like a man than a traditional late Victorian woman. In her drive, perhaps she was not so very different from a man born only eight years earlier than she—the man who found the mine in which she spent her best years. That man was Herbert Hoover.

Chapter 39

The White House in the Wild West

In 1897, a quarter century before my grandfather Victor became involved with the Sons of Gwalia mine, Bewick Moreing & Co hired a twenty-three-year-old American. Herbert Hoover, a recent geology graduate of Stanford University, was to explore Western Australia and look for mining opportunities.

Bright and ambitious, Hoover reported his first impression of Western Australia on his arrival in 1897.

> Finally I arrived at the desert mining camp of Coolgardie, over the 300 miles of newly constructed narrow gauge railway. The town was then at the height of a mining boom. It had all the characteristics of a Western American mining camp, with some special Australian attachments. Government was more rigid, violence was absent, but petty crime, immorality, and good cheer were as generally abundant as in the California of '49. The overriding characteristic of all mining booms is the nth degree of optimism. Everybody in Coolgardie lived in a tinted atmosphere of already estimated fortune—or one about to be estimated—and therefore drank champagne as a beverage.[1]

Quite possibly the miners drank champagne because it was safer and more abundant than water.

Inspecting the company's mines and scouting for others, Hoover was not impressed by the landscape he had to ride through, on the backs of Afghan camels. He reported travelling over land where 'the temperature was over 100 degrees at midnight for days at a time. The rain was little more than an inch per year and most of it all at once . . . we slept on the ground under the cold stars and were awakened by swarms of flies at daybreak'.

His mission for his employers was to find a profitable lode. 'The country is unbelievably flat and uninteresting,' he wrote.

> There is not a fish in stretches of a thousand miles. In fact, there are no running streams . . . The country is covered by a low bush eight or ten feet high with occasional eucalyptus trees so starved for water as to have only an umbrella of foliage. The roads—more properly 'tracks'— that were gradually cut through the low brush extended in straight lines for hundreds of miles.[2]

About 160 kilometres inland from Kalgoorlie, Hoover camped overnight near a 'show' worked by a group of Welshmen. The owners of this mine named it 'Sons of Gwalia'—a Celtic word for Wales. Hoover inspected the mine with growing excitement and, as soon as he could find a telegraph office, contacted Bewick Moreing in London. He 'recommended the purchase of a two-thirds interest for $250,000 and a provision for $250,000 working capital'.

Herbert Hoover created the job of manager of the Sons of Gwalia mine, carrying a small percentage interest himself and taking the manager's job at a salary of $10,000 a year. He also began construction of a handsome house, one that would pass down to future managers of the mine. Indeed, it was to be the finest house in the vicinity. Before he could live in the house, however, Hoover, not yet twenty-five, was recalled to the company's head office in London, then sent to

China, where he played a leading role in saving Westerners during the Boxer Rebellion.

My father discussed Hoover in his writings. He was no fan of his management methods, which involved increasing working hours and lowering wages. When the miners went on strike, Hoover hired scabs, mostly Italians who would work for lower wages. (Mining's incessant need for workers attracted people from Southern Europe long before they flocked to the eastern states, and Dad would have attended school with children from many linguistic and cultural backgrounds. Maybe this early experience made him unusually receptive to migrants as an adult.)

While Hoover defended his approach in the interest of increasing technical and managerial efficiency in the pursuit of profits,[3] my father noted the extravagant house he had built for himself while miners made do with shacks, and the enormous salary Hoover had demanded even before the mine had paid a dividend to its investors.

It appears that Herbert Hoover left Western Australia at exactly the right time to ensure his future. Gold mining was about to dive.[4] My grandfather Victor could not have known that delving into a mess and restoring it to profitability was to become his foremost managerial skill, but this was also about the time he arrived in Western Australia to make his career. Dad wrote:

> By 1908, the year that Hoover left Bewick Moreing & Co., the Western Australian gold industry was over. In 1907, gold production fell for the fourth year in succession. Mines were closing; no new ones were being found. The First World War hastened the decline, and post-war inflation against a fixed price of gold almost finished the industry. From his appointment with Bewick Moreing & Co. in 1912 VTE (Victor) moved from one dying mine to

another, in a firm that had been able to recruit the cream
of mining executives.

Ten years later, Victor was appointed as metallurgist to
the Sons of Gwalia mine at a time when it was, my father
said, 'under sentence of death'. The mine was on the point
of closure because a fire some years before had destroyed
much of the processing plant. Victor kept the operation
going by treating residues, by exploring ever deeper, and by
patenting a method of desalinating water. He also obtained
a government loan that enabled him to steer Sons of Gwalia
through the Depression, as other mines went bankrupt.

In 1927, Victor was promoted to the manager's job at the
mine, the same job Herbert Hoover had held thirty years
before. As manager, Victor, with his family, was entitled to
live in the 'Hoover House'. In its vestibule off the dining
room, a three-piece band played whenever the governor
came for dinner.

The job at Gwalia cemented our grandfather's reputation
as 'one of the outstanding metallurgists of his generation'.[5]
With Victor at the helm, the Sons of Gwalia's fortunes had
prospered, even during the Depression. The price of gold
soared, and a previously tight labour market (in part caused
by 1929 federal government restrictions on immigration)
loosened, with many seeking work. The Sons of Gwalia
repaid its government loan and became Bewick Moreing's
flagship mine. It was the deepest in Western Australia and
the largest outside Kalgoorlie. Over the years, in a country
where the 'resources industry', i.e. mining, still underpins
economic prosperity, this mine proved to be one of Australia's
most profitable, producing 2.6 million ounces of gold.

* * *

Unlike Hoover and our grandparents, who jolted over the
dusty, fiercely hot interior by camel, train or buggy, my

brothers, sister-in-law and I drove to Gwalia in the comfort of an air-conditioned rental car. After the hour's flight from Perth to Kalgoorlie, we picked up the car, and travelled three hours through the red-floored, gum-tree-studded high desert of the Eastern Goldfields. It was an almost-park-like scene. Tall salmon gums, so named for their pink smooth trunks, soared up into the sky with wide spaces between them. The trees exude a toxin that poisons other plants that might compete for water. A light rain swirled on the windshield, though the temperature was warm. As the car rose over hills, we could see kangaroos drinking from indentations in the middle of the road. They looked up at our approach, considering whether to flee, then hopped into the shelter of the scrub. We passed a mob of feral goats feeding on either side of the road, nannies on one side, billies on the opposite. Whether deserted by time and the landscape, or just because it was Easter, the lonely settlements we passed through looked like background sets for Western movies.

Our goal was Leonora, just a mile or two from the Hoover House and museum of the Sons of Gwalia mine. The mine was closed in 1963, but has since reopened. The shanties of Gwalia around it are now preserved as a ghost town. And the house Herbert Hoover built is now nicknamed 'The White House', in commemoration of the job Hoover ultimately took as President of the United States.

We stopped at the mini-mart in Leonora to pick up food, knowing our destination had none. From this sleepy hamlet, a signpost pointed the way. Awed by a sense of abandonment, my brothers and I drove slowly over the rutted road. Pepper trees and a few cacti bordered a track that ran parallel to an old railway line. Around a bend, half-a-dozen deserted iron shacks came into view. Climbing a hill, we passed a shed housing an enormous wooden crane, the winder, which sent the miners up and down the shafts. A nineteenth century wooden building, the museum, sat to its right, and on the hill stood a handsome house built in typical Australian country style with a corrugated iron roof bending low over wide verandahs on all four sides. We'd arrived at our destination—The Hoover House.

We clambered out of the car, wandered over to a shop, and were greeted by the effusive manager. He was expecting us—our stories would add to his store of knowledge about the mine and house.

'I can't imagine how you must feel,' he said, 'to be coming to your grandparents' home after all these years of hearing about it.'

The Hoover House is now a guesthouse, part of the Gwalia Museum. According to a tourist brochure, the Hoover House sits in splendour on top of the hill 'under the shadow of Mt Leonora', while below it, just out of sight, lie the miners' corrugated-iron huts.

My brothers and I stood under a peppercorn tree shading a silent tattered street. How improbable that Gwalia was once a vibrant company town, home to a thousand people. Emus and feral goats now nibble the coarse weed-stalks stubbornly erupting in the unpaved streets where, in the 1920s, the first electric tramcar in the state ran between the mine at Gwalia and the larger township of Leonora. On weekends, loud parties of young people engulfed the wide verandahs of the privileged houses on Staff Hill and, down in the even louder miners' town, men jostled elbows in the pub. The state school capped the year at Christmas with a performance of Gilbert and Sullivan and, on Saturday nights, the town sat together under the stars to watch a moving picture show. There were scout trips, a public swimming pool, motorcycle races, school concerts and plays, church fundraisers and dances, at which the paper reported on 'the ladies' frocking'.

For the family, the life in Gwalia was full, and fun, too. There were children aplenty and they made their own amusement. The township's remoteness formed the unsentimental character of its inhabitants. My father's move to Guildford Grammar School in Perth was a shock, not least because it was the first time, at the age of thirteen, he had to wear shoes. To get to boarding school, Dad had to make two consecutive, twelve-hour journeys by himself, sleeping on the station platform between trains, being chastised by the station master for 'loitering'.

Thinking about how our family had lived in these same rooms long ago, my brothers and sister-in-law and I made dinner from our store-bought supplies. Popping cold beers on the wide verandah, we looked onto the pretty front garden with its astonishing strip of green lawn. Intruders on this ancient land, we were also, quite literally, home. Eating in our granny's house, the presence of family seemed palpable, their photographs on display in the dining room.

Given the modest circumstances in which he grew up, and his sudden success at so early an age on the other side of the world, it is perhaps not so surprising that on being given a blank chequebook, so to speak, Herbert Hoover built a magnificent mansion in the middle of the desert. Not so surprising either that, years later, my grandmother, also of modest background, luxuriated in the house's large master bedroom, its Oregon pine floors (resistant to termites), the shade of its twelve-foot-wide verandah, and its startling rose garden. The roses were watered, as was the entire house, by two enormous iron rain tanks, circled by the native bright pink coral vine. Later, we went for a stroll. My brothers and I looked about us, at the ancient wooden winder, the outdoor bathtub under a tree, the red desert landscape stretching to the horizon.

A museum. An old house, a steam engine, an open pit like a gash in the landscape, and hideous, hideous miners' shacks are all that remain of Gwalia. Like most visitors, we were shocked at the poverty of the miners' shacks. The mostly Italian workers used old explosive boxes, filter cloth and tin to cobble together shelter. Roofed with corrugated iron, freezing in winter and blazing in summer, the shacks were walled with whitewashed hessian cloth and lacked gas or electricity or running water. Even in April, the huts, rusted and overgrown with vines, were oven-hot, still and silent. Furnished as they had been in my grandparents' day, the shacks had sagging beds, rusting kitchen implements, and ancient stoves. A rough man's outpost, the town of Gwalia had a brothel, operating openly, and huts that housed numerous pubs. A sign at one hut designated as a pub gives the flavour of the place. 'Beer, wine', it announced on a board over a sink, 'Population: drunk'.

In Victor and Eva's era, houses with tin ceilings and interior walls lined with whitewashed burlap were the norm, and even the wealthy had no indoor heating or cooling or toilets. But seeing how the miners lived struck me viscerally. Gwalia represents to the modern eye a sickening contrast in standards of living between poor miners and the apex of outback society: the mine manager and his wife.

It is in the contrast in dwellings between management and workers at Gwalia that the values of the corporation are most evident. In this far-off place they seem to sock you in the face because there is nothing else there, in the desert, but this blatant emblem of capitalism in all its forms—rags to riches, envy and greed, environmental pollution, the promise of happiness through material gain, the reality of despair and its alleviation at the grog-shop.

After many years of hardship, deprivation even, because they too had once lived in primitive miners' shacks, Gwalia was to become the pinnacle of my father's parents' achievement. Realising this, as I looked over the ghost town of Gwalia, made me uncomfortable. Our grandmother had her greatest moments here, queening over a population of desperately poor miners. Had she, above ground and gazing over a horizon of rocks, revelled in the labours of the ants below, furrowing and burrowing to bring up the buried treasure?

We slept like angels in the comfortable, now air-conditioned bedrooms of the Hoover House, the earth silent, the air clear, the night sky black and domed with stars. Taking our tea to the verandah in the morning, we saw a flock of emus charging off into the distance. We needed to set off too. Remembering Granny's rigid domestic standards, we cleaned up scrupulously and left the house as immaculate as we found it. A maid was coming, but the Hoover House doubles as a museum exhibit, and we wanted to honour it by leaving it beautiful. As we piled our bags into the car, the first tourists came up the path.

Visiting the Hoover House helped me understand something about Eva I had never understood before. Gentleness, my mother's primary characteristic, had no place in our grandmother's life. The conflict between the two women was actually a conflict between opposing values. Ambition, drive, endurance, adaptability, ingenuity and independence met compassion, idealism and meekness. My father's values had been shaped by his parents' beliefs and by lived experience of growing up in a mining camp. My mother's had been shaped by early loss and by the warmth of a large, loving family.

This attraction of opposites, so strong yet so full of mutual misunderstanding, framed my childhood. Eva's life in the goldfields, away from the life she might have had if she'd remained in England, gave her a husband she adored and four healthy children, things her sisters could only imagine. But there was something else, too. A sense that what she did mattered. She had faced adversity and triumphed. Before her vision and health gave way, she may very well have had a sense of invincibility.

Chapter 40

Four O'Clock

Human invincibility is an illusion. Victor died, as did Eva's beloved youngest son, John. Her only daughter Mary had left to live on the other side of the country, assuming the role Eva herself had once enjoyed: mine manager's wife. A triple loss, at a time when society was barely coping, trying to recover from the war's long years of deprivation and fear. Left alone and friendless, Eva turned to her eldest son for solace, only to find him absorbed in his family and a wife with whom she had nothing in common.

I was eighteen and already in my second year at university when Granny died. She lived for only a few months in the small flat my parents finally bought for her. A nurse–housekeeper came every day and, I think, stayed pretty much full-time. Evangeline Louisa Litchfield Edquist died in her sleep at the age of eighty-two. At the funeral, attended only by family members, the celebrant could not remember her name. Instead of referring to 'Eva' he simply called her 'Mother'. I don't remember anyone shedding tears.

Chris's anecdote says it all.

> I was eleven when my grandmother died. I remember that
> I cried for about ten minutes. This is not a random guess. I
> had been watching the *Jetsons* on the little black and white
> television in the sunroom when my mother came in with

her eyes full of tears to tell me the news. I went back to the kitchen with her. After a few minutes someone else came in and I was allowed to leave. I naturally went back to the TV. The *Jetsons* were still going. I have often recalled this episode, but have never reproached myself. I devoted about as much time to Granny in my life as she did to me. As you sow, so shall you reap.

Perhaps Dad's mother Eva—cold, formal and very British—was aware that her life, and that of her husband and children, would have been as strange to us as if she had come from Mars. Instead, she had tried to instill in us outdated English formality from the Victorian age.

As an adult, I asked my mother why she had never complained to Dad about her ceaseless burden. She simply said, 'I couldn't. It was his mother, after all.' Nevertheless, after Granny died, Mum started eschewing her dresses in drab blues and greys in favour of rebellious reds. She never went as far as nail polish. But she did have the dining room painted lavender.

In her quiet but persistent way, Mum was determined. Some time after our grandmother's death, the Kew Council began removing trees on public land. Outraged, my mother began a letter-writing campaign. It went nowhere. So, she decided to run for election as a councillor. She went to the Town Hall to register herself as a candidate, only to be told that she could never run for elected office because she did not own property in Kew.

John Edquist explained:

> Apparently, she was not a Joint Tenant with Dad in the house at Grange Road. It was solely in Dad's name. I can only hypothesise that Granny willed the property exclusively to Dad. But of course, to Dad, this wasn't a problem. It was only a problem for Mum.

Even in death, Granny had the last word.

Our mother became active in cultural causes, raising money for the university library and enjoying her new freer time with friends. Despite my father's objections, she went on studying. She continued her original research on the Flemish printmakers for years, corresponding with the few experts on the subject in the world.[1]

* * *

Of the generation that had fought in World War I, Great-uncle Bill Rudd's health was the first to give way. As Bill grew sicker over the years, the shrapnel in his gut causing him constant pain,[2] our mother was Kit's confidante. Kitty came to our mother the day Bill died, but Mother was out that cold Saturday afternoon. When I came into the house from my tennis lesson (I was a teenager at the time), I found my father helpless with embarrassment at Auntie Kit's obvious emotion.

'Bill waited till I got there, and then he went,' Kitty said. 'He didn't say anything, just smiled at me and put his arms out to me, and died,' she kept telling us over and over. Bill was a lucky man, I realised, dying quietly in his loved one's arms. Then Mum came home. She went into the kitchen and, putting on the kettle, made a tremendous rattle with the cups. Kit slumped against the sofa. I handed her more Kleenex and gave her a kiss.

Kitty died in 1975. My mother, father and Aunt Nan would all face the final frontier before the twentieth century ended.

* * *

My mother recorded in her memoir that diphtheria when Nan was six years old had left her sister 'with damage to a heart valve so that she was never from that time as strong as I, although she packed her life with incident'. So, it was no surprise when after a visit to the doctor one day, Nan let herself into our kitchen, crossed her legs in her slim skirt on a stool at the old wooden table, and gave us his report.

'He told me to stop drinking and smoking,' she said indignantly. 'He'll want me to give up sex next! What does he want me to be? A nun?'

In her sixties, Nan developed cancer. In the hospital just before she died, she balanced her lipsticks and bottles of nail polish on the wheeled tray above her abdominal tumor stretching the sheet tight across her belly.

'Are the nurses doing your nails?' I asked.

'I'm doing my own nails, dear. Hand me that brush, please.'

Whether for shame, or to protect Kristy, no one talked about the reason Nan had left her husband so precipitously and later fled the country and hid her child in the hills. Kristy found out as an adult. 'I found old letters between my parents,' she said. 'When we were in Tasmania my father had tried to strangle me. And my mother.'

Today, Kristy remains as sweet natured as ever, without the slightest bitterness. Mum, characteristically understated, said in her memoir that 'Kristy would always have a special place in my affections'. Nan and Geoff were in love every day of their thirty-two-year marriage, which ended with Nan's death in 1984. Geoff seemed to lose interest in life after Nan passed away, and died eighteen months later. People said he died of grief.

Nan's death unmoored my mother. She had grandchildren by that time, and more to come, yet she told me, 'Now there's nothing to look forward to.' She tried. My parents started looking at smaller houses. Dispiritedly trudging through many a brick veneer 'home unit' they eventually gave up. After hating the house in which she had lived under the thumb of her mother-in-law, Mum conceded that they could not find a house as gracious, as roomy, and with as lovely a garden as that at 5 Grange Road.

My mother developed Alzheimer's disease at sixty-eight; later we realised the signs of forgetfulness and confusion had been there for a while. For a long time, Dad denied there was anything wrong. But on receiving a definitive diagnosis, he took on her care heroically. He pored over cookbooks to make interesting meals and made lemonade from our lemons. He filled the closets with lavender from the garden and, after finding the old bottling set, made marmalade. Paying back in spades the unselfish care Mum had given his mother and the family, our father looked after our mother at home. It was only when she was far gone with Alzheimer's that he had a change of heart about her studies. He found he missed his wife's keen mind. He remembered she had submitted her thesis to the University of Melbourne Press, and asked a friend who worked there to see if she could find it. Irene Kinsman made enquiries about my mother's manuscript and found it buried in the press's archives.

'This is quite good,' a staff member told my father. 'You should have it reevaluated.'

Dad sought out the professor who had supervised my mother's master's degree, which should, of course have been a PhD. Twenty years after the event, the professor looked embarrassed. 'I'm sorry,' he confessed. 'This was terrific and original work. I gave her low marks because of professional jealousy. And,' he added, 'because she was just a housewife.' A shocking admission. After that, the press could not refuse to publish my mother's thesis.[3] By the time that happened, she was unable to speak or walk or give any signs of recognition.

Such was life in the sexist fifties, sixties and seventies in Melbourne. I can only conclude that because of her thwarted ambition, Mum suffered from depression, and envy of women who achieved academic success. She lived a life of continual emotional and intellectual frustration. By the time she was in her fifties, the strain had elevated her blood pressure and, I think, contributed to her death.

Dad only gave up when he developed bowel cancer in late 1995. At eighty-two, when he learned he had the same cancer that had killed his father and his brother Bill in their sixties, Dad decided to have surgery, but no further treatment. I flew to Australia, and we four siblings all took on roles suited to our abilities. We arranged the sale of the house and packed it up, managed Dad's finances, and found a nursing home for our mother. Chris and his family took our father into their home and he died within five months of his diagnosis.

John Paterson was the last person to see my father conscious. It was typical of John that, despite his frenetic schedule, he found time to visit our dying father in the hospital, to talk about books with him, and to laugh with him. After that visit, he called me in Boston to tell me to 'get my skates on' and fly back to Melbourne. I boarded the next plane, but missed my father's death by an hour.

In February 2003, John Paterson died of a massive stroke. He was sixty years old. Just before his death, he was consulting for the Farmhand Foundation, a program aimed at assessing and preserving Australia's scarce water resources. My brother Chris served as master of ceremonies at John's funeral and my brother John as one of the pall-bearers. Mourners included ministers and past ministers of the Victorian government, past and present members of parliament, judges, and heads of government departments. Taking the podium, Chris said he was there only by the circumstance of family friendship. He said, 'John has been a star in the universe of every living Edquist from the cradle.'

A year and two weeks later, on 5 March 2004, Mark died. As with John, he was felled by a massive stroke. He was a few days shy of his sixtieth birthday. Mark and his wife

Chris lived in Canberra, close friends with John Edquist and his wife Deborah. My brother remembers Mark as an inveterate scientific experimenter, a questioner of authority, and someone who fashioned his house to be a model of sustainability. Just before midnight on 4 March, Chris Paterson called and asked my brother to meet her at the hospital emergency room where the ambulance had taken Mark after he collapsed. John sat with Chris throughout the night as doctors placed Mark on life support. John went home at 5 am. By late afternoon the next day, Mark had died. On getting the call, John rushed back to the hospital. He sat alone with his oldest friend for a few minutes, took his still hand, and said goodbye.

These two bright beacons of how to live a good life under difficult circumstances were gone. Their lesson remains.

* * *

Our mother died in March 1997, eleven months after our father. It took years for Alzheimer's to kill her, yet people did not forget the woman she had been. If she could have looked down at her funeral, she would have been surprised at how the church was packed. My Aunt Marjorie was there, the last of my mother's immediate family. She held my hand tightly as her son Peter Casey read the eulogy. Peter could not contain an edge in his voice when he told the story of my mother's—and his mother's—childhood.

During the eulogy we heard—for the first time—the full story. How one school vacation their little sister, Marjie, only in kindergarten, had been sent to stay with an aunt—and never came back. How, when their mother died, Ruth and her sister Nan had been made to stay home alone while the adults attended the funeral. How the sisters returned to school the next day, and no one, neither teachers nor students, mentioned the reason for their absence. How, after the funeral, their father had made a bonfire of everything their mother owned. Photographs, books, letters, and all her beautiful clothes. How their father then sold the house, moved into a boarding house, let their eight-year-old sister be adopted by one of their aunts, and sent the older girls to live with his relatives, who then rejected them.

The little sister, Marjorie, was more or less lost to her sisters. Her Aunt Jinny, who adopted her, had married a Catholic man, and Marjorie was schooled by nuns. This religious division in the family was as deep a social divide as could be imagined in the homogeneous society of their generation. The three sisters remained devoted, but my mother Ruth and her sister Nan had the deepest and most unbreakable bond.

As Joseph Campbell said (I paraphrase): 'When you get to be about sixty years old and you look back on your life, you see it had a kind of inevitability.'[4] I was much younger when I heard that, and I looked forward to the day when I would understand some of my actions. But Campbell meant, of course, that our behaviour is founded in the forces that shape our childhoods. I wonder now if all that happened between Ruth and Nan was inevitable. The whole thing: Nan saving her salary so Mum could go to university; Mum sending Nan's wartime letters to the press, thus jumpstarting her journalistic career; Nan leaving her husband Dick Nicholls, coming to live with us, and then moving less than a mile away. Perhaps it was all meant to be. Two sisters, abandoned after the death of a mother, the loss of a sister, and the apparent inability of their father to care for them, could never again be parted for long.

* * *

My godfather Mac's influence on my life has been stronger than he could have realised. I knew my mother had worshipped a man who spoke truth to power his whole life, even when it had adverse effects on his career. While she could never defy someone close to her, Mac's example helped her make her own small rebellions against conformity. She sent us to a progressive school, she ordered season tickets to the Musica Viva with her Czech friend, and she sometimes saved the housekeeping money to buy an abstract painting from an emerging artist. How brave she was to face the jeers. It is no coincidence that for my first house, with my first husband, in Lincoln, Massachusetts, I was drawn to the neighbourhood of Valley Pond, where, as in Eltham, a group of politically liberal professors and creatives had built houses on hilly farmland and, in carving out a swimming and boating pond in the valley, created a neighbourhood. Later, in California, John Spence and I married at our house next to a farm where gum trees grew and horses grazed on the hill we could view from our kitchen.

For years after leaving Australia, I yearned for the painting of cherry blossoms that hung in my parents' dining room. Painted by Peter Glass, who lived in the Eltham compound, it had been willed to me in memory of Mac and Katrine. It is the painting I loved as a tiny child when I first saw it at the Ball's house. Now it sits in pride of place in our house.

Before our parents died, they left no instructions about where they wanted to be buried.

'That's your problem,' Dad said, when asked at the end of his life. When I suggested to my brothers that we find a nice quiet cemetery for our father, with room for our mother, whom we knew would soon follow, they did not object. We found a public cemetery run by the town of Eltham. It is a serene, park-like place with a duck pond, just below the artists' compound, Montsalvat. A year after our mother's death, we four siblings gathered again at this peaceful resting place to lay the gravestone. After we spent time admiring the inscription John had placed on the headstone, we decided to go up the hill to the Ball's. Mac and Katrine, of course, were long gone, but we knew that Jenny and her husband Brian Ellis had taken over the old house.

We had difficulty finding the old road among the usual unsightly mix of fast-food outlets, billboards and housing developments now blighting the once semi-rural lower reaches of the town. But when we drove up hilly York Street to the adobe house, the sprawling plumbago over the gate was as blue as ever, seeming to tell us everything would be as we remembered it. We knocked on the door. A surprised Jenny invited us in to sit in comfortable chairs with a view of a cornfield. Except for their grey hair and lined faces, she and Brian appeared as they had years before.

'I feel they are safe now,' I told them. 'Mum and Dad are up here in Eltham with you.'

'How about I open a bottle?' said Brian.

It was only four o'clock. But it was time.

Chapter 41

The Industry of Women

After he retired, my father began work on his magnum opus on Australian industry. He typed it on a desk in our parents' old upstairs bedroom, now his study. I read parts of it when I visited, and I encouraged him to get it published. He did not, and I can only assume that he thought its criticism of the status quo—a status quo he had maintained actively throughout his life—would make the book unpublishable.

My father, like his father before him, was a company man. He had little patience for my contemporaries' career choices of law, journalism, politics or government work, describing them as 'paper-pushers'. How Australia should develop its resources became an obsession for him. Considering his wife and Kitty's continued regret at the loss of Colantet, the Lord family home, Dad wrote about Australia's first white settlers' misplaced priorities. My father recognised that small-farm agriculture was not going to make Australia the green and promised land. It was not fertile enough. So, as my grandfather gutted the earth for its minerals, my father replaced other minerals in an attempt to provide nutrients for soil in Australia's challenging agricultural conditions. Both thought they were doing the right thing for the development of the country. Phosphates and ammonias are now eschewed by organic gardeners, but dry lands like Australia would remain habitable by only a few hundred thousand people without their addition to agriculture.

Dad taught me to take pride in your work. He truly believed in his product. That the corporation could be a force for good was an article of faith for him. He could not understand the Australian labour force's attitude to work, which seemed to mean 'as little as possible'. He told us that if labour, through union action, forced management to its knees, then the company would fold and unemployment would ensue. My father's views today seem right wing and outdated, but they were of the times. The mismatch in goals between unions and the companies that employed them offended his sense of national purpose. He believed a homegrown industry creates national pride and makes a country less dependent on imports. In *A History of Australian Technology*, the manuscript he wrote after he retired, he told of his frustration.[1] Beyond the usual 'tyranny of distance', the Australian mindset prevented native ability from bringing actual products to market, he believed. The idea of respect was at the heart of my father's thesis: without actually being a republican, his writings imply that Australia would have done better to be independent from the British Commonwealth. He was a true nationalist, passionately loving his country and its lifestyle. I think he found it frustrating that his countrymen did not share his confidence.

With regard to the Australian home, he agreed with Robin Boyd, one of Australia's leading domestic architects in the fifties and sixties, that while the design of the single-family house with its three standard bedrooms, large windows and white walls was as avant-garde as anything of its type built overseas, its labour-saving appliances lagged far behind those in the United States.

Dad wrote: 'Australian industry's contribution to the working equipment of the home, such as it was—for cooling, cleaning, heating, refrigeration, ventilating, waste disposal, garden maintenance—was not impressive.' He was not the only one to notice this. Beverley Kingston wrote in *My Wife, My Daughter and Poor Mary Jane*: 'gas was available for industrial purposes and municipal lighting many years before it was adapted to lighten the burden of female domestic labour.'[2]

My father continued:

> the causes of this lacklustre performance of Australian industry are not to be found entirely in the boardrooms and factories, they are chiefly in the minds of the consumers themselves. It is through household appliances that the consumer interacts most directly with her country's manufacturing industry. This is where she has the greatest freedom of choice, whether to take the local product, or an import, or to do without like her grandmother. This is where she meets the results of her preferences and prejudices— for in the long run it is the consumer and nobody else who sets the standards of acceptance. And if these were low compared with American standards at similar income levels, as they were in Australia, it was because Australians didn't expect any better. Australians did not expect or demand to be well served by their manufacturing industry.

As my father perceived, the relationship between industry and the Australian home is complicated. It helps explain attitudes to women before the twenty-first century, is an indicator of who held the family purse, and it also reflects Australians' stoicism and 'make-do' adaptability. To paraphrase Dad's argument, British working people who poured into Australia in the second half of the nineteenth century and the first half of the twentieth wanted to throw off the shackles of the class system and the Industrial Revolution—the factory lifestyle infamous for dangerous, repetitive, mind-numbing work. The newcomers abandoned these restraints when they found plenty of fresh food and air and sunshine and generally full employment. Manufacturing held little appeal.

Second, they were not used to having at their disposal technologies that made everyday life easier. That unfamiliarity cut across class lines. The English gentry has always acted as if convenience was somehow too American and, therefore, decadent.

Thirdly, when ordinary Australians only a generation or so away from England's dreaded caste system achieved unaccustomed power in the new country, they acted like the upper classes in thinking housework should happen behind the scenes, performed by invisible beings. That attitude is not unique to Australia. As my late dear friend Susan Moller Okin wrote in her book, *Justice, Gender and the Family*, all societies have to deal with this problem.[3]

'We have,' she told me, 'inherited social systems in which all the power is held by people who do not do the hard, physical labour associated with living. The Greeks had slaves, and even today in most places the lawmakers have servants—though they might be given the more glamorous name of "staff". None of the influential ever had day-to-day charge of the children.'

No slaves existed in Australia at this time—or more accurately, Melbourne—and no servants, either. The situation was exacerbated, according to Dad's theory, because the ideal of egalitarianism, so central to the country's vision of itself, did not allow for a subservient underclass. It seemed a matter of pride to do it all yourself. Self-sufficiency was also a matter of cost. In egalitarian Australia, no one would work full time at a servant's wages. The 'cleaning lady' is a completely different matter. Mistress of her own schedule and able to dictate her rates, she was, and is, an independent businesswoman.

Drilling down to the particular, my father and his mother had never lived with any kind of convenience, except, in Dad's case, the car. As far as I know, Granny could not drive. Granny's childhood in her large Victorian home, which she and her sisters had to maintain after their father's death, and then her life in the outback in conditions so primitive they bordered on privation, and her sudden elevation to the peak of that society, where she did indeed have help, made her oblivious to the fact that our mother had grown up more comfortably. Mum's early childhood home in Malvern was more middle-class than Granny liked to think and, in Ruth Lord's home, where Mum spent her adolescence, there were always hands to help.

Perhaps she just wanted our mother to suffer as she had, to make plain to her that anyone who complained about a house with a wooden floor laid with carpets as opposed to tamped-down earth under a tent was too much a sissy to take seriously.

In his writing, my father tried to make a more general point, possibly to avert blame from his mother. The Australians were no longer British, he argued, and had different ideas about class; and they were not American either. The driver for home innovation—the much more severe North American climate—did not exist in Australian coastal cities. He'd be surprised at the appliance-heavy homes of his grandchildren.

It's interesting that Dad wrote his manuscript after he retired and, therefore, spent time in our old-fashioned house. In the prime of his life as the breadwinner, he seemed oblivious to what happened in his own home. At that time my mother literally ran through her days, cooking, shopping, scrubbing and washing. She was not alone. This was an age of big families. On our street, with its large, unrenovated, Edwardian houses, many mothers coped with five, six, seven or more children. The Billings family, husband and wife gynaecologists, lived at the top of our street, opposite the Genazzano Convent. They popularised the Billings method of rhythm birth control, the only method endorsed by the Pope. They had eleven children. This speaks to the efficacy of the rhythm method. Not that non-Catholic women had it much better. The contraceptive pill came to Australia in 1961—but only for married women—and abortion was illegal.

It's perhaps no surprise that a man named Barry Humphries became the most popular Australian comedian of the 1960s and 70s. His humour satirised the Australian housewife. Edna Everage, Humphries' most famous character—who metamorphosed into Dame Edna—revelled in a devotion to household appliances, which Humphries mocked. Audiences laughed uncomfortably as they recognised in themselves her middle-class aspirations. Humphries satirised the suburban malady of material consumption and competition. But he mocked only the distaff side and what he considered its pretension to power in the home. In our 'lucky country'[4] any attempt to lighten the housekeeping burden was seen as unnecessary, even something to be laughed at.

My father's strong personality and his extraordinary childhood made him blind to my mother's distress. I have to emphasise that he never consciously hurt her. He relied on her and loved her very much. She, on the other hand, was so clearly unhappy at 5 Grange Road that it coloured all our lives. She must have realised that, kind as he meant to be, her husband did his mother's bidding still, even as he prized self-sufficiency. He expected a level of physical work from his wife that he must have remembered from his early outback life rather than from his mother's later role as 'duchess' of Gwalia.

My father had grown up in an atmosphere of make-do and

material deprivation, without luxuries. He did not desire them, nor did he understand the desire for them in others. From his point of view, what women did at home was an honoured profession because of the hard work it entailed. That the world did not agree did not occur to him. There is a larger point here. The obliviousness to my mother's wants and needs that caused such distress in our household was and, in part, still is endemic to the culture. It derives from Australia's unique history. History creates myths, and Australian myths don't account for women. Among these myths, mateship, the platonic bond between males, endured well into the twentieth century. Mateship is formed around the campfire, on the diggings, in the trenches of warfare, at the pub, or in the union meetings. It excludes women.

I've dwelt on my three Irish great-great-grandmothers. They all arrived around 1850, drawn—or pushed—towards this far-away colony because it needed women. It needed women to provide for the needs of men. To the colonial masters, women were a commodity. While we know that my great-great-grandmothers—Ann, Jane and Margaret—and my great-grandmother, Eliza, all went with their men to the Victorian diggings, there is little mention of women's role in official mining histories.

The needs of women, for support when they reared children in primitive conditions, for spending money to buy a piece of lace at the shops, or for quiet time to read a book—these needs were dismissed as unimportant. Far more important in this masculine culture were battles for equality between bosses and workers, for the right to work fewer hours for more money so the men could go to the football, the races, or the pub.

Brought up at 5 Grange Road, where one just got on with it, it took me years to realise that lack of recognition of women's efforts at home undermined their self-esteem as well as limiting their career choices. This realisation, called the women's movement, could have been mine at its inception at the start of the 1970s. Women gathered together in 'consciousness-raising' groups. I was invited to join one. I refused, unwilling to rock the boat in my new marriage. I had learned my mother's lessons well.

I had a nagging sense that my Australian 'egalitarian' values were both supporting me and holding me back. As it turned out, my friends were in the same throes of self-doubt. When we needed help the most, with young children and unhelpful husbands, we still felt guilt at being the 'mistress' and hiring domestic help.

The dilemma I faced in the busy years of my late twenties and early thirties is still one of the central conundrums of our time. How can we live lives of productivity, bringing in enough income to support our families, without exploiting others or the environment—and at the same time give adequate emotional care to our children? This conflict between career and children has been at the centre of the muddled role-modelling I received from the two most important women in my life as a child—Mum and her sister Nan. Nan's dramatic insistence on the former at the expense of the latter when she put Kristy in foster care caused tremendous heartache.

Looking back, it seems the issue was more complicated than a simple lack of childcare for working mothers. The key to the situation from my mother's point of view was her relationship to power—my father's perceived power—versus women's right to a life outside the home. Perhaps even the right to love. Nan risked so much for love. In 1951, she could well have faced losing her daughter in a custody battle if she attempted to take the child out of the country, especially if she lived with another man while not yet divorced.

My mother's action in refusing Kristy signalled her

disapproval of Nan, still married to Dick Nicholls, going away to live in sin with another man. Mum believed in sacrifice and expected others to sacrifice themselves as she did. Mum's message to me was clear: self-fulfillment at the expense of one's children is tantamount to a crime. The other side of that coin, the exploitation of those whose saintly nature is taken for granted, she never openly expressed.

As an adult who has had her share of difficult child-rearing choices, I now wonder if Mum and Nan could not have arrived at a more creative solution when Nan faced the choice of whether to go to England or to stay with Kristy, instead of the stand-off which had such hard consequences for a little girl. Perhaps Nan could have used some of the money she spent on foster care to provide more help for Mum at home, a nanny perhaps—though at the time I had never heard of an Australian woman hiring one. A part-time housekeeper would have helped. But given Granny's scathing assessment of our mother's abilities, hiring a housekeeper at Nan's expense to help care for Kristy was something that, if it occurred to our mother, she would never suggest. She could never inject money into a sisterly relationship. And so, Kristy was sent away.

Losing our cousin / sister for those months, temporary as the situation may have been, was the most traumatic experience of my early childhood. But putting children in care was not, in fact, unusual. Cousins of the Wilkins family were sent to an orphanage on Sackville Street during the week while their single mother worked. I walked over to visit them sometimes and rage rose in me as I saw children punished for routine pranks in the playground. At the time I vowed to grow up to rescue children like this. As with many of my goals, I failed, but it did inform my adult career choices.

Today, childcare facilities are ubiquitous and maternity leave is sometimes company policy. But the burden on parents is tremendous. In Australia, as in Europe, paid maternity and paternity leave are taken for granted, as are subsidised crèches that allow working parents to leave preschool children safely while they work all day. Still, it's harder than it should be. There are never enough spaces in the crèches, waiting lists are long, and pay for carers is poor. Especially in the United States, where I live, the effort to raise children in a two-career family is intense, and the personal cost is not recognised in any practical, universal way. We must do better.

In theory, the multi-generational family in which I spent my childhood represents an ideal. A lost paradise, in which 'the village' raises the child. Lucky for those for whom it works. In reality, power relationships within a family still mean that one person can be exploited while others are fulfilled. My mother, the eldest child in her family, took on an eldest daughter's role in spades. That is, she took care of others while they got on with their lives. The freedom to have agency is related to a sense of entitlement deriving from an inner sense of self-worth. That, in turn, springs from experiencing a mother's unconditional love. And when a mother dies when a girl is on the cusp of adolescence, all the independence just waiting to unfold—the wings of a butterfly emerging from its chrysalis—is squashed, muffled and prevented. My mother, so warm and intelligent, so compassionate and unselfish, wanted to contribute to the world of scholarship, but she could not overcome her childhood, her marriage, or her time and her place.

I believe the choices set before me as a girl growing up in the 1950s and 60s can shine a light on the still-confused aspirations held out to girls today. Personally, I have little time for the prevailing narrative that girls should overthrow convention and become strong by being disobedient and disruptive. Happiness is also a worthwhile goal in life and, for me, the traditional female role of making sure others are happy has been deeply satisfying. Women have so far done most of the work in this regard. The seesaw tips dangerously at times with the well-documented double burden on mothers.

In the end, with Granny, my mother and her sister presenting, like a spinning top, alternate visions of my future, I chose both adventure and tradition. The little girl who desperately wanted a Betsy Wetsy 'sleepy-eyed' doll for her birthday, emulating an adored mother, eventually took the lessons of all three women to heart; moving across the world like her grandmother; trying, like her beloved aunt (but less successfully) to combine a writing career with a family; and, like her mother, choosing parenthood as a fundamental aspiration.

* * *

The issues of class, exploitation, gender roles and ambition are all exemplified in this story. And, that rock of quartz, with its hard-to-get-at ribbons of gold, symbolises, too, the ceaseless human quest for buried treasure. It seems that as long as there are markets to buy the minerals, ways will be found to get at the treasure locked up in the earth. With climate change upon us, is that disruption of earth's balance about to cause the end of human history? More likely, new ways of living will replace our own, just as our striving, materialistic society replaced one that had survived for eons.

Driving the vast distances of Western Australia, it seems as though this tremendous commercial effort to retrieve the treasures in the earth, the gold for our watches and rings, the titanium in our mobile phones, the uranium that can fuel an electricity supply, will become insignificant in the face of the timeless outback.

A hundred years is a tiny moment in Earth's history. The

town of Gwalia is already a ghost town. The distant townships, the romantic names, already forgotten except by those directly associated with them: Day Dawn, Marvel Loch, Big Bell, White Feather and Red Hill have returned to the red dust. Like the once-filled lakes, this ancient landscape will retain only a memento of our presence. But kangaroos still pause in their foraging to listen for danger, the ungainly emus run with their necks stretched out in front like commuters hurrying for the train, lizards lick the rocks lazily, and birds squabble as the sun goes down.

Fortunes gained, lives lost. Memories crumbled like biscuits. The Earth remains; our time on it but a shadow. This is the human story. It is my family's as well.

Acknowledgements

I am grateful to my brothers John and Christopher Edquist, whose memories corroborate my experience. I wish my late brother Andrew could have contributed his, but have enjoyed reminiscences by his wife Philippa. In addition, I have been fortunate to find letters and memoirs of my paternal grandmother, Eva Edquist; her daughter, my Aunt Mary; my mother, Ruth Edquist; and my great-aunt Kitty Rudd. My aunt, Nan Hutton, left no letters to me (at least none that I can find), but she did leave a public record of her thinking in her newspaper and magazine columns. I am grateful to her daughter, Barbara Hutton, who owns the copyright, for allowing me to extract passages from Nan's work. Most recently, Aunt Mary's daughter, my cousin Kate Marshall in Perth, sent a trove of letters saved by our grandmother from her sisters, her son John while serving in the RAAF, and friends and extended family. These provided great insight into Eva's life and character.

Shona Dewar, also a descendant of the Lord/Constables, progenitors of our Australian family, created the Lord Family archives and continues to find family references in contemporary newspapers, sourced through *Trove*. Without Shona's research, I never would have known that Ann Williams Lord remembered the Eureka Stockade rebellion at Ballarat, a seminal moment in Australia's colonial history.

I also thank another archivist cousin, Sophie Garrett, for her research into Colantet.

Research by Judith Constable on our mutual great-great-grandfather, Thomas Constable, is also included in this narrative.

My late husband John Spence supplied information on his father's role in some of the events mentioned in this book.

I thank my cousin Harriet Edquist for permission to quote her passage about our grandfather's prolific desert garden in her article 'The Abomination of Desolation Spoken of by the Prophet What's His Name', which appeared in *Australian Humanities Review*, 1 July 2005.

Thank you to distinguished historian Beverley Kingston for allowing me to quote from her book, *My Wife, My Mother and Poor Mary Ann*. Bev's encouragement meant a lot to this amateur historical sleuth. I also thank Janet McCalman for permission to quote from her book, *Journeyings*.

I am grateful to the Wilkins family and to Mary Paterson for allowing me to share their immigrant stories. And to Rebecca Driffield for her knowledge of the Preshil parents who were communists when I was at school there.

The writing of a book begins with an idea, a few scribbled passages, and a sprawling manuscript that needs to be pruned. I wrote this from the perspective of someone who has lived most of her adult life in the United States. I needed fact checking from my Melbourne friends as well as comments on how the story would be understood by my American community. Thank you to my beta readers, Gail Gaylard and Iola Mathews in Melbourne, Christine Phillips in Phoenix, and my brothers John and Chris. And my beloved husband John, my first reader and biggest supporter, whose passing has impressed upon me the importance of getting memories down on paper. First edits were done by Ann Videan. For the enormous developmental edit undertaken by Marylee

MacDonald I am forever indebted. And for fact checking, copyediting and proofreading, I thank Margaret Geddes in Melbourne. Julia Beaven at Wakefield Press has been enormously helpful in making the manuscript read smoothly and correcting my American-acquired spelling or grammar errors. Finally, I thank my literary agent John Timlin for his good humour and anecdotes, in addition to his efforts to provide insight into the Australian publishing world.

Notes

Chapter 3   A Suit of Pale Blue
1   Letter from Muriel Hobbs in wartime England to Eva Edquist in Melbourne, 14 November 1943. Collection of letters of Eva Edquist, curated by her granddaughter Kate Marshall.

Chapter 5   Phosphorus and Father Christmas
1   *Herald*, Melbourne, 29 June 1945, p. 3 'Explosion at Yarraville Was Accident'.

Chapter 6   A Bookie's Daughter
1   Ivan Ralph was the son of Cedric Ralph, an active member of the Communist Party of Australia. In *Memoirs*, Scribd, 1993, Ralph discusses his friendship with Alec Whitelaw, pp. 2, 82, his involvement with Preshil, pp. 147–167, becoming a communist, p. 162, and birth of his son Ivan, p. 233.

2   John Wren ran the lucrative Collingwood Tote, an illegal betting ring, from 1893 to 1906 from the back of a teashop on Johnston Street, Collingwood.

3   Our driver could have been Mary Wren, but more likely it was Angela Wren, my mother's exact contemporary, who, according to electoral rolls, was living at home at the time; https://en.wikipedia.org/wiki/Movement_Against_War_Fascism states that Mary Wren was a communist.

4   For an article on how Dights Falls, at the border of Collingwood and Kew, became a dividing social wall, see: https://www.theage.com.au/national/for-little-fish-swimming-upstream-is-a-lot-of-garbage-20040111-gdx3c2.html.

5   For more on industrial unrest in this period, see Douglas Jordan, *The Communist Party of Australia and the Trade Union Movement, 1945–60*, p. 29, PhD thesis, Victoria University School of Social Sciences and Psychology, Faculty of Arts, Education and Human Development, 2011; *The Party*, by Stuart McIntyre, Allen & Unwin, 2022.

Chapter 8   Lords and Ladies

1   Three sons of Sam and Ruth Lord enlisted in 1914. Members of the Light Horse had to provide four remounts at their own expense, so Kit's grey mare would have gone with her oldest brother, Arthur. None of the horses that went with the Light Horse came home. They were not permitted to return to Australia because of quarantine concerns. The Army proposed to leave the horses in Egypt, but the Light Horsemen shot their own horses rather than leave them, fearing they would be mistreated.

2   *Barefoot and Pregnant? Irish Famine Orphans in Australia*, by Trevor McClaughlin, p. 41, lists Ann Williams among the orphans on the Elgin. On her grave, this first name has been amended to the more ladylike 'Anne'. However, since I was told by my mother that I had been named for her paternal and maternal great-grandmothers, I use the version without the 'e' in this narrative.

3   Letter from Doris Draffen to Kit Rudd, 18 July 1954.

4   Selection and the Lords: Under the Land Act of 1862, amended 1865, selectors rented the land for up to seven years. Within the first two years, they had to improve it, and after three years, could buy it for £1 an acre, according to Edwin Carton Booth in *Another England: Life, Living, Homes and Homemakers in Victoria*, first published by Virtue and Co., 1869, p. 197; Geoffrey Blainey, in *The Tyranny of Distance*, Sun Books, 1966, p. 166, points out that settlers had to pay 'at least eighty times as much as USA farmers for new land and Australian farmland was probably less rather than more productive of a comfortable living'.

5   Nan Hutton, *Age*, 16 September 1961.

6   *Camperdown Chronicle*, 16 November 1908: 'In conjunction

with J.G. Johnstone and Co., we held a highly successful sale on account of Mr. S. Lord, on his farm at Colantet homestead, which property has been recently sold.'

7   Nan Hutton, *Age*, 19 May 1961.

Chapter 9   Shaped by Early Grief
1   All extracts in this section are from RME Tale: *Transcriptions from Family History Papers,* collected by Ruth Edquist (nee Charlholmes).

Chapter 11   Cherry Blossoms
1   W. Macmahon Ball: From my memories and from Alan Rix, ed. *Intermittent Diplomat: The Japan and Batavia Diaries of W. MacMahon Ball*, Melbourne University Press, 1888; Christine de Matos, 'Diplomacy Interrupted? Macmahon Ball, Evatt and Labor's Policies in Occupied Japan', *Australian Journal of Politics and History* 52, no. 2, 2006. For general information on Japan at the time of Occupation, Takemae Eiji, *The Allied Occupation of Japan,* The Continuing International Publishing Group, 2002; National Library of Australia summary of Mac Ball's life. https://nla.gov.au/nla.obj-327787426/findingaid.

2   Takemae Eiji, *The Allied Occupation of Japan*, pp. 101–103, 342–344, discusses Mac Ball's appointment in April 1946 as the British Commonwealth member on the Allied Council for Japan and his subsequent clash with General Douglas MacArthur. Mac Ball was perceived as too antagonistic to the aims of General MacArthur to be effective, and he was dismissed by Australia's Minister for External Affairs, Herbert Evatt, in August 1947. For more on this period, see Denis Warner, *Wake Me If There's Trouble*, Penguin Books Australia Ltd, 1995.

3   The Australian Impressionist Painters: https://en.wikipedia.org/wiki/HeidelbergSchool

Chapter 12   The Family Grows Sideways
1   General MacArthur directed the war in the Pacific from headquarters (GHo/SWPA) in Melbourne, then Brisbane, from 1942. It appears Nan worked here first in Melbourne before being transferred to the US Forces Headquarters in Brisbane.

Chapter 14   From Spinifex to Suburbia

1   The extract below, and all others in this section, are from R.C.
Edquist, *Career of VTE*, unpublished family papers.

*Bewick, Moreing & Co. was a London-based organization of
mining engineers, managers and entrepreneurs which dominated
the Australian mining world about the turn of the century. In its
day it influenced international relations and it must be credited
with a highly beneficial influence on Australian mining.*

2   Mary told me this rather self-deprecating story. Peter told it too,
many times. It was, he often said, a marriage of convenience,
but it turned out to be a remarkably happy one.

Chapter 16   Battle of Ideas

1   Peter Londey, in *Other People's Wars*, Allen & Unwin, 2004,
explains the conflicting political interest of Australia in
the battles for independence of the Dutch East Indies. The
Labor government believed that colonies should be given
independence, and, on the other hand, that their Dutch
wartime allies should not be thrown under the bus.

2   Sondra Silverman, 'Australian Political Strikes', *Labor History*,
no. 11, November 1996, pp. 28–29. Quoted in Jordan, *Conflict
in the Unions*: *The Communist Party of Australia, Politics and
the Trade Union Movement*, p. 15.

3   Peter Londey, in *Other People's Wars*, describes the four-man
Australian peacekeeper mission to Java sponsored by the
UN; John C.H. Spence, in *Spitfire Pilot Louis Spence: A Story
of Bravery, Leadership and Love*, Brolga Publishing Pty Ltd,
2021, p. 177, tells how at the conclusion of the United Nations
military mission to Java, Sukano, the first president of the
independent Indonesia, presented John's father, Lou Spence,
with a beautiful wooden carved head. It remains with the
family. Wing Commander Louis Spence was killed in action in
the Korean conflict.

4   The Australian War Memorial on the Malayan Emergency,
https://www.awm.gov.au/articles/atwar/malayan-emergency

5   W. Macmahon Ball, *Nationalism and Communism in East Asia*,
Melbourne University Press, 1952. The book is remarkably

prescient about the long-term prospects of communist rule in China, about the prospect of Korea being divided for a very long time, and about what was then called Indo-China's struggle to free itself from French control under the leadership of Ho Chi Minh. One can see how nothing in history should come as a complete surprise.

6   *I Stand by White Australia*, pamphlet, 24 October 1949, by Arthur Calwell, Minister for Immigration, in Museums Victoria Collection. The pamphlet publicly demonstrates Calwell's commitment to the White Australia policy, which called for deporting prohibited immigrants. The Museum's statement adds that the pamphlet 'is also significant for the way in which it demonstrates the public debates of 1948/49 over the forced deportation of non-British aliens from Australia'. https://collections.museumsvictoria.com.au/items/. On Calwell's views on the Japanese, see Takemae Eiji, *The Allied Occupation of Japan*, p. 135.

7   This was Elizabeth Kata, the best-selling author of *Be Ready with Bells and Drums*, a novel about an inter-racial relationship renamed *A Patch of Blue* when it became a movie. I had the privilege of spending a day with Elizabeth Kata when she visited her publisher Penguin Books (Australia) in 1966. I was working there at the time, and during the course of the day this amazing woman told me her story. As the war worsened, she was interned by the Japanese authorities in a small mountain village, cold and weakened by near starvation. Three weeks before an atomic bomb levelled Hiroshima, Elizabeth gave birth to her son. The baby struggled to survive and remained sickly. After the atom bombs finally forced the peace, Elizabeth's battle continued. She fought the Australian government for two years before she was allowed to return with her son. Once back in her homeland, she and her child faced hostility because of their association with the enemy. The baby's black hair and eyes aroused particular anger. Twenty years on, here she was, a public figure, a world-famous author. It was not just her fortitude and perseverance that impressed me. She told me, 'I don't believe in national or colour boundaries. I consider myself to be a citizen of the world.'

8 Phillip Deery, 'Scientific Freedom and Post-War Politics: Australia 1945–55', in *Historical Records of Australian Science*, B (1) 2000, pp. 1–18.

Chapter 17 Left and Right in Kew

1 John Perceval, painter, and Sunday and John Reed, art patrons, were among the most influential people in the development of art in twentieth century Australia. In a series of complicated, close, rivalrous relationships that are now the stuff of legend, John Perceval married Mary Boyd, members of whose large family were also iconic artists, and she later married Sidney Nolan, the most famous painter of them all. Nolan was previously married to Cynthia Reed, the estranged sister of John Reed and the mother of my dear friend, Jinx Nolan. My classmate, Sweeney Reed, was adopted by the Reeds. He was actually the son of Joy Hester and Albert Tucker, artists who also lived at the Reed's home, Heide, now a museum.

2 Peter's 1975 book, *Animal Liberation*, launched him onto the world stage of philosophical debate about the rights of non-human species. He popularised the term, 'speciesism'.

3 Sylvia Martin, 'The Lost Portrait', *Inside Story*, 23 April 2018. https://insidestory.org.au/the-lost-portrait/ The Kew Branch of the CPA 'determined which doctor you consulted, which lawyer you went to, which trade union you joined, even in some cases which business you dealt with'. Email from Penelope Ralph Pollitt to Sylvia Martin.

4 Cedric Ralph, *Memoirs*, p. 257. In another of those amazing coincidences I discovered in writing this book, the person who cut Cedric Ralph in the street was Ron Haig-Muir, husband of my mother's first cousin, Kathleen Lord. They lived around the corner from us, and not far from the Ralphs. In his memoir Ralph reported the incident as an example of his social difficulties once he became active as a communist, yet the fact that he persuaded Ron Haig-Muir to end hostilities with a drink in the pub suggests that Cedric Ralph had considerable charm.

5 'Attempted exclusion of Egon Kisch from Australia'. Wikipedia says that Kisch jumped from the boat at Station Pier. Our

mother said she was at the demonstration on Princes Pier, which adjoins Station Pier.

6   A.W. Martin, *Robert Menzies, A Life, Volume 2, 1944–1978*, Melbourne University Press, 1999, p. 144; David Horner, *The Spy Catchers: The Official History of ASIO, 1949–1963, Vol. 1*, Allen & Unwin, 2014, kindle edition, loc.2979.

7   Martin, *Robert Menzies*, p. 154; Cameron Forbes, *The Korean War: Australia in the Giants' Playground*, p. 113; John C.H. Spence, *Spitfire Pilot Louis Spence*, pp. 185–204.

8   Martin, Robert Menzies, p. 169.

9   'Red Act Moves Start in Court', *Argus*, 21 October 1950; Cedric Ralph, *Memoirs*: 'After the Party was made illegal, the Party issued proceedings in the High Court to challenge the validity of the legislation', p. 288.

10   'From the Archives, 1950: Police raid Communist offices across Australia', staff writers, *Sydney Morning Herald*, 21 October 2019, republishing, 'Raids on Red Offices', first published in *Age*, 24 October 1950. https://www.smh.com.au/national/from-the-archives-1950-police-raid-communist-offices-across-australia-20191021-p532r5.html ; Cedric Ralph, *Memoirs:* ASIO trails communists, p. 261, and his phone tapped, p. 263.

11   Obituary of Cedric Ralph: https://www.search.org.au/cedric_ralph; *Communism in Australia: A Resource Bibliography*, compiled by Beverly Symons, with Andrew Wells and Stuart Macintyre; *The Party*, by Stuart Macintyre.

12   The Communist Dissolution referendum, 22 September 1951: Reason in Revolt-Source Documents of Australian Radicalism: 1951 Referendum (Communist Party Dissolution) 22 September 1951. http://www.reasoninrevolt.net.au/biogs/E000351b.htm

13   Gerard Henderson, *Santamaria: A Most Unusual Man*, Miegunyah Press, Melbourne, 2015, p. 294.

14   Mary Elizabeth Calwell, 'How We Survived the Movement', *What Did You Do in the Cold War, Daddy? Personal Stories from a Troubled Time*, New South Publishing, 2014, pp. 202–223.

15   Mark Aarons, with John Grenville, *The Show: Another Side of Santamaria's Movement*, Scribe Publications, 2017, p. 24.

16   John McLaren, in *Writing in Hope and Fear*, University of Cambridge Press, 1996, p. 82; David McKnight, *Broadcasting and the enemy within: ASIO's political surveillance of the ABC*, online article, 19 July 2006, https://www.davidmcknight.com.au/archives/2006/07/broadcasting-and-enemy-within-asios-political-surveillance-abc/

Chapter 18   Gaslighting

1   Beverley Kingston, *My Wife, My Mother and Poor Mary Ann*, Thomas Nelson, Melbourne, 1975, p. 15.

2   Glenn Stevens, *Inflation and Disinflation in Australia, 1950–91*, Conference 1992, Reserve Bank of Australia Publications, https://www.rba.gov.au/publications/confs/1992/stevens.html/

Chapter 19   Our Cousin, Our Sister

1   A divorce was hard to obtain in Victoria in 1951: http://www5.austlii.edu.au/au/journals/ANZLawHisteJl/2006/7.pdf/

Chapter 20   Running Through Her Days

1   Andrew Leigh, *Battlers & Billionaires: The Story of Inequality in Australia*, Black Inc. Books, 2013, p. 226.

2   Kingston, *My Wife, My Daughter and Poor Mary Ann*, p. 15.

3   ibid.; Simon Leo Brown and Matthew Crawford, 'Your grandmother did more housework in a week than you do in a month', ABC Radio National, *Life Matters*, 28 May 2018. On the reality television show, *Back in Time for Dinner*, 'The show's researchers found a 1953 *Australian Women's Weekly* article calculating one typical housewife, Mrs R. Partridge of Pymble, NSW, did 77.5 hours of housework per week'. https://www.abc.net.au/news/2018-05-29/your-grandma-did-more-housework-in-a-week-than-you-do-in-a-month/9806790/

Chapter 21   On Passchendaele Street

1   For a description of the environs of Port Phillip Bay over eons, before the arrival of Europeans, see the study by Dr Shaun Canning and Dr Francis Thiele,

February 2010, https://www.achm.com.au/assets/files/
Indigenous_Cultural_Heritage_and_History_within_the_VEAC_
Melbourne_Metropolitan_Investigation_Area.pdf

2   Damien Murphy, 'Death and despair at the Battle of
      Passchendaele', *Sydney Morning Herald*, 13 October 2017,
      https://www.smh.com.au/national/mud-death-and-despair-at-
      the-battle-of-passchendaele-20171013-gz08hj.html/

Chapter 22   The Stony Rises

1   Letter from Doris Draffen to Kit Rudd, 18 July 1954, in 'Doris
      Draffen's Narrative', *Transcriptions from Family History Papers*,
      collected by Ruth Edquist.

2   Catherine Lord Rudd (Kitty), *Little Girl Grown Old*,
      unpublished memoir.

3   *History of Pomborneit*, Victorian Education Department,
      Jubilee school histories, 1922, Australian Manuscripts
      Collection, State Library of Victoria, accession no. M 3739.

4   'In the 1860s the rabbit infestation of the Stony Rises caused
      the Manifolds to dispose of the north-east portion of their
      Purrumbete property, in the Pomborneit area. Selectors, such
      as the Boyds, Hallyburtons, Lords, Harrisons and McGarvies,
      moved in during 1865 as a result of the sale of this Manifold
      land', *Corangamite Heritage Study* (www.corangamite.vic.
      gov.au) pp. 218, 231–233; The Lords had selected land at
      Pomborneit when the rabbit pest was already underway. But it
      had not yet caused widespread devastation, as Kitty's memories
      show; the historical record reveals that the Manifolds, who sold
      land to the Lords, addressed it. 'I know the rabbits were a real
      problem, as some Manifold documents in the collections of this
      archive include an agreement about building stone rabbit proof
      walls and also digging out rabbit warrens on their properties
      (item 1964.0002.00118)', email, 1 March 2023, from Sophie
      Lord Garrett discussing *The Coorangamite Heritage Study*.

5   Arthur and Frank Lord enlisted as privates in 1914 and rose
      through the ranks to become captains. Arthur won the Military
      Cross, and Frank both the Military Cross and the Military
      Medal, an unusual achievement. In 1958 Arthur Lord collapsed

and died when 'a piece of shrapnel lodged in his body for some forty years, had come loose and blocked a blood vessel', Shona Dewar, *Lord-Constable Family Record Collection*, p. 158.

6 The *Victorian Electoral Act* of 1856 introduced the secret ballot to the world, and required that election officials print the ballots and provide a booth that could be entered by only one person at a time. Ann and Sam Lord were in Ballarat at the time of the Eureka rebellion, which 'she remembered distinctly', according to her obituary in the *Camperdown Chronicle*, 23 November 1918, p. 2.

7 Margaret Kiddle, *Men of Yesterday: A Social History of the Western District of Victoria, 1830–1890*, Melbourne University Press, 1961, pp. 152–153.

8 Registry of Births, Marriages and Deaths, Victoria, death certificate of Thomas Constable, 2 March 1911.

9 Valda Strauss, 'Irish Famine Orphans in Australia', *The Mallow Field Club Journal*, Vol. 11, 1993; https://isaanz.org/wp-content/uploads/2023/04/Famine-Orphans-2020.pdf

Chapter 23   Hardship, Best Forgotten

1 Margaret Connor Crow as a voluntary immigrant; she signed her marriage certificate. Deborah Oxley. *Convict Maids: The Forced Migration of Women to Australia*, Cambridge University Press, 1996, p. 266, states that only 41.7% of Irish free immigrant women could both read and write. Oxley contrasts a comparable literacy rate of 10.3% for convict women, and 21.2% for Irish working women as a whole, remarking that the emigrants, therefore, constituted a brain drain for Ireland.

2 Letter to the editor of the *Bendigo Advertiser* by Thomas Dungey, 6 April 1906. Reported in 'The Centenary of Bendigo', article in *Bendigo Advertiser*, January 1951, p. 7, https://trove.nla.gov.au/newspaper/article/89565378

3 George MacKay, *History of Bendigo*, Melbourne, Ferguson & Mitchell, 1891.

4 Dayne Maxewelle, *Inglewood in the Fifties and Sixties*, a series of articles, editors' notes and readers' letters, which appeared

in the pages of the *Inglewood Advertiser* from September 1906–
August 1907, researched on microfilm by Kevin J. Poysner,
Inglewood & District Historical Society Inc., 2000, p. 50.

5   *History of Immigration from Sweden*, Museum Victoria,
Immigration Museum, Royal Exhibition Building, Melbourne;
E.O. Koivukangas, *Scandinavian Immigration and Settlement in
Australia Before World War II*, PhD thesis, Australian National
University 1972.

Chapter 24   Up Above Comes Down Under

1   Sara Wills, 'Entry-Migrant Hostels', *The Encyclopedia of
Melbourne online*, School of Historical & Philosophical Studies,
University of Melbourne, July 2008.

2   'It would be an act of the grossest public indecency to permit
a Japanese . . . to pollute Australian shores.' Takemae Eiji, *The
Allied Occupation of Japan*, p. 135, quoting Peter Bates, *Japan
and the British Commonwealth Occupation Force, 1946–52*,
Brassey's (UK), 1993, pp. 134–135.

3   'Japan and Australia have enjoyed full diplomatic relations
since 1941 . . . although relations were severed after less than
a year owing to the outbreak of the Pacific War in December
1941. Relations were restored in 1952 and have continued since
then.' https://en.wikipedia.org/wiki/List_of_ambassadors_of_
Japan_to_Australia/

4   David Tokimasa Obituary in the *Honolulu Advertiser*, 29
September 1968. https://www.newspapers.com/clip/38422250/
david-h-tokimasahonolulu-advertiser/

5   Speech by Paul Morawetz on the difficulties facing Jewish
immigrants to Australia after the war, given at the Brian
Fitzpatrick Testimonial Dinner at Melbourne University on 19
June 1964, Gloria Frydman, *What A Life, A Biography of Paul
Morawetz*, Wakefield Press, 1995, p. 73.

6   For ASIO's politicisation during the Cold War, see Justin T.
McPhee, *Spinning the Secrets of State: The History and Politics
of Intelligence in Australia*, PhD thesis, RMIT, 2015. http://
researchbank.rmit.edu.au/view/rmit:161477

7 John Nicholson, *The Long Road Home: The Life and Times of Grisha Sklovsky*, Australian Scholarly Publishing, 2009, p. 135.

Chapter 26   Science at the Dinner Table

1 'Prime Minister Robert Menzies, obsessed with the Cold War in 1952 and an Anglophile, apparently gave permission to the British to conduct these tests in the utmost secrecy', Martin, *Robert Menzies*, Vol. 2, p. 168.

2 Fallout from the bomb at Monte Bello drifted over areas where he spent part of his childhood.' *Report of the Royal Commission into British Nuclear Tests in Australia*, Vol. 1, 5.4.1., Australian Government Publishing Service, 1985.

3 ibid.

4 The Mary Kathleen uranium mine: https://en.wikipedia.org/wiki/Mary_Kathleen,_Queensland

5 Compulsory X-ray screening in Victoria was introduced in 1963 and continued until 1974, *55th Report of the Victorian Commission of Public Health*, 30 June, www.parliament.gov www.parliament.gov.au

6 Albright & Wilson. http://www.chemlink.com.au/albright.htm/

7 Richard Edquist, *'Australia: A Singular Society'*, unpublished manuscript, 1987, p. 47.

8 ibid., p. 28.

Chapter 27   Food of the Past, Food of the Future

1 Harriet Edquist, 'The abomination of desolation spoken of by the prophet what's-his-name', *Australian Humanities Review*, 1 July 2005.

Chapter 28   A Rightward Turn

1 During the 1956 Melbourne Olympic Games, ASIO, fearing the Petrovs would be kidnapped by Soviet agents, spirited them up to Surfers Paradise, Queensland, to stay with ASIO operatives Dudley and Joan Doherty. According to the Doherty's daughter Sue-Ellen, as interviewed by journalist Sandra Hogan, Joan Doherty and Evdokia Petrov struck up a close friendship.

Sandra Hogan, *With My Little Eye*: *The Incredible True Story of Spies in the Suburbs*, Allen & Unwin, 2021.

2   For research on creeping federal control of services: Alan Fenna, 'The Centralization of Australian Federalism 1901–2010: Measurement and Interpretation', *Publius: The Journal of Federalism*, Vol. 49, Issue 1, Winter 2019, 30–56, https://doi.org/10.1093/publius/pjy042. 27 November 2018

3   Lesley Greene's three children were Margaret, Anne and Paul. Her second daughter, Anne (married name Biezanik), became a doctor, and had eight children. A convert to Roman Catholicism, she caused a stir in May 1964 by publicly challenging the Archbishop of Westminster to refuse her Communion because she ran the first Catholic birth control clinic in England. She published a book on the matter in November 1964, asserting that the contraceptive pill is God's will, 'a reprieve for the daughters of Eve won for them by Mary'. According to Mary Wreford, 'Aunt Hilda was shocked by this'. *Recollections of My Mother* by Mary Litchfield Wreford (nee Edquist), November 1992, unpublished family papers. For more on this story, see 'The writings of querulous women: contraception, conscience and clerical authority in 1960s Britain' by Alana Harris, published online by Cambridge University Press, 11 September 2015, DOI: https://doi.org/10.1017/bch.2015.20

4   Letter, 28 December 1956, from Margaret Greene to 'D. Edquist'.

5   The Victorian League of Rights was founded in 1960, and still exists to promote far right policies. It is against government intervention in private and business life. Its founder, Eric Butler, was proud of his anti-Semitism and referred to the 'alleged Holocaust' and 'The Holocaust Hoax'. The League also was against non-British immigration to Australia in general, believing that the monarchy and the British heritage are essential parts of Australian identity.

6   The League of Empire Loyalists was an organisation founded in 1954 to promote such ideas as banning non-white immigration to Britain. Many, though not all, of the

group were openly anti-Semitic, and when the leader, A.K. Chesterton, refused to ban Jews from membership, others left the organisation to form even more right-wing groups, later becoming the National Front. Thus weakened, the League of Empire Loyalists dwindled to a membership of only 300 by 1961.

7   Ben Greene, 1901–1978, was a Quaker and Aunt Mary surmised that this background led him to a belief in pacifism. He ran unsuccessfully for political office with the Labour Party, but as the 1930s progressed, and he became convinced that appeasement would save rather than cost lives, he became increasingly associated with members of the British Union of Fascists, then helped found the ultra-right British People's Party. He was arrested in May 1942 and interned along with other Nazi-sympathisers. After the war he remained involved with far-right causes. https://en.wikipedia.org/wiki/Ben_Greene

8   Letter to Mrs E.L. Edquist from Mary Wreford from Cranbrooke Hotel, Johannesburg, South Africa, 7 April 1961.

Chapter 29   Private School, Public Transportation

1   Janet McCalman, *Journeyings*, Melbourne University Press, 1993, p. 136. For more on Melbourne's unusually strong social divisions marked by schooling see Graeme Davison's Class–Entry in *The Encylopedia of Melbourne online*, eMelbourne.net.au, School of Historical & Philosophical Studies, University of Melbourne.

2   'Victorians were ambivalent toward education and the cultivating of too many who would rise above the ruck', Geoffrey Blainey, *A History of Victoria*, Cambridge University Press, 2006, p. 57.

3   In the past ten years funding for non-government schools increased at twice the rate for government schools. https://www.theguardian.com/australia-news/2021/feb/02/australian-government-funding-for-private-schools-still-growing-faster-than-for-public/

For a view on funding for non-government schools from the Catholic side, see https://australiancatholichistoricalsociety.com.au/history-resources/australian-catholic-education/

Chapter 31   Cultsha

1   The French explorer Nicolas Baudin and the English surveyor
    Matthew Flinders met by chance while exploring the waters off
    what is now called South Australia. Their meeting place on 8
    April 1802 is now memorialised by the name Encounter Bay.
    Napoleon had sent Baudin to explore 'New Holland' and by
    the time the two navigators met France and England were at
    war. However, the meeting of the ships was peaceful. Baudin
    discovered Kangaroo Island https://www.en.wikipedia.org/wiki/
    Baudin_expedition_to_Australia./ The brothers of my paternal
    great-grandmother, Eliza Turner Edquist, were among the first
    white settlers of Kangaroo Island in 1882.

2   'Sidney Nolan's paintings of Ned Kelly transcend his outlaw
    status to make him a symbol of a romantic and rebellious
    aspect of Australian identity', in 'Bushrangers: Ned Kelly and
    Australian Identity' by Bruce Tranter and Jed Donoghue,
    Journal of Sociology, Vol. 44, issue 4 https://doi.org/10.1177/144
    0783308097127https://doi.org/10.1177/1440783308097127

3   Rock paintings in the Kimberley region of Western Australia.
    https://www.bradshawfoundation.com/australia/gallery/index.php

4   Geoffrey Hutton, *It Won't Last a Week: The First Twenty Years of
    the Melbourne Theatre Company*, Macmillan, 1975.

5   While contemporary Australian novels tend to be set in the
    cities and suburbs (though an increasing number speak to the
    Indigenous experience), most of the books of my childhood
    idealised the 'Aussie battler', i.e. a working-class person,
    often in the bush, struggling against relentless nature and an
    unsympathetic political system. Most of the protagonists were
    male. Ruth Park's *The Harp in the South* trilogy, published in
    1948, has since become a classic. For a dated but interesting
    analysis of class and culture in literature, see T. Inglis Moore,
    Social Patterns in Australian Literature. Angus & Robertson,
    1971, reissued by the University of California Press, September,
    2020. For an account of the political aspect of mid-century
    literature and journalism in Australia, see John McLaren,
    Writing in Hope and Fear, Cambridge University Press, 1996.

6 Censorship and the release of *Lady Chatterley's Lover*. From memory—I was working at Penguin at the time—and confirmed by Craig Munro and Robyn Sheahan-Bright, editors, in *Paper Empires: A History of the Book in Australia*, 1946–2005, University of Queensland Press, 2006, p. 212, and by Geoffrey Dutton in *A Rare Bird*: *Penguin Books in Australia, 1946–96*, Penguin Books Australia Ltd, 1996, pp.73–74.

Chapter 33   The Corporate Wife

1 *Life on the Leases—The Woman's View*, an anecdotal 1985 calendar produced by the Perth Branch of the Women's Auxiliary of the Australasian Institute of Mining and Metallurgy.

Chapter 34   The Companionate Wife

1 'A Ring Will Be More Than a Gift', 'Nan Hutton on Thursdays', *Age*, 11 May 1973.

2 'Housewife is not an apt description', *Woman's Day*, 12 December 1955, cited by John Murphy in *Imagining the Fifties*, UNSW Press, 2000, pp.44, 227.

3 'Six to one against', ibid., p. 48.

4 *Argus*, 9 March 1945, (Trove). 'Mr Hutton, whose work in the SW Pacific and European war zones has been of a uniformly high standard, is among the outstanding Empire war correspondents.' These articles appear to have aroused the ire of the FBI, and he was subsequently denied a visa to enter the United States. http://adb.anu.edu/biography/hutton-geoffrey-william-geoff-12677/text22849/

5 Nan Nicholls, 'Inexpensive Luxury for Housewives', *Argus*, 1 August 1950. www.trove.nla.gov.au.

6 'Sydney market prices show some declines but within an underlying upward trend. Conversely, the credit squeeze appeared to be a trigger for the Melbourne market prices to flatten out before picking up strongly in the late 1960s', Nigel Stapledon, 'A History of Housing Prices in Australia 1880–2010', University of New South Wales Australian School of Business, School of Economics Discussion Paper: 2010/18, http://research.economics.unsw.edu.au/RePEc/papers/2010-18.pdf

Chapter 36   A Journey Back in Time

1   *Memories of Her Life* by E.L. Edquist, unpublished family papers. This extract is one of many from these *Memories* included in this narrative.

2   'The Journal of the Reno Cyanide Co., 1 December 1902, refers to a Deed of Partnership of 8 November 1902, the capital of the company being £150, subscribed by the partners Victor T. Edquist (£50) and Jessie Davies (£100). In December 1903, the Reno Cyanide Co. paid Howells Con. G.M. Ltd. £700 for the Prince of Wales Mine, where Will and Victor had been employed. They bought it for the residues, the mine being closed down', in R.C. Edquist, *Career of Victor Thomas Edquist*, unpublished family papers, 1987.

3   'I believe this refers to the treatment of concentrates at Red Hill Gold Mine. A paper by VTE describing the successful treatment process was published in the Chamber of Mines *Monthly Journal*, 30 September 1908', in R.C. Edquist, *Career of Victor Thomas Edquist*, unpublished family papers, 1987.

4   Today the Kambalda nickel mine is owned by BHP Billiton, the world's largest mining company, https://en.wikipedia.org/wiki/Kambalda_Nickel_Operations

5   Heydon, P.R., *Gold on the Murchison*, Carlisle, WA, Hesperian Press, 1986.

6   J.M. Hooper, *Youanmi: The Discovery of Murchison Gold*, Carlisle, WA, Hesperian Press, 1986, p. 85.

7   The Edquist process. The carbon in pulp method is one means of extracting gold. It, too, relies on charcoal, https://en.wikipedia.org/wiki/Carbon_in_pulp/

Chapter 37   Ruination

1   *Looking Back: Gwalia-Leonora, W.A., 1895–1963*, by C.W.F. Turnbull, Leonora Gwalia Historical Museum, 4th edition, 2006.

2   ibid., 26 April 1927, P.102; Janet McCalman, Len Smith,'Family and country: accounting for fractured connections under colonisation in Victoria, Australia', *J Pop Research (2016)*

33:51-65 DOI 10. 1007/s12546-9160-5, published online 9
March 2016, Springer Science+Business Media Dordrecht
2016.

3   Billy Griffiths, *Deep Time Dreaming*, Black Inc, an imprint of
Schwartz Books, 2018, p. 177.

4   Patrick Bertola, 'Undesirable Persons: Race and West
Australian Mining Legislation', in *Gold, Forgotten Histories and
Lost Objects of Australia*, Iain McCalman, Alexander Cook and
Andrew Reeves eds., p. 124.

5   https://www.ancient-origins.net/
ancient-places-australia-oceania/wilgie-mia-ancient-mine-
where-ochre-runs-red-kangaroo-blood-001425/

6   Elfie Shiosaki, Centre for Human Rights, Curtin University,
"They were afraid to speak": *Testimonies of Aboriginal women
at the 1934 Moseley Royal Commission*, Coolabah, No. 24
& 25, 2018, ISSN 1988-5946, Observatori: Centre d'Estudis
Australians i Transnacionals / Observatory: Australian and
Transnational Studies Centre, Universitat de Barcelona, 2018.

Chapter 38   A Daughter of the Empire

1   Edquist, E.L., 'Memories of her life', unpublished. Of all the
collected writings of the family, many of which I had not read
until I started this memoir, I found Granny's the most lively
and empathic. Her description on her bookish father's struggles
to educate himself, his terror at a job interview, his bravery in
crossing the world to sell cookies in South America, all made
me immediately fond of William Litchfield, this never-known
great-grandfather. How I would have liked to have met him!

2   Hilda Frances Litchfield joined the Anglican Order of St John
the Baptist at the age of forty.

3   Eva Litchfield's sisters: *Recollections of my Mother*, by Mary
Litchfield Wreford, nee Edquist, November 1992, unpublished
family papers. A delightful anecdote from these recollections
shows how Eva's sense of adventure contrasted with her sisters'
more apprehensive natures. Mary took a trip with her mother to
England to see the sisters in 1930. 'Mother, Aunt Margaret, her
friend Elsie Kean and I had a week in Paris that summer. Mother

seized the opportunity to fly and she and I flew from Croydon to Le Bourget. Margaret and Elsie went by train and ferry.'

Chapter 39   The White House in the Wild West

1   Herbert Hoover, *The Memoirs of Herbert Hoover, Years of Adventure 1874–1920*, New York, MacMillan, 1951, p. 30.

2   ibid., pp. 32–33.

3   Richard Hartley, 'Bewick Moreing in Western Australian Gold Mining 1897–1904: Management Policies & Goldfields Responses', *Labour History*, no. 65 (1993), pp. 1–18, https://doi.org/10.2307/27509195

4   Decline in gold production beginning in 1908, https://www.dmp.wa.gov.au/Documents/About-Us-Careers/AnnualReport_1908.pdf

5   Lenore Layman and Criena Fitzgerald, eds., *110° in the Waterbag*, Western Australian Museum, 2012, pp. 140–142.

Chapter 40   Four O'Clock

1   For more on our mother's work, see 'Marks and Meanings: Revealing the Hand of the Collector and "the Moment of Making" in two 18th-Century Print Albums', by Louise Voll Box, in *Journal of Eighteenth Century Art and Culture*, Issue 6, Fall 2018.

2   On Bill Rudd's wartime injuries from Gallipoli: https://www.abc.net.au/news/2015-04-24/gallipoli-2015-bone-in-box/6406804?nw=0&r=HtmlFragment

3   Ruth Margaret Edquist, 'The Sadeler Catalogue', https://books.google.com/books/about/Sadeler_Catalogue.html?id=mhtLywAACAAJ

4   Joseph Campbell, https://www.britannica.com/biography/Joseph-Campbell-American-author/

Chapter 41   The Industry of Women

1   R.C. Edquist, *History of Australian Technology*, unpublished manuscript, family papers, 1988.

2   Kingston, *My Wife, My Daughter and Poor Mary Ann*, p. 41.

3 Susan Moller Okin, *Justice, Gender and the Family*, Basic Books, 1989. Susan and I lived in the same suburb of Lincoln, Massachusetts, and as fellow Antipodeans, bonded when our children were small. Her feminism was always polite, but always challenged the status quo. She was gracious, charming, brilliant, and determined. Susan was said to have 'invented the study of feminist political theory', arguing in her book *Women in Western Political Thought*, Princeton University Press, 1979, that gender issues need to be brought to the forefront of political philosophy. Her 1989 book, *Justice, Gender and the Family*, maintained that political theories of justice, including equality and individual rights, must also apply to family systems.

4 *The Lucky Country* is the title of a satirical, best-selling book on Australian culture, first published in 1964. Australians immediately started to use the ironic title as a descriptor of their country in a positive rather than a negative sense. Donald Horne, *The Lucky Country: Australia in the Sixties*, 6th edition, Penguin Modern Classics.

Bibliography

This is a family story, but like all stories, is set in a particular place and time. Casting a wider net beyond our home to the city and country we lived in to understand the social and political environment of the period, I found inspiration from the books listed below.

Books and articles about Victoria, and Australia in general, and family references

Aarons, Mark, with John Grenville, *The Show: Another Side of Santamaria's Movement*, Scribe Publications, 2017

Ball, W. Macmahon, *Nationalism and Communism in East Asia*, Melbourne University Press, 1952

Bendigo's Centenary 1851–1951. Special Centenary Edition of *Bendigo Advertiser*

Blainey, Geoffrey, *A History of Victoria*, Cambridge University Press, 2006

Blainey, Geoffrey, *The Tyranny of Distance*, Sun Books, 1966

Black, Sarah Jane Shepherd, *Tried and Tested: Community Cookbooks in Australia, 1890–1980*, PhD thesis, School of History and Politics, University of Adelaide, 2011 https://digital.library.adelaide.edu.au/dspace/bitstream/2440/649791/8/whole.pdf

Booth, Edwin Carton, *Another England: Life, Living, Homes and*

Homemakers in Victoria, first published by Virtue and Co., 1869, BiblioLife, LLC

Box, Louise Voll, 'Marks and Meanings: Revealing the Hand of the Collector and "the Moment of Making" in two 18th-Century Print Albums', in *Journal of Eighteenth Century Art and Culture*, Issue 6, Fall 2018

Brennan, Niall, *Dr. Mannix*, Rigby Limited, 1964

Brennan, Niall, *John Wren, Gambler*, Hill of Content Publishing Co. Inc., 1971

Brett, Judith, *Robert Menzies' Forgotten People*, Melbourne University Press, 1992, 2007

Calwell, Arthur, Minister for Immigration, 'I Stand by White Australia', pamphlet, 24 October 1949, Museums Victoria Collection

Canning, Shaun, and Francis Thiele, 'Indigenous Cultural Heritage and History within the Metropolitan Melbourne Investigation Area: A Report to the Victorian Environmental Assessment Council, February 2010', https://www.achm.com.au/assets/files/Indigenous_Cultural_Heritage_and_History_within_the_VEAC_Melbourne_Metropolitan_Investigation_Area.pdf

Clarke, Keith M., *Convicts of the Port Phillip District*, CPN Publications, 1999

Clift, Charmian, *Sneaky Little Revolutions: Selected Essays of Charmian Clift*, Nadia Wheatley, ed., New South, 2022

Collingham, Lizzie, *The Taste of Empire: How Britain's Quest for Food Shaped the Modern World*, Kindle edition, 2017

Courthoys, Ann, and Joy Damousi, eds, *What Did You Do in the Cold War, Daddy? Personal Stories from a Troubled Time*, New South Publishing, 2014

Crotty, Martin, and David Andrew Roberts, eds, *Turning Points in Australian History*, University of New South Wales Press, 2009

Davison, Graeme, 'Class – Entry', *The Encylopedia of Melbourne online*, eMelbourne.net.au, School of Historical & Philosophical Studies, University of Melbourne

Day, David, *Chifley*, Harper Collins Publishers, 2001

Deery, Phillip, 'Scientific Freedom and Post-war Politics: Australia, 1945–55', *Historical Records of Australian Science*, 13, 2000

De Matos, Christine, 'Diplomacy Interrupted? Macmahon Ball, Evatt and Labor's Policies in Occupied Japan', *Australian Journal of Politics and History*, 52, no. 2 (2006), 193, https://doi.org/10.1111/j.1467-8497.2005.00414

Dewar, Shona, ed., *The Stuff of Life: Documents and Stories from the Lord-Constable Family Collection, Australia, 1841–2011*, private publication

Dewar, Shona, ed., *The Lord-Constable Family Record Collection*.

Dutton, Geoffrey, *A Rare Bird: Penguin Books in Australia*, 1946–96, Penguin Books Australia Ltd, 1996

Edquist, E.L., 'Memories of her life', unpublished

Edquist, Harriet, 'The abomination of desolation spoken of by the prophet what's-his-name', *Australian Humanities Review*, issue 36, July 2005

Edquist, R.C., *A History of Australian Technology*, unpublished manuscript, 1988

Edquist, R.C., *Career of Victor Thomas Edquist*, unpublished family papers, 1987

Edquist, Ruth, *RME Tale, Transcriptions of Family History*, unpublished, 1980s

Edquist, Ruth M., *Sadeler Catalogue*, master's thesis, University of Melbourne, 1990

Eiji, Takemae, *The Allied Occupation of Japan*, Continuing International Publishing Group, 2002

Emsley, John, *The Shocking History of Phosphorus: A Biography of the Devil's Element*, Pan Books, 2001

Evans, Gareth, *Incorrigible Optimist: A Political Memoir*, Melbourne University Press, 2017

Fenna, Alan, 'The Centralization of Australian Federalism 1901–2010:

Measurement and Interpretation', in *Publius: The Journal of Federalism*, Vol. 49, Issue 1, Winter 2019

Ferber, Sarah, Chris Healy, and Chris McAuliffe, eds, *Beasts of Suburbia: Reinterpreting Cultures in Australian Suburbs*, Melbourne University Press, 1994

Fitzpatrick, David, *Oceans of Consolation: Personal Accounts of Irish Migration to Australia*, Cornell University Press, 1994

Fitzpatrick, Sheila, *My Father's Daughter: Memories of an Australian Childhood*, Melbourne University Press, 2010

Forbes, Cameron, *The Korean War: Australia in the Giants' Playground*, Pan Macmillan Australia Pty Ltd, 2011

Frydman, Gloria, *What A Life: A Biography of Paul Morawetz*, Wakefield Press, 1995

Gaynor, Andrea, *An Environmental History of Growing Food in Australian Cities*, University of Western Australia Press, 2006

Hardy, Frank, *Power Without Glory*, Random House Australia, Vintage Edition, 2000

Heenan, Tom, 'Hutton, Geoffrey William (Geoff) (1909–1985)', *Australian Dictionary of Biography, Volume 17* (MUP), 2007, National Centre of Biography, Australian National University

Henderson, Gerard, *Santamaria: A Most Unusual Man*, Miegunyah Press, Melbourne, 2015

Hogan, Sandra, *With My Little Eye: The Incredible Story of a Family of Spies in the Suburbs*, Allen & Unwin, 2021

Horner, David, *The Spy Catchers, The Official History of ASIO, 1949–1963*, Allen & Unwin, 2015

Humphries, Barry, *More Please: An Autobiography*, Viking, 1992

Hutton, Geoffrey, *It Won't Last a Week: The First Twenty Years of the Melbourne Theatre Company*, Macmillan, 1975

Hutton, Nan, https://en.wikipedia.org/wiki/Nan_Hutton

Ismail, Sah-Hadiyatan, 'Australia and the Indonesian Independence', *Asian Social Science*, Vol. 7, No. 5, May 2011

Johansson, Carl Erik, *Cradled in Sweden*, Everton Publishers, 2002

Jordan, Douglas, *Conflict in the Unions: The Communist Party of Australia, Politics and the Trade Union Movement, 1945–1960*, PhD thesis, Victoria University School of Social Sciences and Psychology Faculty of Arts, Education and Human Development, 2011

Kata, Elizabeth, *Be Ready with Bells and Drums*, Penguin Books, 1963 (reissued as *A Patch of Blue* in multiple editions)

Kato, Megumi, *Japanese Representation in Australian Literature*, PhD thesis, University of SW, 2005

Kelly, Andrew, *ANZUS and the Early Cold War: Strategy and Diplomacy Between Australia, New Zealand and the United States, 1945–1956*, Cambridge, UK, Open Book Publishers, 2018

Kiddle, Margaret, *Men of Yesterday: A Social History of the Western District of Victoria, 1830–1890*, Melbourne University Press, 1961

Kingston, Beverley, *My Wife, My Mother and Poor Mary Ann*, Thomas Nelson, Melbourne, 1975

Koivukangas, E.O., *Scandinavian Immigration and Settlement in Australia before World War II*, Ph.D. Thesis, School of Social Sciences, Australian National University, 1972

Leigh, Andrew, *Battlers & Billionaires: The Story of Inequality in Australia*, Black Ink Books, 2013

Macintyre, Stuart, *A Concise History of Australia*, 2nd ed, Cambridge University Press, 2004

Macintyre, Stuart, *The Reds: The Communist Party of Australia, from Origins to Illegality*, Allen & Unwin, 1998

Macintyre, Stuart, *The Party: The Communist Party of Australia from heyday to reckoning*, Allen & Unwin, 2022

McCalman, Janet, *Journeyings: The Biography of a Middle-Class Generation, 1920–1990*, Melbourne University Press, 1993

McCalman, Janet, *Vandemonians: The Repressed History of Colonial Victoria*, Miegunyah Press, 2021

McKay, George, *History of Bendigo*, Ferguson & Mitchell, Melbourne, 1891

McKernan, Michael, *Drought: The Red Marauder*, Allen & Unwin, Sydney, 2005

McLaren, John, *Writing in Hope and Fear: Literature as Politics in Post-War Australia*, Cambridge University Press, 1996

McLaughlin, Trevor, *Barefoot and Pregnant? Irish Famine Orphans in Australia*, Genealogical Society of Victoria, 2001

McPhee, Justin, *Spinning the Secrets of State: The History and Politics of Intelligence in Australia,* PhD thesis, RMIT, 2015, http://researchbank.rmit.edu.au/view/rmit:161477

Martin, A.W., *Robert Menzies, A Life, Vol. 2, 1944–1978,* Melbourne University Press, 1999

Mathews, Iola, *Winning for Women: A Personal Story*, Monash University Press, 2019

Maxewelle, Dayne, *Inglewood in the Fifties and Sixties*, A series of articles, editors' notes and readers' letters which appeared in the pages of *Inglewood Advertiser* from September 1906–August 1907, researched on microfilm by Kevin J. Poysner, Inglewood & District Historical Society Inc., 2000

Moore, Nicole, *The Censor's Library: Uncovering the Lost History of Australia's Banned Books*, University of Queensland Press, 2012

Moore, T. Inglis, *Social Patterns in Australian Literature.* Angus & Robertson, 1971, reissued by University of California Press, September 2020

Munro, Craig, and Robin Sheahan-Bright, eds, *Paper Empires: A History of the Book in Australia*, University of Queensland Press, 2006

Murphy, John, *Imagining the Fifties: Private Sentiment and Political Culture in Menzies' Australia,* UNSW Press, 2000

Murphy, John, 'Shaping the cold war family: Politics, domesticity and policy interventions in the 1950s', *Australian Historical Studies*, 26:105, 544–567

Niall, Brenda, *My Accidental Career*, Text Publishing, 2022

Nicholson, John, *A Long Road Home: The Life and Times of Grisha Sklovsky,* Australian Scholarly Publishing Pty Ltd, 2009

O'Connell, Jan, *A Timeline of Australian Food: From Mutton to Masterchef*, New South Publishing, 2017

Okin, Susan Moller, *Justice, Gender & the Family*, Basic Books, 1989

Oxley, Deborah, *Convict Maids: The Forced Migration of Women to Australia*, Cambridge University Press, 1996

Parsons, Ronald, *Migrant Ships for South Australia, 1836–1866*, Gould Books, 1999

Podger, Hugh, *Albright and Wilson: the Last Fifty Years*, Brewin Books, 2002

Ralph, Cedric, *Memoirs,* Scribd, 1993

Rix, Alan, ed., *Intermittent Diplomat: The Japan and Batavia Diaries of W. Macmahon Ball*, Melbourne University Press, 1988

Rudd, Kitty Lord, *Little Girl Grown Old*, undated memoir, family papers.

Shaw, A.G.L., *A History of the Port Phillip District: Victoria Before Separation*, Melbourne University Press, 1996

Silverman, Sondra, 'Australian Political Strikes', *Labour History*, no. 11, November 1996

Spence, John C.H., *Spitfire Pilot Lou Spence: A Story of Bravery, Leadership and Love*, Brolga Publishing, 2021

Stevens, Glenn, *Inflation and Disinflation in Australia, 1950–91*, Conference 1992, Reserve Bank of Australia Publications

Strauss, Valda, 'Irish Famine Orphans in Australia', *Mallow Field Club Journal,* Vol. 11, 1993

The Report of the Royal Commission into British Nuclear Tests in Australia, Volume 1, Australian Government Publishing Service, 1985

Tranter, Bruce, and Jed Donoghue, 'Bushrangers: Ned Kelly and Australian Identity', *Journal of Sociology*, December 2008

Warner, Denis, *Wake Me If There's Trouble*, Penguin Books Aust Ltd, Australia, 1995

Wright, Claire, *The Forgotten Rebels of Eureka*, Text Publishing, 2013

Books and articles about Western Australia

Annear, Jan, ed., *Life on the Leases, The Woman's View: An Anecdotal 1985 Calendar*, a tribute to all the 'Mining Women who helped establish and develop the mining towns of Australia', Perth Branch of the Women's Auxiliary of the Australasian Institute of Mining and Metallurgy

Annear, Jan, ed., *More of Life on the Leases, The Woman's View, An Anecdotal 1987 Calendar*, Perth Branch of the Women's Auxiliary of the Australasian Institute of Mining and Metallurgy

Baldasser, Loretta, A., *A Brief History of Italians in Western Australia* https://doi.org/10.1177/1440783308097127 and in *A Changing People: Diverse Contributions to the State of Western Australia*, Office of Multicultural Interests & Constitutional Centre of WA, Perth

Bertola, Patrick, 'Undesirable Persons: Race and West Australian Mining Legislation', in *Gold, Forgotten Histories and Lost Objects of Australia*, edited by Iain McCalman, Alexander Cook and Andrew Reeves, Cambridge University Press, 2001

Bingley, A.N., *Back to the Goldfields: Coolgardie & Kalgoorlie, 1892–1940*, Mobil Oil Australia and Hesperian Press, 1988

Birrell, Ralph Winter, *The Development of Mining Technology in Australia 1801–1945*, unpublished PhD thesis in History, University of Melbourne, 2005

Bull, Margaret, *White Feather: The Story of Kanowna*, Fremantle Arts Centre Press, 1981

Bunbury, Bill, *Timber for Gold: Life on the Goldfields Woodlines*, Fremantle Arts Centre Press, 1997

Cammilleri, F., *Chasing the Weight*, Hesperian Press, 1986

Casey, Gavin, and Ted Mayman, *The Mile that Midas Touched: The Story of Kalgoorlie from 1893–1968*, Rigby Limited, Revised Edition, 1968

Carnegie, David, 'The Outward Journey, Chapter V, Water at Last', in *Spinifex and Sand*, Part V http://en.wikisource.org/wiki/Spinifex_and_Sand/Part_v/Chapter_V (in the public domain)

Crowley, F.K., *Australia's Western Third, A History of Western Australia from the first settlements to modern times*, London, MacMillan & Co. Ltd, in association with University of Western Australia Press

Edquist, E.L., *Letter to Hay Marmion*, 1916, unpublished family correspondence

Edquist, E.L., *Memoirs*, unpublished

Edquist, Harriet, 'The abomination of desolation spoken of by the prophet what's-his-name', *Australian Humanities Review*, 1 July 2005

Edquist, Mary, *Recollections of my mother*, by Mary Litchfield Wreford, nee Edquist, November 1992, unpublished family papers

Edquist, R.C., *Career of Victor Thomas Edquist*, unpublished manuscript

Hartley, Richard, 'Bewick Moreing in Western Australian Gold Mining 1897–1904: Management Policies & Goldfields Responses', *Labour History*, no. 65, 1993

Heydon, P.R., *Gold on the Murchison: A Tale of Twin Towns, Cue and Day Dawn*, Hesperian Press, 1987

Hooper, J.M., *Youanmi: A Story of Murchison Gold*, Hesperian Press, 1987

Hoover, Herbert, *Years of Adventure 1874–1920*, MacMillan Company, 1951

Leyman, Lenore, and Criena Fitzgerald, *110° in the Waterbag: A History of Life, Work and Leisure in Leonora, Gwalia and the Northern Goldfields*, Western Australian Museum Books, 2012

Lozeva, Silvia and Dora Marinova, 'Negotiating Gender: Experience from Western Australian Mining Industry', *Journal of Economic and Social Policy*, Vol. 13: Issue 2, Article 7, 2010

Leuchtenburg, William, *Herbert Hoover: The American Presidents Series*, with Arthur M. Schlesinger, Jr. and Sean Wilentz, eds, New York, Times Books, Henry Holt and Company, 2009

McCalman, Iain, Alexander Cook and Andrew Reeves, *Gold: Forgotten Histories and Lost Objects of Australia*, Cambridge University Press, 2001

McDonald, G.J.C., Ex-Inspector of Police, *Beyond Boundary Fences: Some Incidents of Early Day Life on the Goldfields of Western Australia*, Hesperian Press, 1996

Palmer, Alex, *Field's Gold: The Story of the Yalgoo Goldfields*, Fremantle Arts Centre Press, 1981

Raeside, Jules, *Golden Days, Memoirs and Reminiscences of the Goldfields of Western Australia*, Hesperian Press, 1996

Register of Heritage Places—Assessment Documentation Gwalia Museum Group 1, 23/09/2005

Shiosaki, Elfie, "They were afraid to speak": Testimonies of Aboriginal women at the 1934 Moseley Royal Commission, *Coolabah, No. 24 & 25, 2018, ISSN 1988-5946, Observatori: Centre d'Estudis Australians i Transnacionals / Observatory: Australian and Transnational Studies Centre, Universitat de Barcelona, 2018*

Turnbull, C.W.F., *Looking Back: Gwalia-Leonora Western Australia 1895–1963*, Leonora Gwalia Historical Museum, 2006

Women's Auxiliary of the Australasian Institute of Mining and Metallurgy, Perth Branch, *Life on the Leases—The Woman's View, 1985 Anecdotal Calendar*

Index

A

Adelaide   6, 35, 225, 231
Age, The   214
agricultural conditions   162, 166–167, 237, 269
  home gardens   70–71, 145, 164, 170
Albright & Wilson   16–17, 21–23, 162, 165–166, 208
Apollo Bay   193–195
Argus, The   57, 97
atomic bomb   2
  American   159
  British   159–161
  Russian   159
Austin, Thomas   119
Australian Art & Artists
  Merric Boyd   83
  Charles Condor   53
  Roy Dalgarno   83
  Russell Drysdale   200
  Heide   83
  Indigenous   200
  Michael Meszaros   83
  Sidney Nolan   199
  John Perceval   83
  Tom Roberts   53
  Arthur Streeton   53
  Walter Withers   53
Australian Broadcasting Commission   42, 49, 148
  Radio Australia   42, 52, 147, 149
Australian House & Garden   214
Australian literature & writers
  Mary Durack   199
  May Gibbs   198
  Frank Hardy   26
  Ion Idriess   199
  Ray Lawler   200
  Norman Lindsay   199
  Ruth Park   200
  Ethel C. Pedley   199
  Neville Shute   196
  Ethel Turner   199
Australian Security Intelligence Organisation, ASIO   28, 79, 87, 150, 176

B

Ball
  Jenny   49, 268
  Katrine   50–53, 264
  W. Macmahon   42, 49–53, 75, 77, 147, 266–268
Ballarat goldfields   7, 34–35, 123, 125, 131
Beauvoir, de Simone   219
Bendigo goldfields   7, 130–131
Bennett, Mary   242
Bewick Moreing and Company   64–65, 228, 231, 233, 251–252
birth control   274
Boyd, Robin   270
Bridgewater-on-Loddon   132, 134, 137
British Empire   9, 243–244
Butler, Eric   180

C

Calwell, Arthur   77
Camberwell   44–48, 95
Camperdown   35, 116, 118–121
Casey, Peter (cousin, son of Marjorie Charlholmes Casey)   265

Catholic Social Studies Movement   90–91
censorship   3, 202–203
Charlholmes
  Adolf Louis (great-grandfather)   132–136
  Alwyn Bertrand ('Bert', grandfather)   37–40, 132, 136–140, 265
  Ernst (grandfather's brother)   136–139
  Estelle (grandmother, wife of Bert)   37–39
    see Estelle Lord
  Margaret (great-grandmother)   135
    see Margaret Crow
  Marjorie (aunt, daughter of Bert & Estelle)   14, 31, 37–39, 266
  Maud (grandfather's sister)   136–139
  Nancy ('Nan', aunt, daughter of Bert & Estelle)   3, 14, 37–40, 55, 58,1 17, 267–266
    see Nan Nicholls, Nan Hutton
  Nell (wife of Ernst and a cousin)   138–139
  Ruth (mother, daughter of Bert and Estelle)   3, 12, 37–43, 265
    see Ruth Edquist
Chifley, Ben   28
child care   276–278
China   78, 87, 183, 252
class   8, 185–186, 144, 244, 272–273, 279
Colantet   36, 116–117, 121, 218, 269
Cold War   88, 176–178
Collingwood   25–27
Commonwealth Scientific and Industrial Research Organisation (CSIRO)   78, 152
communists   2, 25–28, 78, 87
  Communist Party of Australia (CPA)   25–28, 85, 87–89, 91
  Communist Party Dissolution Act   88–89
Constable
  Eliza (great-grandmother's sister)   123
  Jane (great-great-grandmother)   122–127
    see Jane Leary

Mary Jane Hart (great-grandmother's sister)   123, 125
Ruth (great-grandmother)
  see Ruth Lord
Thomas aka Michael Hart (great-great-grandfather)   34, 122–125
Council for Scientific and Industrial Research (CSIR)   78
Crow
  Betty Kellett (granddaughter of John Patrick)   137
  Eliza Jane (great-grandmother's sister)   131, 138
  John Patrick (great-grandmother's brother)   131, 138
  John Wilson (great-great-grandfather)   128–132, 137–138
  Margaret (great-grandmother)   131–136, 138
    see Margaret Charlholmes
  Margaret Connor (great-great-grandmother)   127–132
Cue/DayDawn   229, 232–233

D
Davies
  Daniel   225
  Elsie (half-sister of Victor Edquist)   225
  Will (half-brother of Victor Edquist)   227–229
Democratic Labor Party (DLP)   90–91, 177
Depression, the Great   39–41, 75, 139, 253
divorce   98–99, 103
domino theory   78
Dutch East Indies/Indonesia   75–76

E
Edquist
  Alfred (grandfather's brother, son of Eliza & Andrew)   225
  Andrew (brother)   72–73, 81, 92, 102–103, 193, 225

Andrew (great-grandfather)   132–133, 142, 225

Arthur (grandfather's brother, son of Eliza & Andrew)   225

Christopher (brother)   33, 69, 102, 42, 193, 259

Eliza Turner Edquist (great-grandmother)   225, 231

Eva (grandmother, wife of Victor)   3–9, 14–15, 20, 59–63, 64–69, 72–74, 95, 103–106, 141–144, 161–162, 205, 208, 212, 224–261, 279
  see Eva Litchfield

Harriet (cousin)   168

John (uncle)   14, 66

John (brother)   10, 14–16, 18, 30–32, 44–47, 54, 68, 72, 103, 142

Mary (father's sister, daughter of Eva & Victor)   65–67, 222
  see Mary Wreford

Richard (father, son of Eva & Victor)   5–6, 12–13, 16–18, 20–23, 29, 59, 63–64, 67, 78–79, 88, 141, 193, 198, 203, 208–212, 224–238, 263–264, 269–271

Ruth, (mother, wife of Richard)   3, 9–13, 30–32, 44–48, 51–63, 72–74, 86, 92, 101, 161–162, 202–212, 260–267, 276, 279
  see Ruth Charholmes

Victor (grandfather, father of Richard)   4, 6–9, 64–66, 136, 225–258

Education, Victoria
  Fintona Girls' School   185, 189, 219–222
  funding   186–189
  Genazzano Convent   60, 186
  history   186
  MacRobertson Girls' High School   39, 186
  Melbourne University   41, 185, 205
  one-room schoolhouse   37
  philosophy & discipline   189
  Preshil   23–24, 29, 81–86, 184–185
  sectarianism   186–189
  snobbery   186
  teaching as a profession   41, 248
  unequal opportunity   185–189, 226

Education, Western Australia
  Guildford Grammar School   6, 154, 256
  Gwalia   255
  Youanmi   238

Eltham   49–53, 267

Eureka Stockade   123–124

Evatt, Herbert Vere   75, 89, 177

explorers   129, 197–198

F

Ferber, David   152

friendship with foreigners   2, 45–48, 145, 147–152

G

Geelong   35, 36, 37

Greene
  Anne (daughter of Lesley & Ben Greene)   296
  Ben (husband of Lesley Greene)   180
  Graham (cousin of Ben Greene)   180
  Lesley (adopted daughter of Margaret Litchfield, grandmother's sister)   179
  Margaret (daughter of Lesley & Ben Greene)   179, 181
  Paul (son of Lesley & Ben Greene)   180

Gwalia   4, 65, 229, 238–243, 244, 254–258, 274, 280

H

Hampton   30–32, 43, 107–114

Hardy, Frank   26

Heidelberg   53

Hobbs
  Elizabeth (great-grandmother)   245
    see Elizabeth Litchfield
  George (great-great-grandfather)   244–245
  Muriel (cousin of grandmother Eva Litchfield Edquist)   14

Hoover, Herbert   249–253, 254, 256
Hoover House, The   251–252, 253–258
Humphries, Barry   274
Hutton
  Barby (cousin, daughter of Nan &
    Geoff)   213
  Geoff (uncle, husband of Nan)   97, 102,
    201, 213–218, 261–262, 265, 266
  Nan (aunt, wife of Geoff)   102–103, 201,
    209–210, 213–218, 224
    see Nan Charlholmes, Nan Nicholls
  articles by Nan Hutton   214

I

immigrants & immigration
  assimilation difficulties   149–150
  foodways   3, 108, 145, 173–174, 234
  government encouragement of   17, 128,
    144
  housing   145
  Immigration Restriction Act   77, 86
  labour relations   164
  New Australians   9, 145, 146, 164
  wartime internment   234
Imperial Chemical Industries (ICI)   17,
  152, 208
Indigenous people
  in Victoria
    conflict   1, 7, 129, 240
    decline in population   239–240
    nutrition   129
  in Western Australia
    antiquity and cultural   240
    mining   241
    Mt Margaret Mission   242
    rock painting   200, 240
    Stolen Generations   241–243
industrial action (strikes)   27–28, 31, 75, 94,
  164, 270
  effect on women and children   28, 93–95
inflation   27, 94, 164
Inglewood   132, 137–138
Irish Famine orphans   33–35, 126–127

J

Japan
  Allied Occupation of   50
  attitudes towards   50, 77–78, 147–149,
    159
  in World War II   9, 12, 42, 77–78, 148,
    159

K

Kalgoorlie   6, 229–230, 251, 254
Kambala   229
Kew   5, 8, 16–20, 27,59–63, 68–74, 80–81,
  87, 89, 92–96, 103–106, 141, 159–168,
  172, 174
Kingston, Beverly   93, 104, 271
Kinsman, Arthur   152
Kinsman, Irene   263
Kisch, Egon   86
Korean War   78, 88

L

Labor Government   17, 27, 88
Labor Party
  Australian Labor Party (ALP)   89, 90–91,
    177
Lake Austin   233
Lake Lefroy   229
League of Empire Loyalists   180–181
Leary, Jane (great-great-grandmother)   34,
  122–127
Leonora   4, 229, 244, 254–255
Liberal Government   87–89
Liberal Party   76–77, 89
Litchfield
  Agnes (Nessie, grandmother's
    sister)   248
  Annie Marguerite ('Margaret',
    grandmother's sister, adoptive mother
    of Lesley Greene)   179, 248
  Elizabeth (great-grandmother, mother of
    Eva)   245
    see Elizabeth Hobbs

Eva (paternal grandmother)   230
see Eva Edquist
Hilda (grandmother' sister)   246,
248–249
Horace (grandmother's brother)   246–
247
William (great-grandfather, father of
Eva)   245–248
Lord
Ann Williams (great-great-grandmother,
mother of great-grandfather Sam Lord
II)   34–36, 121
Annie ('Sis', twin of Sam III,
grandmother's sister, daughter of Ruth
& Sam Lord II)   122
Arthur (grandmother's brother, son of
Ruth Constable & Sam Lord II)   34,
122
Doris Lord Draffen (grandmother's
cousin, daughter of Will)   35, 115,
121, 139
Estelle (maternal grandmother, daughter
of Ruth & Sam II)   33, 37
see Estelle Charlholmes
Frank (grandmother's brother, son of
Ruth & Sam II)   34, 40–41, 122
Jack (grandmother's brother, twin of
Kitty, son of Ruth & Sam II)   33, 116,
122, 187
Jean ('Jinny', grandmother's sister,
daughter of Ruth & Sam II)   140, 266
Kitty (grandmother's sister, daughter of
Ruth & Sam II)   33, 116–122, 187
see Kitty Rudd
Ruth (great-grandmother, married to
Sam Lord II)   33, 36–37, 116, 121,
139–140
see Ruth Constable
Sam I (great-great-grandfather, married
to Ann Williams)   34–36, 121
Sam II (great-grandfather, son of Ann &
Sam I)   36, 116

Sam III (grandmother's brother, twin of
Sis son of Ruth & Sam II)   34, 122
Tom Draffen (son of Doris Lord Draffen,
cousin of Kitty)   118–121
Will (great-grandfather's brother, son of
Ann & Sam I, father of Doris)   115
Lyttle, Margaret   82

M

MacArthur, General Douglas   50
Malayan Emergency   76–77
Mannix, Daniel, Archbishop   26, 90
manufacturing technology in
Australia   17, 21–23, 104, 162–163, 270
Marvel Loch   231–232
mateship   235
McCalman, Janet   186
Meekatharra   233
Menzies, Robert   12, 52, 78–79, 87–88,
155, 159
mines
Big Bell   238, 280
Fingalls Mine   231
Mary Kathleen   160–161
Mountain Queen   231
Queen of the Hills   233
Red Hill   229–230
Reno   227–228
Sons of Gwalia,   4, 6, 229, 238–240,
250–251, 253–254
Warriedar   233
Youanmi   228, 234, 236–238
mining
contribution to prosperity   1, 7, 161
end products   1, 7
environmental impact   1, 7, 161, 235
family relations effect   225, 231–238,
275
housing   232, 256–258
Indigenous   241
methods   228, 236
Victor Edquist Career   225–240

Morawetz
    Dita & Paul   149–150
Movement Against War & Fascism   86
Murchison goldfields   160, 232

N

Neville, Auber Octavius   241–142
New Australians   9, 145–146, 164
    see immigrants & immigration
Nicholls
    Dick (first husband of mother's sister
        Nan)   55–56, 98–100, 103
    Kristy (cousin, daughter of Nan and
        Dick)   54–58, 61, 72, 81, 97–103, 262,
        276–277
    Lady (mother of Dick)   55–56
    Nan (mother's sister)   3, 54–58, 61, 92,
        94–95, 97–100, 276–277, 279
        see Nan Charlholmes, Nan Hutton
    articles by Nan Nicholls   94–95

O

Okin, Susan Moller   272

P

Paterson
    John   153, 264
    Mark   153, 264–265
    Mary   178
    Peter   153–154, 156–157
    Shirley   153–157
Penguin Books   202
Pentonville Convicts   122, 124–125
Perth   6, 229, 231, 233, 238
pesticides   165–166
Petrov Affair   176–177
Pomborneit   35, 36, 120
Port Phillip   10, 127, 128, 133
Portsea   218
Powlett Plains   135
Preshil   23–24, 29, 81–86, 184–185
    see Education, Victoria

Q

Queensland   28, 55, 57

R

rabbits   119–121
radiation   39, 159–161
Ralph
    Cedric   85–90
    Helena   84
    Ivan   25, 81
    Penelope   85–86
rationing
    in Australia   17, 25, 28, 31
    in UK   17
referendums
    1948   27
    1951   89
refugees   47–48, 149–150
Reserve Bank of Australia   94
Royal Family   69, 142–143, 244
Rudd
    Bill (Kitty's husband)   30–32, 107–115,
        145–146, 261
    Kitty (grandmother's sister)   30–34,
        107–122, 145–147, 162, 209, 261
        see Kitty Lord

S

Sadeler Brothers   205
Santamaria, B.A.   90, 177
selection   35–36
Singer, Peter   83
Skibbereen   34, 123, 126–127
Sklovsky
    Anna   151, 195
    Celia   150–152
    Grisha   150–152, 178, 194
    Jane   151
    Michael   151
Sons of Gwalia Mine   4, 6, 229, 238–240,
    250–251, 253–254
South Africa   181

South Yarra   20, 66

Special Broadcasting Service (SBS)   151–152

Spence
  Louis   76
  John   45, 76, 267
Sputnik   182
Stolen Generations   241–243
Stony Rises   35, 115–121
Swedes in Australia   33,132–134, 203
Sydney   196–197

T

Talbot   132–134, 225
Tasmania   54–56
Tokimasa, David and Lebe   147–149
  Toorak   64–65, 95
  unions   27–28, 75–76, 91, 93, 164, 270

U

United Kingdom
  atomic testing in Australia   159–161
  attitude to Australians   9, 159, 197
  Australian attitudes to Britain   142–143, 147, 197–198, 203
  books   197–198, 202
  London   6, 7
  rationing   17
United Nations   75–76
United States
  armed forces   12, 57, 152, 183
  atomic bomb   159
  attraction   197
  books   166, 200–202
  education   186
  friends   152
  science and technology   182–183, 273
Uruguay   245
USSR
  athletic prowess   182
  atomic bomb   159, 187
  Hungarian uprising   177–178
  Stalin   178

V

Victorian League of Rights   180

W

Western Australia   7, 61, 67, 228–244, 250
White Australia   77
  Immigration Restriction Act   77
Whitelaw
  Elizabeth   25
  Margaret   16, 25
Wilkins
  Charlie   44–48
  Peter   45
  Stephen   45
  Suzette   45
Woman's Day   58, 2, 14
Wreford
  John (brother of Peter Wreford)   224
  Mary (father's sister)   181, 212, 224
    see Mary Edquist
  Peter (husband of Mary Edquist)   67, 224
Wren
  John   25–27
  Miss Wren   25, 81
World War I   34, 12, 45
World War II   2, 9, 12–13, 42, 75, 112

Y

Yalgoo   160
Yarraville   21
Youanmi   228, 234–238

Wakefield Press is an independent publishing and
distribution company based in Adelaide, South Australia.
We love good stories and publish beautiful books.
To see our full range of books, please visit our website at
www.wakefieldpress.com.au
where all titles are available for purchase.
To keep up with our latest releases, news and events,
subscribe to our monthly newsletter.

Find us!

Facebook: www.facebook.com/wakefield.press
Twitter: www.twitter.com/wakefieldpress
Instagram: www.instagram.com/wakefieldpress

Printed in the USA
CPSIA information can be obtained
at www.ICGtesting.com
CBHW051737131024
15802CB00020B/858

9 781923 042438